M000166731

Baxter's Boys

(They came. They scored. Then played a match!)

Enjoy the Madness!

Best wishes,

Patrick O

ORLA
KELLY
PUBLISHING

Patrick Osborne

Orla Kelly Publishing
Kilbrody,
Mount Oval,
Rochestown,
Cork,
Ireland

Dedication

This book is dedicated to every lunatic who has ever donned a football jersey and trudged around a mucky field, chasing a ball while dreaming of scoring the winner in the last minute of the Champion's League final. This book is also dedicated to the poor souls who've had the misfortune of watching these lunatics in action from the sidelines.

Acknowledgements

To my incredibly patient wife Liz and my three children, Robert, Rebecca & David who have had to put up with me over the years repeatedly telling them that I was going to write a book.

To my Mam, Joanie, who has encouraged me from day one to follow my dreams.

I would like to thank my publisher, Orla Kelly for getting the ball rolling & helping to bring my story to print & to my editor, Jean O'Sullivan for making sense of my Dublinese.

Contents

Contents

Chapter 1

"The pitch was a rough green area with a surface that wouldn't have looked out of place on the moon. Jaded, sickly grey, concrete tower-blocks surrounded it on three sides, loitering with intent. It had been christened locally the Stadium of Light because of the hundreds of brightly lit flats shining down on it when darkness fell. The Council workers who cut the grass had a less affectionate name for the place, however. Due to the fact that at any moment they were liable to be hit with a dirty nappy tossed from one of the many overhanging balconies they called it the Stadium of Shi..., well, ye can guess the rest. A forty-foot, battered and graffiti covered truck container that acted as a makeshift dressing room sat alone in a far corner. Someone had tried to set fire to it twice within the first few days of its installation but fortunately it had survived. This was the harsh reality of our new home ground but we couldn't afford to be choosy. Before this season our best ever run in the cup was almost a draw in the first qualifying round. But this year things were different. We were Sporting Les Behans', Sunday league's finest."

Fran Reilly

The camp photographer, dressed in a figure-hugging sparkly top with matching hot pants that were barely legal in the western world let alone anywhere else on the planet, was doing his best to herd the lads into position for the official team photo. The players were delighted to be togged out in their spanking new yellow kit, courtesy of their generous sponsor, Frank the Publican, the owner of the local boozer. The Assassin, bald-headed and built like a shithouse, wore his jersey the wrong way around so that the back of his massive, wrinkled head, faced the photographer. Just as everyone was settling into place to have their image captured for posterity, banging could be heard coming from the boot of the gleaming taxi that was parked next to the pitch. The team turned as one towards the racket.

"For fuck's sake!" cursed the Assassin. He stormed over to the car and popped open the boot. "Ye better keep it down, I'm tryin' to have me bleedin' picture taken. D'ye hear me?" he warned before throwing in a few digs, "And if ye make a mess ye'll be fuckin' payin' for that as well." He slammed the boot closed, strode back to his curious teammates and retook his position.

Baxter, the Scouse manager, wrapped in a worn, tan sheepskin coat and topped with a tweed cap, turned and looked questioningly at his agitated player.

"The little bollox tried to do a runner," the Assassin replied indignantly.

Baxter nodded. In his late fifties and being that bit older and supposedly wiser, he knew better than to probe any further. As things began to settle once again, a Hitler speech came ranting into life. Everyone looked at Podge, the short, pot-bellied goalkeeper whose hand was heavily bandaged and held up in a sling. Podge retrieved his mobile phone from inside the sling.

"It's me new personalised ringtone for Sharon. Got it off the History channel," he explained, giggling like a schoolboy.

Trigger reached across and snatched his teammate's phone and said, "Give me that," before hitting the decline button and handing it back.

Podge, his mouth agape, was momentarily frozen with fear. Sharon was going to kill him for hanging up. Another player, Davey Byrne, who was fully togged out in his football gear and yet still wearing his motorbike helmet, turned to his pal, Mick. "His mot will batter him if she ever finds out about that ringtone," he predicted.

Mick wasn't aware that he was being spoken to. He was too busy fixing his perfectly quaffed, long blonde mane, wrapped up in his own world whereas per usual he was the centre of the universe. At this stage the photographer was almost hyperventilating with the lack of co-operation from the assembled players. He clapped his hands briskly together, schoolteacher-like.

"Righ', youse," he said, the pitch of his voice almost high enough to shatter glass. "On the count of three, say knob cheese. One, two, three..."

Five weeks earlier...

Mick lay asleep on his back, stretched across black silk sheets that covered his king-sized bed while a beautiful young woman's head rested on his toned, muscular chest. He had of course boasted to his date that the sheets were one hundred percent Mulberry silk imported all the way from Singapore but she wasn't in the least bit interested. As well as the opulent bed coverings the entire surface of the ceiling was covered with a large mirror, capturing the naked couple in its reflection. Empty champagne flutes sat on a bedside locker next to an ice bucket and a classy Art Deco style radio alarm clock. The clock read 7.28 a.m.

Several streets away, Mick's teammate, Fran Reilly, was also in the land of nod. He was lying in a single bed with his infant daughter, Laura, dressed only in a nappy and babygro, snuggled into his bare chest. Over the child's cot hung a colourful 'Winnie the Pooh' mobile, a present from her doting paternal grandmother. A half empty feeding bottle, teething medicine and plastic spoon were piled up on an old stool next to a radio alarm clock, an exact replica of the one back at Mick's place. It was 7.29 a.m.

In another house close by, Davey Byrne, fully clothed in a dark tracksuit, was sprawled across the top of his double bed. Sounds resembling someone changing the gears of a truck without using the clutch escaped from his open gob. He was grasping an empty can of cheap lager against his chest for dear life. A large Star Wars poster of Luke Skywalker fighting Darth Vader was Sellotaped to the ceiling while a third identical radio alarm clock sat on the floor surrounded by even more empty lager cans. Davey's Ma quietly entered the room carrying a tray with a mug of piping hot tea and freshly buttered toast. She looked around at the numerous cardboard boxes that were cluttering the room. They were all labelled as 'Art Deco Electric Clock Radios'. She shook her head despondently, knowing only too well that they weren't the result of earnest endeavour. The alarm sounded at 7.30 a.m. She deftly knocked it off with her slipper-clad foot before carefully setting down the breakfast tray.

"Did ye somethin' small, love," she half whispered to her only son.

Davey stirred. "Righ', Ma, thanks."

Mrs. Byrne eased the empty can from Davey's reluctant grasp, ruffled his hair and headed for the door.

3

"Have a blast," he mumbled.

His Ma paused momentarily, giving a sad smile. She was well aware of her son's many faults, but he was also an extremely kind-hearted person and she was really going to miss him.

Mick flicked off his alarm. The beautiful girl who was asleep next to him let out a gentle sigh as she instinctively gathered the sheets closer to her bronzed skin and rolled away onto her own side. Mick casually brushed aside the girl's long, auburn coloured hair from her flawless cheek, checked her out but quickly lost interest. He stared at himself in the ceiling mirror, his mind beginning to wander. It was far too easy picking up these gullible, young wannabes, telling them exactly what they wanted to hear in his sophisticated accent while flashing the cash at the same time. Sometimes he was a talent scout for a well-known television company, whose name of course he had to keep secret. Other nights he pretended to be a major stakeholder with a very prominent fashion house where he regularly partied with the lead designers. Once again, discretion was essential and he couldn't on pain of death reveal any names but needless to say, everyone who was anyone was wearing their creations.

He couldn't help it. If he was being honest with himself, he was most probably a sex addict. Although the lack of a real challenge when it came to the chase was frustrating, he still needed to satisfy his desires. In the meantime, he would just have to be content bedding gorgeous women like the one next to him. Life could be tough. A niggling thought inside his head came to the fore reminding him that his father had rang, yet again. That had to be at least the fifth time in as many days, definitely not the norm. His dad had left numerous messages too on the answering machine, none of which he had bothered to reply to thus far even though each call sounded more urgent than the last. The fucker could wait.

Fran, still dozy from the lack of sleep, fumbled about trying to switch off his alarm, knocking over his daughter Laura's feeding bottle and medicine in the process. The child woke and began to cry. It was easy to see why sleep deprivation was up there as a preferred method of torture by clandestine organisations throughout the world. Fran gave a tired smile but he wasn't angry. He adored his only child and knew from talking to some of his pals that kids weren't long growing up. They also gleefully informed him that that was when the real sleepless nights began.

Mick powered his Porsche 911 through the deserted, early morning streets narrowly avoiding a badly parked van along the way. The roar from the engine startled a mangy fox that was scavenging for food from an overturned wheelie bin. The once mainly carnivorous mammal, who now had a penchant for pizza, cautiously watched the car as it sped past before resuming its foraging. Less than a minute later, Mick yanked the handbrake bringing the car to an abrupt stop outside Davey's house, jolting Fran, who was half asleep upright in the passenger seat. Mick belted the car horn several times as Fran gave an enormous, disinterested yawn, barely aware of his surroundings.

"Bet you anything he's still in bed," Mick said in his posh accent, belting the horn again, "I'm not hanging around here all day waiting for the little runt."

Fran raised an eyebrow.

Mick looked at his pal and narrowed his eyes. "What? I said runt not cu..."

"Give him a chance, will ye. He's probably been up all night, workin'," Fran interrupted.

"Working? The man has no concept of the word. Surely you mean thieving," said Mick, more than a little frustrated.

"Ye know wha' they say? One man's stroker is another man's liberator," Fran said, knowing too well that this would really wind his friend up.

"You're getting worse, you do know that?" said Mick. He glanced at the bedroom window of the red-bricked, two up two down terraced house and saw an animated Davey appear, holding up five fingers. "Only out of bed. Now there's a complete and utter surprise." He slumped back in his seat, folding his arms like a petulant child.

A few minutes had passed when Davey came rushing out through the front door, carrying a kit bag, his long hair all over the shop. Fran climbed out of the two door car to allow his mate gain access into the back. It was a bit of a pain in the arse every time someone wanted a lift. Fran had asked Mick why he'd even bothered buying a four seater sports car in the first place but Mick had smiled and replied 'that sometimes his latest conquest had friends who wanted to tag along for the ride.' Enough said.

"Well, good mornin', ladies," Davey cheerfully said, once he'd got settled.

The lads looked him up and down, their eyes coming to rest on his unfortunate choice of footwear. Davey also glanced down only to discover that he was still wearing his puppy dog slippers with the moving beady eyes, a birthday present from his mother.

"Suits you," Mick said, his compliment knee deep in sarcasm.

"Fuck. Back in a sec," said Davey but before he had the time to even lean forward Mick slammed the car into gear and sped off. The backseat passenger was knocked off balance, tumbling awkwardly much to the delight of the other two lads.

"Yis pair of bastards," Davey cursed, trying to right himself.

An elderly cyclist pushed his bicycle along the freshly raked pebble pathway, pausing to pet the head of his half-crippled dog. He didn't want to have to put the poor creature down and he had no problem spending the few bob on tablets to help ease the pain caused by the arthritis but if things got any worse… His wife called out from an upstairs window, "Don't forget the messages on your way back, love," she said, reminding him for the one hundredth time.

He felt like shouting back up to her that he didn't have Alzheimer's, not yet, but wisely decided to give a complying nod instead. Anything for a quiet life. Securing the holdall to his bicycle carrier with elasticated bungees, he threw his leg over the crossbar and set off on his travels.

Davey was curled up sound asleep in the cramped back seat of a car more designed for speed than comfort. Mick, wearing designer shades, was content to drive while Fran fiddled with the stereo, bored out of his tree. He opened the glove compartment and before the driver could stop him, pulled out the skimpiest, lacy thong he had ever seen in his life.

"Ye dirty bastard. Anyone I know?" Fran asked.

"No. Just some piece of skirt I pulled the other night," Mick curtly replied.

Fran held the knickers up for further inspection. "Not a dental nurse by any chance? Cause this thing looks like somethin' ye'd use for flossin'?"

Mick gave his passenger a withering look. "Philistine."

Unfazed, Fran turned around and placed the micro panties on Davey's head, sat back and admired his handiwork. He decided to route further into the glove compartment.

"Shut that and don't be so bloody juvenile," Mick said.

Fran ignored his pal of course and pulled out a woman's designer purse. "Are ye a handbag snatcher now as well?" he asked, suspiciously.

"Put it back, please and stop the messing. And for your information it's called a clutch."

Fran wasn't surprised that Mick knew these things especially if it helped him to get his leg over. He took no notice of his friend's request however and began to rummage through the bag or clutch or whatever it was called. He retrieved a red lipstick, opened it and pursed his lips. He contemplated what to do with it for a split second then turned his head in Davey's direction and grinned.

"Don't be an A-hole, cosmetics are seriously expensive," said Mick.

Fran gave him a questioning look.

"I'd imagine," Mick added but didn't elaborate further.

The elderly cyclist rode leisurely away, whistling an old tune that he'd heard way back but hadn't the foggiest who it was by. Maybe his wife was right, maybe he was getting old timers.

Back in the car, Fran looked behind him, a mischievous grin on his face. Mick checked his rear-view mirror. Davey was still asleep, blissfully unaware that his face was now plastered with makeup. It looked as if an epileptic 'Cure head' had done the job, mid fit.

"You can be an awful spaz at times," Mick said, definitely not impressed.

"Spaz?" said Fran, "Who says shit like that?"

"I do," Mick said, leaning over to his passenger's side, snatching back the lady's clutch and shoving it into the glove compartment.

"Watch out!" shouted Fran.

The car walloped the elderly cyclist sending him flying over the roof. Mick was caught totally unawares and bounced his head against the rear-view mirror as the car shuddered to a stop. At the same time Davey was thrown forward, almost impaling himself on the gear stick.

"Fuckin' potholes," he said, rousing from his slumber not quite sure if he was having one of those dreams where you fall but never hit the ground or else you'd be dead and then you'd never wake up.

Fran and Mick jumped out of the car leaving their pal behind. Mick went straight to the front of his Porsche, bent down and carefully examined the damage while Fran raced over to where the outstretched cyclist had ended up. Davey scratched his head and was baffled to find something resembling women's knickers resting on top of his head. He casually turned around and looked out the rear window. "Holy shit," he said. He clambered out of the car and joined Fran who was now bent down over the cyclist, his ear almost touching the prone man's lips, listening hard for breathing.

"Is he brown bread or wha?" asked Davey with childlike curiosity.

"Shut up for a minute, will ye," Fran replied.

Davey moved in closer and slipped his hand into the cyclist's pocket, stealing his wallet without his pal noticing.

"Will I give him CPR?" he asked, helpfully offering his services.

"There's no need, he's breathin'," Fran answered, feeling very relieved.

"Are ye sure?" Davey asked, somewhat peeved, "That's an awful shame."

Fran looked at his friend with arched eyebrows.

"I mean it's just that I know how to do it properly after the labour sent me on a course and I haven't gotten the chance to work on a real person yet, only the dummy."

Thankfully the cyclist began to come around. Davey put his disappointment behind him and gave the elderly man's forehead a gently rub.

"Yer alrigh', buddy. Just after fallin' off yer bike. Hit a dirty big pothole," he said, attempting to comfort the injured man, "The council should be ashamed of themselves and all the road tax we have to pay."

The cyclist stared at Davey, horrified. "Get away from me, ye pervert," he just about managed to say.

Davey looked at Fran, confused. "Does he want a slap or wha'?"

"Take no notice, doesn't know wha' he's sayin', probably concussed."

The cyclist slowly got to his feet just as Mick joined them.

The elderly man pointed at the driver. "Ye shoulda been watchin' where ye were goin', ye feckin' eejit," he said, scolding Mick.

"I don't care for you accusatory intonations, Grandpa," said Mick, his right hand clenched into a fist.

"I'm warnin' ye, I was a boxin' champion in the army," the older man said, trying to make his aging frame appear bigger.

Fran stepped between the two men. "Cool it, gents." He was just calming things down when Davey pointed at Mick's forehead. "Yer bleedin', bud."

Mick dabbed his skin with his index finger and inspected the smallest trace of blood. "If I'm left scarred, I'll fucking decapitate you," he shouted, lunging at the cowering cyclist.

Fran grabbed hold of Mick. "Relax the cacks, will ye, it's only a scratch," he said, trying his best to stop his friend from completely losing the rag.

"More than can be said for me poor bicycle," complained the cyclist.

"Your bike!" Mick roared, "I'll show you what you can do with your pitiful little bike." He charged over to where the mangled bicycle lay, picked it up and flung it over the hedgerow. He then returned to his car to examine his forehead in one of the wing mirrors.

The elderly man was almost in tears. "That was an anniversary present from herself."

Fran turned to Davey. "Get it for him, will ye?"

"I will in me brown," Davey protested.

"Please?" begged Fran.

His teammate reluctantly made his way over to the hedgerow, found a gap of sorts and disappeared through it.

"I'll have to sit down. I don't feel well," the old man meekly said.

Fran helped him into a sitting position just as Davey left out a roar. Fran, Mick and the cyclist all looked towards the hedgerow as Davey emerged carrying the damaged bicycle in one hand while covering the left-hand side of his face with the other.

"Fuckin' thorns, nearly took me bleedin' eye out," he swore.

The cyclist placed a hand on his head in total dismay. "Look at the state of me bicycle! It's completely bandjaxed."

"It's not that bad. A little bit of manipulatin'..." said Davey, already forgetting about his facial injury. He stood on the front wheel rim and pulled hard on the handlebars with all his strength. There was a groan from the metal and then the wheel snapped off. "Eh, nothin' a professional can't sort out," he said, quickly backtracking.

A loud, diesel engine vehicle rumbled into earshot catching the attention of all four men present.

Davey looked in the direction of the approaching noise. "Time to go, boys," he said, sensing a whole lot of shit coming their way.

Mick marched over to where the old man was slouched. "You haven't heard the last of this," he said in an unveiled threat.

Fran grabbed Mick by the shoulder and started to pull him towards the sports car. "Leave it, it was an accident," he said.

Davey let the rest of the broken bicycle fall to the ground. He then pulled his sleeve down over his hand and hurriedly ran it over any areas he may have touched in case forensics dusted the bike for fingerprints before running back to the car. Fran was doing his best to force Mick into the driver's seat. Once he had achieved this he raced around to the far side.

"Ten minutes with a pro, have it as good as new," shouted Davey as Fran shoved him the rest of the way in and followed suit.

Mick started the engine, revving it loudly several times. He then leaned out the window. "Don't worry, old man, I'll be seeing you around." The car sped off leaving the bewildered cyclist sitting alone in the middle of the road wondering what the hell had just happened.

Chapter 2

The imposing Victorian prison was nicknamed 'The Joy', not that it brought much pleasure to its six hundred plus residents. It housed some of the country's most dangerous criminals as well as the occasional T.V. license dodger. Richie, average build and wearing thick, health-board type glasses, entered the smoke-filled cell. The cigarette ban prohibiting smoking in the workplace didn't include prisons. This pleased the vast majority of warders as they'd enough on their plates without having to deal with nicotine deprived inmates kicking off.

"Mr. Kelly, your new roommate will no doubt bring you up to speed as to how things work around here," the warder said. He promptly turned on his heels, leaving Richie standing in the middle of the cell holding his folded towel with toiletries resting on top. The new man surveyed his surroundings and noted that almost every inch of the walls were decorated with glossy pictures of scantily clad women. 'Less is more,' he thought.

Kelly, his muscular arms heavily coated in colourful tattoos, lay on the top bunk, his face hidden behind a girlie magazine, cigarette smoke lazily rising from behind it.

"Alrigh', buddy, so which bunk is mine?" asked Richie in a friendly sort of way, wanting to make a good first impression.

The inmate slowly lowered his magazine. His head was shaven tight to the scalp and his face boasted several jagged scars. The remains of a cigarette hung from his surprisingly luscious lips. Richie knew women who would pay an absolute fortune to have a mouth like that. Kelly glared at Richie, sizing him up before raising his glossy booklet.

"Coupla house rules," said the convict. "One, I'm not yer buddy. Two, top bunk is mine. Three, ye give me five smokes a day..." he lowered the magazine, "...for the rent. And four..." He paused for a moment taking a long, last drag on his cigarette, "I'll have to think about four." He took the remains of the butt from his mouth and flicked it at Richie, narrowly missing him. "Crystal?"

Mick's car shot past a sign that read Newton Rangers F.C. with an arrow pointing left. The vehicle braked hard and reversed at speed sending loose pebbles flying in all directions then turned as instructed. A few hundred yards up the road two teams were fully togged out on a second pitch that was being used for the pre-match warm up.

Newton Rangers were immaculately dressed in red jerseys, black shorts and matching red socks. They jogged up to the halfway line in unison then turned and sprinted hard towards the goal line in a tight formation that would have even impressed the Red Arrows acrobatic flying team. In contrast Sporting Les Behans' were in disjointed groups, scattered all over the pitch, wearing white tattered jerseys with Murray's Pub printed on them. Podge, Charlie and Yoyo were sharing a large spliff. The Assassin and Jigsaw were sipping cans of lager while injecting vodka into oranges using syringes. Trigger was on his own, furiously doing push-ups while Huey was at the far sideline bent over trying to puke his guts up. Paddy Power was oblivious to everyone as he leant against a goalpost studying the form of various nags in the newspaper. Gitsy was sneezing in between bouts of blowing his nose like a trumpet into his off-white, cotton hanky. Split the Wind was jumping about like a distressed helicopter, practising his karate kicks, while Birdy, sallow skinned and athletically built, was walking on his hands along the top of the crossbar.

Mick and the lads pulled in next to Baxter who was chomping hard on gum. Fran lowered the passenger window. "What's the story, Pa?" he greeted.

Baxter removed his tweed cap and scratched his head. "No sign of the referee. What kept you?" he asked in his strong Scouse accent.

"Ran into someone," Fran partly explained.

"Alright, lad. Anyone I know?" the manager asked.

"Wouldn't say so."

Mick pointed towards Birdy who was now walking along the top of the crossbar as if it was a tightrope, with arms stretched out horizontally to keep his balance. "Who's the clown, then?"

"That lads, is Birdy, our newest signing and you're never gonna believe this but he really is a clown. His family owns a circus," the gaffer revealed, brimming with excitement.

"Is he any good?" asked Mick.

"Heard the kids love him," Baxter innocently replied.

"What?" said Mick.

"I think he meant at football," Fran offered.

"Bugger if I know but anyone's gotta be better than this lot," said Baxter. He blew a large bubble as he surveyed his motley crew. The bubble eventually burst leaving pieces of chewing gum stuck to his face. "Right, hurry up and get changed, the referee might still make an appearance," he said, scraping the gum back into his mouth with a nicotine stained fingernail. He then did a double-take on noticing Davey slouched in the back with the makeup all over his face. "Soft lad."

Podge, Charlie and Yoyo looked on as Birdy continued with his high wire act. The circus performer then stepped off the crossbar but caught it smoothly with his vice-like hands as he dropped towards the ground. He swivelled around the bar several times before dismounting with a double somersault, landing perfectly upright, his arms raised in the air. Charlie and Yoyo clapped wildly, blown away by the impromptu performance. Birdy bowed politely to his small but none the less appreciative audience. The lads were convinced that if it had been the Olympics it would definitely have been a gold.

"That was bleedin' rapid," said Charlie.

"Must be on the good gear," Yoyo said but he was still mightily impressed.

Podge spat on the grass and said, "Piece of piss."

"Wha'? Love to see you try," said Charlie, throwing down the gauntlet.

"Righ'!" replied Podge, stupidly accepting the challenge. He threw off his goalkeeping gloves revealing a gold ring on his stubby wedding finger.

Inside the away dressing room, Fran, Mick and Davey were togging off. Fran was lacing up his polished boots while Mick tugged at a large hole in the sleeve of his jersey.

"This is simply unacceptable. You'd think that codger Murray would buy us a new set," he complained.

"We did well even gettin' these yokes out of him in the first place," said Fran.

Davey walked into the adjoining toilet area to take a leak.

Fran nudged Mick. "Hurry up before he sees his reflection," he whispered.

Davey finished his slash, shook himself a few times. "More than two shakes is a sin," he muttered to himself, tucking his flute back into his shorts, remembering the saying from his Catholic schoolboy days. He was about to leave when he spotted his reflection in the stained mirror. "Wha' the..."

As Fran and Mick scarpered out of the dressing room they could clearly hear Davey roaring behind them. "Fran Reilly, ye little bollox!"

Over at the goal, Charlie and Yoyo were in fits of laughter with a bemused Birdy standing next to them. Podge was making pitiful jumps in an attempt to grab hold of the crossbar. Charlie and Yoyo could take no more and decided to give their pathetic teammate a helping hand. They hoisted him up and after swaying back and forth like a drunken rugby lineout Podge eventually managed to latch onto the metal bar. Charlie and Yoyo broke free and collapsed to the ground, panting heavily from the excessive load, leaving Podge dangling in mid-air. The overweight player wriggled about, swinging his short, stumpy legs in a feeble attempt to get on top of the crossbar but was failing miserably. By this time Davey had caught up with Fran and Mick who were glued to the epic struggle.

"What's that ape up to?" Davey asked, referring to Podge.

"Auditioning for a role in the next series of The Zoo by the looks of it," answered Mick.

Fran noticed that a stud on his left boot had come loose. "Any of youse got a spanner?" he asked, twisting the cog.

Davey pointed at Podge. "Try him for size."

Fran pulled a face.

"There's one in me bag," Davey said.

"Sound. Back in a minute," said Fran.

As Fran rooted through Davey's kit bag back in the dressing room, the elderly cyclist's wallet fell to the floor opening up on a photo of him and his wife. Fran picked it up, slightly puzzled, flicked through it and found two well handled, fifty euro notes.

Outside on the pitch, Podge was still hanging from the crossbar having had no luck climbing up on top much to the amusement of his gathered teammates.

"Help me down, lads, will yis?" he pleaded.

The players weren't queuing up to offer their assistance. It wasn't that they didn't like Podge, it was just better craic watching him make a complete arse of himself, again. Hashish heads, Charlie and Yoyo, continued to drag on their shared spliff in between bouts of silly laughter. Podge finally dropped to the ground and started rolling around, screaming in agony.

The rest of the team cautiously edged closer.

"What's the matter with you?" asked Baxter, the suspense killing him.

Podge held up his bloodstained hand minus his wedding ring finger. Charlie and Yoyo laughed hysterically while Huey threw up. The rest of the team immediately backed off, absolutely disgusted.

"For Christ's sake," cursed Baxter, scowling at his sick player, "When your auld mare named you Huey, she was spot fucking on."

Fran arrived back from the dressing room and was curious to find almost the entire team bent over searching through the grass while Podge was sat down smoking a freshly rolled spliff, giggling away and muttering to himself.

Davey crouched lower to the ground, swept the pale green blades apart with the palm of his hand before picking up the pudgy keeper's finger with the buckled wedding ring somehow still attached. He held it aloft. "Bingo," he proudly announced as if he'd just found the lost Ark of the Covenant itself. "Better get it wrapped in ice or something. And I need a volunteer to drive that divvy to the ozzy, he's doing me 'ead in," said Baxter, glaring at Podge.

Fran turned to Mick.

"Not on your life," replied his teammate.

Fran helped Podge to his feet and they headed for the dressing room with Davey in tow, carrying the severed digit. Davey gave a mischievous smile then pretended to pick his nose with Podge's finger.

"Give over," said Fran, trying to hold in the laughter.

"Sorry, couldn't help it," Davey apologised. He then immediately pretended to stick the finger up his jacksie.

Fran shook his head pretending to be appalled but in truth found the entire scenario very funny. He knew it was childish, but it would make for a very entertaining story back in the boozer later on.

A short while after Podge had been escorted to the dressing room, a tractor and trailer pulled up next to where several opposition players were hanging around, complaining about the delayed kick-off. They didn't need to spell out the real reason for their grievances, everyone knew the score. This was Sunday League and valuable drinking time was being lost. The tractor driver, a hardy looking boyo with a dense mop of black curls, dismounted and helped an elderly man down from the cab. Mick looked on in horror, realising that the old man was the very same cyclist that he had earlier knocked down. Curly took the smashed bicycle off the trailer, setting it gently onto the grass. He then handed over the bag which had been attached to the carrier and shook the cyclist's hand, got back into his tractor and drove off, sounding the horn twice. Mick immediately slid away towards the dressing rooms.

Fran, Mick and Davey hid behind a pebble-dashed wall, peeping around the corner. Podge stood next to them, looking from his hand, now wrapped in a bloodstained towel and held together with insulation tape, to a clear plastic bag which was tucked under his arm. The bag contained his severed finger surrounded by a half dozen cans of chilled coke, acquired from a machine located in the small clubhouse. Improvise, adapt and overcome as the marines would say. Davey had also managed to liberate about twenty euros worth of coins in the process. Baxter noticed the lads spying and waved them over but they point blankly refused to budge. Instead, Fran beckoned for the manager to come to them.

You'd have needed a chainsaw to cut the atmosphere in Mick's car it was that thick. Davey and Podge were in the back looking at one another with neither man daring to say a word. Mick gripped the steering wheel tightly with both hands, staring straight ahead. All of a sudden he whipped his head around and pointed at Podge.

"I'm warning you. If you get so much as a speck of blood on the seats, I'll pull the rest of your fucking fingers off," he threatened.

Fran and Baxter stood outside the dressing rooms, deep in conversation.

"The cyclist is the ref?" exclaimed Fran, finding the coincidence hard to believe. "Is he not a bit old?"

"He was telling me that he'd retired from the game, but they were badly stuck and he was only doing it as a favour," said Baxter.

"I see."

"Lucky to be alive by all accounts," the manager said, "And as if knocking him off his bike wasn't bad enough, the scallies stole his wallet as well. Had a ton inside it to pay for his messages, the poor aul fella." He shook his head in disbelief at the depths that some people would sink to.

Fran looked sheepish, realising for the first time just how bad the whole incident sounded.

Fran and Davey stood on the garage forecourt, their kit bags resting at their feet. In the background Mick was showing a mechanic the damage to his beloved car. Fran thought that the grease monkey resembled a seabird plucked from a serious oil slick with the amount of black stuff smothering his overalls.

"I reckon he was that close to throttlin' the old man on the bike," Davey said, demonstrating with both hands.

"It's all about the car alrigh'," replied Fran, thankful that things hadn't escalated any further.

"Wha' did he mean by accusatory intona – wha'ever the fuck he said to the cyclist?"

"Accusatory intonations? The way the aul fella was blamin' him for the accident I think," said Fran.

Davey spat on the ground. "And why couldn't he have just said that? He can be a righ' tosser at times."

"Suppose," Fran agreed.

The mechanic cleaned his hands slowly on an old rag and although his face remained neutral, Fran thought he could make out the slightest hint of a grin. This was going to be a nice little earner for him.

Mick returned to where the lads were patiently waiting. "Thing's going to cost me an absolute fortune to get fixed," he revealed.

"Sure yer loaded anyway and it only looks like a small dent," said Davey, trying to make light of the situation.

"It's a classic car, not that I'd expect you to understand," Mick replied. "I could do with a stiff bloody drink."

Chapter 3

Sitting at the counter in Frank the Publican's bar sipping cool pints, Fran, Mick and Davey watched as their teammates, with the exception of Birdy and Podge, bounded in.

"Championes! Championes, are we, are we, are we!" they boisterously sang.

"You won? And without me?" Mick asked, not really believing such a feat possible.

"Good as," said Baxter, hardly able to contain his delight. "The new lad, Birdy, was superb in goal and the referee played a blinder. Replay is next Sunday."

The team headed down the back of the pub still singing followed by their ecstatic manager. Fran, Mick and Davey exchanged incredulous looks.

"I'll get the drinks in," Davey said.

His companions didn't need to be told twice and quickly hurried down the back to join the rest of the lads.

Davey hailed the publican. "Same again, head," he ordered.

The publican acknowledged Davey's request and began pulling the three pints. Davey opened the referee's wallet but there was nothing inside. He scratched his head, perplexed. There was definitely money inside when he'd lifted it from his victim. The publican set the drinks down and politely waited for payment. Davey looked at him, cautiously studying his face before deciding to take Podge's buckled ring from his pocket and setting it on the counter.

"This any good?" he asked.

The publican had a swift look around before taking a bookies pen from behind his ear and giving the ring a poke. "Is that blood on it?" he asked in an accent with a hint of a Kerry lilt.

Davey picked up the stained piece of jewellery, leaned along the counter and deftly dipped it into the pint of an unsuspecting customer who was preoccupied with his newspaper. He gave it a quick rub with his thumb then held it up for inspection. "Not anymore."

The publican took the gold wedding band and dropped it into his shirt breast pocket. He then held his hand out. "The name's Frank by the way."

"As in above the door?" said Davey, accepting the man's offer of friendship.

"Same as. Are ye a football team?"

"Rumour has it."

The publican smiled. "Haven't seen ye in here before?"

"No. One of the lads was though, a few weeks ago, said it was a decent enough shop," Davey explained. "We used to gargle in Murray's down the road but don't get me started about that miserable aul bollox."

"Yeah?" said the publican, hoping to hear some juicy gossip about his rival.

"Pulled the plug on the aul sponsorship deal we had goin', not that it was anythin' to write home about in the first place."

"I suppose I could help your team out. Wha' are ye called?"

Davey took a slow sip of his pint, weighing up in his mind how he was going to play this. It wasn't every day that a sucker jumped out of the water and straight into your boat and tried to impale himself on your un-baited hook. He spotted a heading out of the corner of his eye on the other customer's newspaper reporting that Sporting Lisbon had been beaten two-one in the Portuguese cup final.

"Funny ye should ask," said Davey, still taking his time. "We decided to change it from Murray's to... Sporting... Les Behans'," he proudly announced.

"Sporting Les Behans', strange name that," Frank said.

"Not really when ye come to think about it. See, there was this bloke who used to play for us called Lesley, Lesley Behan," Davey lied.

"Lesley Behan," repeated the bar owner, his interest piqued.

"Les to his mates."

"I see."

"And his favourite team was Sporting Lisbon, from Portugal?" said Davey.

"I've heard of them. Fair play. So what happened to Les?"

"Ah ye know, stopped breathin' and his heart gave up. That kinda thing."

Down the back of the pub the team was gathered around an assortment of tables pulled together, listening to Baxter as he gave a rundown on the match.

"The la was like a bleeding kangaroo on Gary's."

"Gary's?" asked Split.

"Gary Abletts," replied the Liverpudlian manager.

Split shook his head, none the wiser.

"Tablets," Baxter added. "Does no one speak English around here anymore?"

A few of the lads smiled.

"Didn't he use to play for the 'Pool?" said Trigger.

"Everton as well, if I'm not mistaken," Fran replied, "a good player."

"Where's he now?" Gitsy asked.

Paddy Power blessed himself. "Died of the big C."

"Ah fuck, remember him now," Gitsy said. "Always seemed like a decent skin."

The majority of the lads shook their heads out of respect.

"I see Baller Murphy got the message, was only given a few months to live," said Trigger.

"Jaysus, I didn't hear that," Fran said, genuinely shocked. Baller was one big solid bloke, always doing triathlons and the likes. "Only seen him a couple of weeks ago, he looked great."

"I know. Got it in the stomach and thought it was an ulcer for ages before finally gettin' it checked out," Trigger informed the lads.

"As sad as it is, d'ye know wha' he should do now?" said Charlie.

The lads remained silent, waiting for their teammate to continue.

"Hit the credit union for a massive fuckin' loan, leave somethin' behind for his mot," Charlie suggested.

"They've copped onto all that. Ye'd have to give the money back," Split said.

Charlie shook his head. "There's fuck all they can do about it when yer six-feet under."

"His partner's only young," said Fran, pitying what lay ahead for the poor girl.

"A real beauty," Trigger remarked but in a respectful sort of a way.

"Must call around, see if I can help her out with anything," Mick said but his quip wasn't best received. A joke was a joke and there weren't many things sacred amongst the lads but they had no time for that kind of cheap shot.

"Anyhow," said Baxter, breaking the awkward silence, "Birdy was jumping this way, that way, made at least half a dozen world class saves."

"Where is he by the way?" asked Fran.

"Headed off straight after the game. Said he'd a show to do this evening," the manager partly explained.

"You said that the referee did you a favour?" Mick said, trying to recover from his earlier faux pas.

"Too right. Yoyo went bombing up the wing and cut inside the box but your man never touched him, tripped over himself he was going that fast. But fair play to the ref, gave us the peno without a moment's hesitation," Baxter said.

The team cheered and Yoyo raised his drink in acknowledgement of the rare praise.

Baxter turned to Fran and said, "He's a real speed merchant."

"No surprise there, he has pedigree," Fran said.

"Was his auld fella an athlete or something?" asked Baxter, the curiosity getting the better of him.

"Nope. But back in the eighties Yoyo's Da was the fastest handbag snatcher this side of the Liffey."

Although Baxter knew the lads a fair few years now, he was still learning stuff about them every other day. "By the way, thanks again for doing that today."

Davey appeared carrying three pints and set them down on one of the tables. "Wha' did I miss?" he asked.

"I was just thanking Fran for the hundred quid he gave me for the ref after the poor man was robbed. I gave it to him at half-time. He was made up," the manager revealed.

Fran and Davey exchanged glances. Davey smiled sheepishly, not for stealing the money but for being sussed. In his world of reasoning the old bloke could easily have died as a result of being knocked down and the money would have been of no use to him then, would it?

"The ref said the other team never offered him a penny. The miserable shower of shites," added Baxter, shaking his head in disappointment.

The Assassin stood up and pulled a tenner from his pocket. "Come on, girls, don't be shy. We're not havin' Fran stump up the money on his own, especially when he doesn't have a regular job."

"Ah, it's no hassle," Fran said, absolutely mortified by his teammate's suggestion.

"Shut it," ordered the Assassin but in a friendly sort of way. "We're makin' a collection and that's the end of it."

There was no point in Fran arguing with Al Caffrey, he'd only have to explain that he took the money from the referee's wallet, hanging Davey into the bargain. Instead, he decided he would leave the cash behind the bar for a few celebratory scoops for the team later on. With a bit of luck, they'd be too well-oiled to ask any questions.

Pedestrians dodged cars that were desperately searching for parking spaces outside the busy city centre hospital. There were talks of relocating it to some green-field site on the outskirts but the various political parties and their respective advisors couldn't agree so the plan had been shelved for the time being. Inside the outdated building, an Indian doctor with an impressive set of teeth and a pleasant face, stood at the end of Podge's bed. The patient was propped up with several starched, white pillows strategically placed behind his back for support and added comfort. In fairness, Podge had been amazed at how quickly he'd been dealt with once his teammates had abandoned him at A&E with his severed finger and the bag of cans.

"We will know in a few days whether or not the surgery was successful, Mr..." the doctor explained, flipping through his notes.

"Podge," offered Podge.

The doctor looked up from his clipboard, making a strange face. "Ok, Mr. Podge."

"No, that's me nickname," said the plump patient.

The doctor was even more confused.

"Doesn't matter, bud," said Podge. His expression suddenly turned serious. "I heard they're goin' to have to shut down the maternity ward."

"This is news to me," the doctor said, genuinely shocked.

"Yeah, too many cracks in the buildin'," Podge revealed.

The doctor looked at his patient who had started laughing to himself like a lunatic. 'This wasn't good,' he thought. 'It was a very serious matter when any part of a hospital had to close. And then for a patient to find it funny just isn't normal.' The medic took a ballpoint pen from his pocket and scribbled a note reminding him to ask about the head injuries that surely must have been sustained in the fall.

"By the way, where's me ring?" Podge managed to ask as his fit of laughter finally subsided.

"Sorry?" said the doctor.

"Me weddin' ring? It was on me finger, that's how I ripped the fuckin' thing off." Podge re-enacted the incident to eliminate any further misunderstandings due to the language barrier.

The doctor shook his head apologetically. "Unfortunately, Sir, there was no ring handed in with your finger."

"That robbin' pox," Podge vehemently exclaimed knowing too well who the culprit was. He laid into one of the pillows with his good hand while shouting a string of profanities that would have made even the toughest of sailors blush.

Inside his prison cell, Richie lay stretched out on the top bunk, his face hidden behind a soccer magazine.

"Finished?" offered a weak voice from another corner of the confined room.

Richie lowered the magazine and stared at Kelly, his cellmate, who was sporting a swollen nose stuffed with bloodstained tissues, a cut just below the eye and a bandage wrapped around his head. Gone was the sweaty vest look and he was now dressed neatly in a crisply ironed prison shirt, wearing an uncertain smile. In his hands he held a roll of Sellotape which he was subconsciously fiddling with. A large football poster had recently been fixed to the wall behind him. Every one of the pictures of the semi-naked women had also been replaced with various soccer posters.

"That's grand, thank you," Richie pleasantly said. "Now don't get me wrong or anythin'. I love a bit of gee meself but just not in me face twenty-four-seven, especially when there's no chance of gettin' the ride. And who knows wha' migh' have happened if I'd gotten the urge, these springs mightn't have been up to the job." He slapped the thin, fire retardant mattress on his bed, giving Kelly the eyes. "Know wha' I mean?"

His cellmate nodded eagerly while at the same time taking several small steps backwards. Richie resumed his reading. Moments later he heard a match being struck. He peered over the top of his publication only to find Kelly with a cigarette in his mouth and a lit match in his hand. Richie frowned. His flustered cellmate immediately removed the cigarette from his gob.

"Sorry, sorry..." he apologised, hurriedly extinguishing the flame, "...old habits and all that."

Richie smiled.

"I'll just nip out to the landin'," Kelly said.

Richie gave the lag a nod granting him leave. Kelly quickly departed the scene allowing the new top dog to get on with his reading.

The polished, gold-plated plaque on the Georgian building read Horatio Lawson & Associates. Real estate in this part of town was at a premium and only the most affluent of companies were facilitated. A motorbike ridden by Davey, who was dressed in typical courier attire, pulled up outside. He parked the bike and retrieved two small parcels from an over the shoulder satchel emblazoned with the logo 'NO MESSIN' COURIERS'. He examined the parcels before tossing one of them into the storage box located at the rear of the gleaming machine, locking it away.

The prim and proper looking receptionist sat bolt upright behind her desk as Davey ambled in. He plonked the parcel unceremoniously down onto the counter with a bang having scant regard as to whether or not the contents were any bit delicate.

"Need yer scribble there, darlin'," he said, giving her a cheeky wink. While appearing only half interested his eyes were scanning the place, taking in every minute detail and backing-up the info to his computer-like memory.

The receptionist looked at the courier as if he was a piece of shit on her shoe. Davey couldn't help but notice her contempt. The way things were going in the world today he wouldn't be surprised if she reported him for sexual harassment just for breathing.

"And where's the other one?" she abruptly asked.

"What's that?" asked Davey, playing dumb, something he had perfected to a T over the years. He had learned from past experiences that when people thought you were thick, they invariably lowered their guard. Believing in their own intellectual superiority made it an awful lot easier to fool them. And that was definitely a good thing in his line of work.

"There are supposed to be two packages," the receptionist insisted.

"Don't think so, love," replied Davey, keeping up the pretence and knowing well that addressing her as 'love' would only further rile her.

The receptionist placed the palms of her manicured hands flat on the desk and pushed herself to a standing position, leaving out an exaggerated sigh as if she was expected to walk the Camino in six-inch heels. She then moved a full two yards over to a sturdy looking metal filing cabinet. While she was diligently searching through the paperwork Davey quietly leaned over the counter, surveyed the table surface below, noting where her handbag was situated. He then discreetly disconnected the telephone line from its socket.

The receptionist selected a document from the filing cabinet and quickly read through it.

"Just like I said. There are supposed to be two," she smugly spouted, waving the piece of paper in the air for dramatic effect.

Davey gave a goofy smile while shaking his head 'no'. He really had this fuckin' eejit thing down to a fine art. The receptionist returned the document to the cabinet drawer and slammed it shut. She strode over to the phone, lifted the receiver and jabbed at a button. Davey would have loved nothing more than if she'd broken one of her precious fingernails. Instead he had to content himself with chewing on one of his own mangled nails while casually observing the proceedings. The receptionist pulled a face, looked at the receiver then tried again getting the same unsatisfactory result.

"Mustn't have paid yer bills, wha'," said Davey, enjoying winding up the snotty bitch. "I'm a hundred and ten percent sure that there was only the one package."

The receptionist shot him daggers before hanging up and reluctantly making her way over to a door marked Stuart Lawson. Knocking gently first, she opened it and disappeared inside.

Once the receptionist was out of the way Davey got to work. He leaned over the counter and opened up her handbag. He toyed with her purse but let it go, trying to think of the bigger picture before stealing her pen instead and reconnecting the phone wire. An extremely irritated, male voice bellowed from inside Stuart Lawson's office.

"Tell him he better find that second parcel prompto or I'll sue their asses off!" the boss man shouted.

The receptionist emerged from the adjoining office. Her face said it all, 'I told you so, you big thick'.

"A few anger management classes wouldn't go astray there," Davey said, nodding towards the head honcho's office.

The receptionist remained stern.

"I'll see wha' I can do," Davey said, not giving a fiddler's how it made him look. He turned on his heels having successfully completed the first part of his mission and was gone.

The small fish and tackle shop was situated on the north side of the quays bang in the heart of the city. Davey had been going there since he was a kid and the place hadn't changed much even though it had gone through several different owners. Back in the day this was where he and his pals used to buy their snares for catching gicknas, the type of down and out pigeons you found mooching around the streets, train stations and the likes for scraps of food. Snaring a pigeon was a great challenge for a young fella and it was also cheap entertainment too in a time when money was scarce. The lads would always release the birds unharmed, removing any thread or catgut they found wrapped around the feet and toes, usually the result of some amateur using the wrong type of line.

Sometimes, but not often enough, Davey would manage to catch a thoroughbred pigeon which had dropped out of a race. The racing pigeons were snare-wise and would have to be on the brink of starvation before they would risk being captured. If he was successful in outsmarting one of these birds there was no point in contacting the rightful owners as they seldom ever wanted them back, deeming them failures. This gave Davey the opportunity to make a few bob selling the pigeons on to young, local loft owners who couldn't afford to take the chance of shelling out large sums of money on prized chicks. Instead, they would have to be content to breed the dropouts with their own stock in the hope of one day producing a champion.

Davey exited the fish and tackle shop carrying a long, thin, canvas bag containing his latest purchase. He slung the bag over his shoulder, lit up a cigarette and took a long, slow drag, a mischievous look spreading across his face. He then climbed onto his motorbike, kick starting it into life.

After dropping off the canvas bag, he continued on the relatively short journey till he arrived at his chosen destination, across the busy road from Lawson & Associates. He parked his powerful machine, pushed his helmet up so that it now rested on the top of his head and checked the time on his digital watch. It was 16:50 pm.

"Base, Davey here, over?" he said into his two-way radio.

The reply came back through static. "Go ahead, Davey," ordered the base controller.

"I'm runnin' late. Need to know wha' time Lawson and Associates shuts. Over?"

"Hold on…"

Davey lit up another cigarette and sucked in the nicotine hit with relish. He liked this job and the opportunities it presented, legal or otherwise. On his first day in work he had told his boss that he couldn't have a tracker on his bike. He pretended that he'd had a run in with some heavies, owed them money and feared being whacked if he didn't pay up. The boss had initially explained to Davey that it was company policy to have a tracker and that he'd have to let him go if he wasn't willing to have one installed. But that all changed when Davey had told him that if he couldn't pay back the cash, he'd have to inform the gangsters and the debt would then be automatically passed on to his employer. He knew it was unfair he'd said but that's the way these guys worked. Davey also revealed that sometimes the criminals would get bored waiting for the full amount to be paid back and could just decide to take you out early as an example to others. The terrified boss had a sudden change of heart and told Davey that as the head of the company he could make special exceptions when the need arose. As a result Davey kept his job, there was no more talk of a tracker being fitted to his bike and his boss had kept his distance, presumably in case of a bad shot.

"Davey. Over." said the base controller.

"Go ahead. Over."

"Five sharp. Receptionist says she won't wait a minute longer. Over."

"Sound. I'll do me best but the traffic's chocca. Over," Davey lied.

The receptionist sat behind her desk, liberally applying her newest favourite red lipstick, 'Lustful Inferno' while checking her appearance in a decorative, handheld mirror. Two secretaries entered the reception area through an adjoining door, both buttoning up their respective coats.

"We're heading over to Cassidy's for one, coming?" the taller of the two asked.

The receptionist glanced at the wall clock. It was five minutes to five. "I'll follow you over. I am just waiting on a package," she explained. "Not that I expect the courier to show. He was an awful looking gobdaw."

Davey was slouched on his motorbike, chilling, yet still keeping a close watch on the entrance to Lawson and Associates. The main door opened and out walked the two secretaries engrossed in scandalous gossip about some celebrity caught with her skirt up so to speak. Davey bolted upright in anticipation. As the office workers descended the stairs and headed towards Cassidy's pub, he realised that the receptionist wasn't one of the pair and sunk back down onto the leather saddle. Inside the office the receptionist had her coat on with her bag in hand ready to depart. She was staring furiously at the wall clock, drumming the tips of her polished nails against the top of her desk. It was now five past five.

"Fuck this for a game of soldiers," she declared, letting her posh facade slip. She exited the building, glanced up and down the street before double locking the door.

Meanwhile Davey was coolly observing the proceedings. He shoved his helmet back down onto his head and started up his bike. The receptionist began to walk away just as Davey apparently only arrived, pulling up next to her. He flipped up his visor and retrieved the second parcel from his satchel.

"Yer other package, sweetheart," he proudly announced.

"We're closed," the receptionist curtly replied, clipping Davey's enthusiasm.

He slowly put the parcel away. "No skin off my nose. Just that yer boss seemed to think it was important."

The receptionist hesitated, her bravado dissipating.

Davey spoke into his two-way radio, "Base? Davey here. Over?"

"Go ahead, Davey. Over," replied the tired sounding base controller who was coming to the end of a twelve-hour shift.

"Yer wan is refusin' to take the..."

"Look, just give it to me," said the annoyed receptionist.

"And wha' about the package?" Davey cheekily asked.

The receptionist gave a derisive snort.

"Hold on. She's had a change of heart. Over," Davey said, laughing into his radio. He handed the receptionist the parcel and she began to walk away without so much as a thank you.

"Signature?" Davey reminded her.

She stopped and exhaled loudly then began to rummage through her bag. "I don't believe this." She could have sworn that there was a biro in there earlier on. She glared at the courier. "Have you got a pen?"

Davey shook his head. "Fuck all use to me, love. Sure I barely know the alphabet." He discreetly checked over the receptionist's shoulder as she punched in the code, disarming Lawson and Associate's very expensive security system. Halfway through the process she spun her head around. Davey was looking up at the decorative cornicing on the ceiling pretending to be only casually interested. The receptionist resumed disarming the alarm allowing Davey to carry on with his spying.

There was very little traffic at this hour of the night, the area being mostly made up of offices with the staff long gone home if they'd any sense. Davey, dressed from head to toe in black with the canvas bag from the fish and tackle shop strapped over his shoulder, hurried up the steps to Lawson and Associates. Checking to make sure that the coast was clear first, he slipped off the canvas bag and unzipped it. He took out several pieces of a dismantled fishing rod, began to screw the parts together while at the same time pushing the assembled pieces of the pole carefully through the letterbox of the solid Georgian door. Inside the deserted reception area the rod was slowly fed forward towards a hook where a bunch of keys hung tantalisingly. Any security guard worth their salt would have flagged the habit of leaving the keys in open view as a serious risk. However, people were human and convenience was king, and no receptionist in their right mind was going to waste time going back and forth to some locked box every time a co-worker needed keys. It was this kind of thinking that kept Davey in work and ahead of the posse.

The carbon fishing rod wavered slightly as Davey attempted to snare his prey. He was sweating mad like that time the lads were away on a stag do and had gone to an Indian for a spicy Vindaloo. Afterwards some bright spark had come up with the idea of having a bet to see who could last the longest back in the hotel's sauna. Paddy Power had fainted and had to be carried out while Davey had won but lost about a stone in weight in the process.

"Come on, ye little fucker," he quietly cursed, trying to keep the rod steady and look through the letterbox at the same time. He gently wriggled the pole about and eventually managed to unhook the keys. "Yes. Now come to papa." After easing the rod out slowly, he collected his prize and promptly opened the door.

Once Davey had gained access to the building, he punched the numbers on the keypad that he had spied from the receptionist earlier in the day, successfully knocking off the state of the art alarm system. He then retrieved a cheap, pay as you go mobile from his pocket and dialled a ten-digit number from memory.

"All clear," he whispered into the phone, delighted with how well his plan was going so far.

A large removals truck was parked in front of Lawson and Associates, its hazard lights blinking brightly in the dark night. Davey and three accomplices, all sprouting fake facial hair and wearing identical overalls with matching baseball caps, hurriedly loaded various pieces of office furniture and equipment into the back of the truck. Davey happened to raise his head and spotted a Garda car cruising towards them. One of the accomplices also noticed the approaching lawmen and immediately alerted the two other lads. They glanced at Davey with growing concern and he knew too well that they were contemplating doing a legger.

"Relax the cacks, lads. I'll sort this out," he calmly said, his brain kicking into overdrive, trying to conjure up an excuse.

The Garda car pulled up next to the men and the passenger window was lowered.

"Alright, lads, working late?" asked the skinny, pimpled faced Garda.

"Ye know yerself, Guard. Have to do everythin' at night now, wha' with the parkin' restrictions and all that malarkey," Davey offered.

The Garda nodded. "You've plenty of help with you all the same," he said, sizing up the other men.

"Is that wha' they call it," laughed Davey. "I was gonna ask ye to arrest them for loiterin'."

The Garda was doing his best to remain serious in front of his colleague, but the edges of his upturned mouth were betraying him. "I'm sure they do their fair share. Don't overdo it," the young Garda advised.

"No fear of that," said Davey. "Shouldn't be much longer, we've almost cleared the place out."

"Night so," said the unsuspecting lawman.

The window was raised and the car pulled away. The pretend removals men broke into nervous laughter once the squad car was out of sight, feeling very relieved.

"Yer a mad bastard, don't know how ye kept a straight face," said one of the impressed accomplices.

Davey shrugged his shoulders, dismissing the compliment and said, "There wasn't a pick on yer man all the same, was there? D'ye remember years ago, all the coppers seemed to be big mad bastards from Kerry or Mayo, just waitin' for any excuse to bate the shite outta the Jackeens?"

The lads nodded in a kind of nostalgic agreement although they definitely preferred the modern, softly, softly approach. Thank God for those bleeding-heart liberals.

Chapter 4

The sun rose slowly over Mountjoy prison, doing its best to warm the gloomy, cold morning. Richie stood in line in the prison canteen waiting for feeding time at the zoo to begin. In fairness, the grub was a lot better than most people imagined and although it wasn't Michelin Star quality, what was on offer was far superior to anything the majority of the inmates had ever experienced at home.

Richie glanced to his left where a minor disturbance was taking place. A pumped-up inmate who obviously lived in the gym and swallowed steroids like they were going out of fashion was in a heated conversation with Richie's cellmate, Kelly. Richie was drawn to the wiry looking man standing next to the gym bunny. There was something unsettling about his appearance and stance, like a python poised to strike. Richie had heard about this bloke, a Mr. Quinn, and a nasty piece of work by all accounts. Kelly raised a finger and pointed it directly at Richie. Mr. Quinn glared over at Richie who brazenly stared back until a lag standing next to him in the queue discreetly kicked his shoe.

"I wouldn't if I was you, bud. The bloke ye gave the hidin' to just happens to be one of Quinn's cronies," he warned.

Maybe Richie's insistence on Kelly redecorating their cell with the football posters hadn't been such a good idea after all. He remembered a saying that he'd read somewhere one time about 'Hindsight being the foresight of an ignorant man'. Fuck it. What was done was done. He knew he better watch his back though from now on and he'd have to go see the governor about banging in for yet another transfer.

The receptionist flung open an office door inside Lawson & Associates and was stunned to find that the room was completely bare.

"This one's empty as well!" shouted a shocked female voice from an adjoining office. "Call the police!"

An unmarked Garda car with a flashing siren thrown on the dashboard was abandoned outside Lawson's, its front right wheel mounted on the footpath. In the reception area, detective Lyons, middle-aged, plump and wearing a grey skirt suit, stood next to her younger colleague, detective Cartland. In contrast, he was tall, athletic and business like. Lyons questioned the receptionist while Cartland took notes. The receptionist seemed to be more interested in the handsome Cartland's physical appearance rather than aiding the investigation much to the annoyance of Lyons'.

"Right, if you can think of anything relevant – no matter how trivial, call us immediately," Lyons said, emphasising the word 'relevant' while making no attempt to disguise her contempt for the silly little office girl. She knew she was being catty with the receptionist and the younger woman's tidy figure wasn't helping matters. She was well aware that she was carrying a few too many pounds for her own liking but she'd lost that lust for life and food had rapidly become her new best friend.

Cartland snapped his notebook shut and pocketed it before retrieving a business card from his inside jacket pocket and handing it to the office worker. The detectives then turned, making their leave.

"The courier..." muttered the receptionist, slightly unsure.

The detectives both turned.

"It's just that he came across as, you know, a bit of a scanger," she explained.

Cartland was seated behind the wheel of the unmarked car with Lyons sat next to him. She was busy on her mobile.

"Yes, m... e... s... s... i... n..., No Messin' couriers, based at Grand Canal Place," she said. Out of the corner of her eye she noticed that her colleague was eyeballing her legs, but she didn't let on. Even with the extra weight she'd put on over the years, her legs, to their credit, were standing the test of time.

"Find out the name of the biker who dropped off a package yesterday evening, just after five," she told her subordinate back at the station.

Fran gently placed his daughter, Laura, who was fast asleep, into her cot. He carefully pulled the colourful blanket, which her granny Reilly had lovingly crocheted, up to her shoulders then kissed his daughter softly on the forehead.

"Sweet dreams," he whispered.

He plodded back into the living-room, flopped onto the couch and attempted to switch the T.V. on using the remote but nothing happened. Davey had recently given him a gift of a 'dodgy box' which allowed him to access all the latest movies and sporting events for free. If he could get the damn thing working, that was. He suddenly remembered that he was supposed to pick up new batteries. He unclipped the back of the remote hoping that if he removed the batteries and switched them around, he might be able to squeeze the last bit of life out of them. He tried turning on the T.V. again and this time had more success. Scrolling through the movies that were available, the latest offering from your man with the wonky nose and the mallet head, whose name Fran could never remember, caught his eye. Just as he was getting settled the doorbell rang. He let out a sigh and reluctantly rose to his feet. Outside on the step a man's finger kept the doorbell engaged.

"Relax, will ye," Fran said, pulling open the hall door, fearing that the noise would wake Laura. He froze.

"Well, are ye gonna invite yer bro in or wha'?" asked the man who was dressed in a silky, multi-coloured shirt and pants, several sizes too big for him.

That man was Richie, Fran's younger brother and he had just escaped from the nick, not bothering to wait for a transfer in the finish.

Richie, now dressed in a skinny legged, track bottoms and tee-shirt belonging to his brother, towelled his hair dry. As he was doing this he bent forward and inspected a framed photo of Laura, his one and only niece. She was pictured with her late mother, Vicky, splashing about in a swimming pool in some sunny hotspot, all smiles and inflatable armbands. Fran entered the sitting room carrying two mugs of tea.

"Was there enough hot water for ye?" he asked.

"Ah, plenty, thanks," said Richie, taking one of the piping mugs from his brother. "She's a ringer for her Ma," he said, referring to the photo.

Fran half smiled. "She is indeed. It'll be Vicky's anniversary soon."

"Yeah? Is it a year already?" Richie asked.

"Two," answered his brother, his sadness barely diminished despite the amount of time that had passed.

"Didn't realise," Richie apologised. "Bein' locked up messes with your sense of time."

"I'll take yer word for that," Fran said.

"Are ye seein' anyone?" asked Richie.

"No," Fran answered defensively, the bluntness of the question catching him off guard.

"No?" pushed Richie, not one to be fobbed off so easily.

"I've been too busy."

"Ye did yer best for Vicky, ye know."

"Wasn't good enough though, was it?" Fran replied.

"It wasn't as if you were stickin' the gear into her veins. Ye can't keep livin' in the past. Gotta get on with it, even if it's just for the sake of the babby."

"Wish it was that easy," said Fran, taking a sip of his tea. "Don't know how I'll ever repay ye for wha' ye did that nigh'."

"Ye can start by findin' me somewhere to kip while I sort things out in me head. Seems how I can't stay here," Richie said, sulking.

"That's not fair. I'd let ye stay under any other circumstances but with Vicky's aul wan still fightin' for custody of Laura it leaves me with very little choice."

"I know, bro, that was below the belt," said Richie, immediately regretting his smart arsed remark.

"Look, I'll ring Mick. He should be able to organise somethin'," Fran suggested.

"If he's not too busy waxin' his car or shaggin' some bird," said Richie. Both men laughed.

"Suppose there was no way ye could have side-stepped the aggro inside, for a change?" asked Fran, "I mean ye were only in the Joy how long?"

"Ye sound like me Ma. I was gonna be banged up for the next few months with the big ape, had to show him I was nobody's lackey."

"Not that I probably want to know but how in the name of Jaysus did ye escape?"

"D'ye remember Johnny Dunne? From the old flats just off Dorset Street?" asked Richie.

"Ginger headed lad?"

Richie nodded, "That's him."

"The two of youse were as thick as thieves when ye were nippers," Fran said.

"A gas young fella," said Richie. "Hadn't seen him in donkey's years until I spotted him workin' on the bin lorry, collectin' the prison waste. He copped me straight away and sussed that I was to tryin' to do a bunk. Fair play, he let go of one of the big wheelie bins, lettin' it roll down the slipway and smash into the fence. It drew the screw's attention away long enough for me to be able to scale a fence and bail into another bin. Johnny then tipped me into the back of the lorry and the job was Oxo."

"Do the screws not check the waste?" Fran asked, amazed at the basic lapse in security.

"Would you stick yer nose in there?"

"Probably not. So that's wha' the bleedin' smell was when ye got here."

"Well ye hardly think it was me new cologne. Eau de Joy, wha'?" laughed Richie.

"Ye wouldn't know with you lot. Yis make yer own gargle after all."

"The hooch? Rot the bleedin' teeth outta yer head that stuff. Full of sugar."

"Are they dressin' yis like MC Hammer in prison as well?" Fran jokingly asked, referring to the colourful, African dashiki suit that Richie had been wearing when he first arrived on the doorstep.

"Snatched it off some line in a back garden on the way here. I was in a bit of a hurry."

Large ornate gates guarded the entrance to the impressive turn of the century manor property. Immaculately landscaped gardens with manicured lawns framed the sweeping pebble driveway while an empty child's swing gently swayed in the warm breeze. Mick's sports car was parked next to a second tasty motor opposite the big oak hall door. A woman's voice could be faintly heard drifting down from an upstairs window where the curtains fluttered in the wind.

"Hmm, oh..." moaned the woman. She was dressed in stockings, high heels and a blindfold and was straddling Mick, who was completely naked, on the four-poster bed. The walnut panelled walls were adorned with paintings of stern-faced pilgrims all of whom appeared to be glaring condescendingly down at the cavorting couple.

"Oh God, oh, oh..." babbled the woman, completely caught up in the moment.

Beads of sweat had formed on Mick's contorted face. His eyes were shut tight as he grasped the pristine white sheets. Outside, an approaching car crushed the loose limestone pebble beneath its tyres as it made its way towards the grand house. Mick's eyes shot open. He turned his head towards the open window, listening intently. Children's playful laughter, followed by car doors slamming shut rose up from below.

"Careful, Simon, don't push her too high," warned a posh female voice from outside.

"Yes, yes, oh yes!" screamed the woman who was now bucking wildly on top of Mick oblivious to the impending aggro.

He grabbed her by the shoulders and shouted, "Oh fucking no!"

The startled woman was then unceremoniously dumped onto the floor on her backside. Mick scampered to the window, peeking out through the flapping curtains. The woman tore the blindfold off.

"What the fuck is she doing back?" Mick asked himself aloud. "Shit."

The well-dressed, posh speaking lady balanced two small schoolbags under one arm while inserting a key into the front hall door. Inside the upstairs bedroom Mick and his female companion were frantically running around trying to collect their scattered clothing.

"Come on, come on," Mick urged.

The posh lady entered the empty kitchen, glanced around and left. She opened a cupboard that had been cleverly designed to fit under the stairs and put away the schoolbags before climbing the expensively carpeted stairs. Pausing momentarily outside a closed door, she made a strange face then turned the brass knob. The door eased open. Mick and the woman were now both fully clothed and standing casually in the centre of the room with Mick pointing to the paintings on the walls.

"All of which are included in the price of course," he informed his nervous companion.

Mick turned towards the woman standing in the open doorway. "Oh there you are, Lady Wallace," he continued without missing a beat. "This is Miss Richardson. I've just finished giving her the tour of your splendid home and she's become quite excited."

Both Mick and Lady Wallace observed Miss Richardson from the bedroom window as she hurried towards her car and almost lost her footing such was her haste to escape. She jumped into her car and sped away, past the children who were still playing on the garden swing oblivious to the carry on inside the great house. Lady Wallace positioned herself directly behind Mick and slipped her arms around his waist.

"She was anxious to get off," she whispered into his ear, giving the lobe a gentle nibble.

Mick deftly slipped from her hold, making for the door. "I have to go, there's this merger I must hammer home," he said, apologising profusely, clasping his hands together prayer-like.

Lady Wallace gave a long, exaggerated sigh as if she'd heard it all before.

Mick paused. "Look, I'll ring you later, I promise."

The lady of the manor folded her arms not believing a single word out of the scoundrel's mouth. Mick walked back to her and kissed her full on the lips while giving her pert posterior a gentle squeeze and said, "I swear."

Mick sprinted towards his car as the children looked on.

"Bye, Uncle Michael," they called out in unison.

"Cheerio, kids," he replied, waving up to Lady Wallace at the same time.

She coyly waved back but Mick had already hopped into his Porsche and was gone. Sniffing the air, she noticed the discarded blindfold lying on the floor. She picked it up, held it to her breasts and shook her head. He was such a rascal, she knew that. She also knew that she should have nothing more to do with him, but the truth was that he was a terrific fuck who'd never once shown even the slightest interest in her money, a rarity in her circles.

The Porsche raced along the narrow country road in pursuit of Miss Richardson's vehicle. Aided by his car's powerful German engine, it didn't take Mick long to catch up and he spotted his prey a short distance ahead. With a risky manoeuvre he just about managed to overtake on a tight bend, forcing his latest conquest to pull into a deserted lay-by. Miss Richardson exited her car slamming the door, her face fit for murder. Undeterred, Mick climbed out of his motor, wearing a hopeful grin.

"You're an estate agent?" she yelled.

The rogue shrugged his muscular shoulders.

"You lying pig," she added, trying to strike him across the face.

Mick caught her hand and held it with the minimum amount of pressure. "I never actually said that I lived there," he softly replied.

She made a feeble attempt to pull away but with no real conviction. "Yes, well..." she said, having calmed down somewhat.

Mick wrapped a powerful arm around Miss Richardson's waist drawing her closer. "Don't tell me you didn't enjoy it, the thrill of almost getting caught?" he teased.

A spark flickered in her eyes which Mick picked up on almost immediately. He took this as his cue to continue where they'd left off. He guided her onto the bonnet of her car without resistance, began kissing her passionately while sliding her skirt upwards with a free hand.

The city centre estate agents was a hive of activity. Sales chatter from the commission driven staff reverberated throughout the open-plan space. Mick waltzed in as if he hadn't a care in the world. One of the new junior employees, an impressionable lad name Keith who was barely out of college, put down the phone receiver, scratching a name off the list sitting on his desk.

He glanced up at Mick. "You look like the cat that got the cream!"

"A gentleman doesn't kiss and tell," Mick said, pretending to be offended.

Before Keith could delve any further into Mick's legendary sexploitations, the owner, the bespectacled Mr. Watts, rapped on the glass wall of his cube-like office at the far corner. He pointed to his wristwatch, throwing his hands into the air in exasperation.

Keith immediately picked up the phone and began scribbling, trying to look busy. "The old man's going to give you an earful," he said out of the side of his mouth.

Mick threw a casual shrug then sauntered up to Mr. Watts' door, gave a polite tap and entered.

Watts retrieved a large envelope from a filing cabinet and tossed it to Mick. "I want you to handle this one. You won't have far to go, it's right up your street, literally."

Mick caught the envelope and although curious to see which one of his neighbours was leaving for pastures new, he didn't look inside.

"Are we any closer to finalising the sale of Lady Wallace's place?" the older man asked. He stared over his solid framed glasses and said, "You seem to be spending an awful lot of time up there lately."

"Wanted to make sure I knew the entire place inside and out and that I'd covered everything," Mick replied, giving nothing away. "And I'm getting there."

"Well, try and get there a little bit quicker. The commission will be massive," his boss ordered. He had his suspicions as to what was likely going on but if Mick could flip the property, he didn't really give a toss what else he was flipping.

Mick remained silent, choosing to give a slight nod of the head by way of a reply. Mr. Watts removed his glasses, giving the bridge of his nose a gentle massage. "You know, Mick," he said, "You've got that certain something that just can't be taught in this business, especially when it comes to the ladies. And if you tried even a smidgeon harder you could make a very decent living out of this game."

The unmarked Garda car eased up outside Davey's house. Detective Lyons turned to her partner, Cartland. "Let me handle this. Myself and the toe-rag have history," she said.

Cartland made no reply but was more than happy to comply.

Davey stood in his rear garden wearing a stern expression, his mobile phone pressed tightly against his ear. Behind him was the entrance to a large concrete shed with the reinforced metal doors slightly ajar.

"Ah Jaysus, Jacko. The Ma's due back next week," he complained. He turned and looked into the shed, shaking his head. It was full to the brim with the stolen office furniture from Lawson's & Associates. "I've no choice now, have I? Yeah, I'll have to find somewhere else to stash it then." The doorbell rang and he gave a look in its general direction. "I've gotta go." He hung up on Jacko. "Fuckin' amateurs."

Cartland pressed the doorbell again. As he was doing so, Lyons was discreetly checking out his muscular ass, not realising that she was also slowly tracing the circumference of her mouth with the tip of her tongue. Davey pulled open the front door and was surprised to see the two detectives. He mentally chastised himself for not looking through the spy-hole first.

"Hello, Mr. Byrne and how are we today?" Lyons said, pleasantly greeting Davey as if they were old friends but knowing only too well just how uncomfortable her unannounced visit was going to be for him. "Let's have a chat about some missing furniture, shall we?"

Davey was made of sterner stuff and although caught on the hop he wasn't one to lie down without fighting his corner. "Well, if it's not Ireland's answer to Cagney and Lacey," he said, referring to his Ma's favourite eighties detective show. "Kick Me and Lick Me. The country can sleep soundly in its bed tonight knowin' that the force's most intelligent operatives are hot on the case."

The police were suitably unimpressed.

"At least yer not the fat ugly one," Davey added, blowing Cartland a kiss.

The detectives ignored his antics and brushed past him into the house. Davey knew by the scowl on Lyons' mush that he had already pressed the right buttons.

Cartland poked around the assorted ornaments that were lined up along the mantelpiece in the living-room, pausing to look inside a vase decorated in a flowery, oriental style pattern much to Davey's annoyance.

"I have a receipt," the homeowner challenged.

Cartland smirked.

"Didn't know you were into fishing?" Lyons said, probing for a weakness.

Davey was at a loss for a split second until he saw the detective looking at the canvas bag sitting on the timber floor. The bag was partially open with the dismantled fibreglass rod pieces exposed. He knew he should have dumped it on his way home last night but he was going to give it to the young fella living down the road who's Da had only recently been made redundant.

"Fishing?" repeated Lyons, snapping the suspect from his thoughts.

"In a big way, Ms. Lyons," Davey answered.

"You have a license, I presume?" She also enjoyed playing the game.

"I've been rehabilitated and am now a law abidin' citizen, as well you know. Will I get it for ye now? I keep it next to the one I have for the telly and under the one I have for me dog."

Lyons dismissed him with her hand. "There's no need, for the time being."

Davey had never owned a dog but when he heard a rumour that the social welfare gave you twelve quid a week towards its upkeep, he was all over it like a rash. Proof of ownership was a license which only cost a score for the year. It was a no brainer except it wasn't fucking true. Not one to be conned, especially not when it benefited the government, he applied to the social for an Exceptional Needs Payment to have his imaginary dog neutered and micro-chipped. Unbelievable as it was, he recouped his license fee and more than doubled his money.

"Freshwater or salt?" Lyons pursued.

"Wha'?" asked Davey.

"Do you fish in rivers or in the sea?" Lyons said, mouthing the words slowly in a fish-like kind of way.

"Ah the sea, definitely the sea. Find it a bigger challenge, especially them pikes, vicious bast..." he noticed Lyons' stern expression, "...yokes."

After twenty minutes of looking about and repetitive questioning and getting absolutely nowhere in the process, the detectives were done.

"We'll be keeping a close watch," Lyons informed Davey.

"Watch away, yer highness but ye'd wanna be careful, this sounds a lot like police harassment to me. I migh' even have to get onto the Ombudsman," replied Davey, more than a little relieved that nothing had been found in the raid.

Lyons stuck her face into the suspect's. "I know it was you who stole that furniture and I'm going to reel you in by the balls, no matter how long it takes."

Davey took a step back. "Got the wrong man. Like I told ye already," he said, "I'm after gettin' meself a small bit of work and I'm on the straight and narrow now."

He followed Lyons and Cartland to the front door, ushering them outside as quickly as they would allow.

Lyons paused and turned. "By the way, pike are freshwater fish," she said, correcting his earlier mistake.

The detectives got into their car and drove off at speed.

"Shite," Davey cursed as the car disappeared from sight, annoyed that he'd made such a basic slip up. If only he'd listened more when he was at school besides always acting the maggot, he might have learned something useful.

The day after Richie's prison escape, Fran rang Mick hoping that he could sort his brother out with somewhere to lay low until some semblance of a plan could be concocted. Mick hadn't exactly been brought up to speed with regards to Richie's newfound freedom, i.e. doin' a leggin' job from the nick until he'd collected the two lads by which stage it was far too late to back out. He wasn't one bit happy about the situation, but Fran had somehow coaxed him into becoming an unwilling accomplice. This was a talent that Fran possessed and had used on Mick many times before in the past. Carefully steering his newly repaired car, Mick looked at Fran who was sitting next to him and shook his head.

"Thanks again," said Fran.

His friend didn't reply.

"Well, Mick, how's the ridin' goin'?" asked Richie from the back seat. "Still gettin' yer fair share?"

"Up to my eyes, as a matter of fact. I was actually thinking of taking a lad on," Mick answered.

"Good to hear. Any chance of sortin' yer man out?" Richie said, playfully clipping Fran across the back of the head.

"Lost cause, I'm afraid," Mick answered.

"Give it a rest," laughed Fran, disguising his true feelings. He was getting fed up with how much interest everyone else seemed to be taking in his love life or lack of it. He knew they meant well but he wasn't ready to get involved with anyone new. He wasn't sure if he'd ever be ready.

The lads drove up to closed wrought iron gates that looked as if they weighed a ton if you had the misfortune of them falling on top of you. Mick, using some sophisticated App on his mobile was able to open them without getting out.

"Harry Potter eat yer heart out," said Richie, as if the whole process was some sort of black magic.

Mick was going to show him another App on his phone that allowed him to see what was inside the fridge but thought better of it. He didn't want to blow the poor fucker's mind altogether. They drove past a 'For Sale' sign, pulling up next to a circular fountain type roundabout. Fran and Richie followed Mick out of the Porsche, pausing to admire the stylish property while Mick unlocked the front door.

"This is some gaff. Yer man must be sellin' the gear big time, wha'?" commented Richie.

Mick forced a smile, discreetly catching Fran by the arm and allowing Richie to enter the house first.

"I could get dismissed for this," Mick warned his friend.

"I know, bud, appreciate it," Fran said. "But it's not as if he'll be throwin' any wild parties now, is it?"

As if on cue loud noises came blaring from the living-room. Mick glanced at Fran who could only manage a shrug of his shoulders by way of a response. They went inside the house and followed what seemed like hundreds of voices cheering loudly until they came to a room where they found Richie stretched out on a tan leather couch, shoes and socks already kicked off, engrossed in a computer soccer game.

"Right, Richie. The clients are due back in the country at the end of the month to check how things are proceeding so you'll have to be gone by then," Mick explained, almost having to shout above the racket. He was already regretting helping his friend's brother out.

"Gooooal!" roared Ritchie. He leapt up from the couch, pulled his top over his head and ran around the sofa in celebration. Mick caressed the purple coloured vein that had popped out on the side of his forehead. The stress was starting to overwhelm him.

Fran, sensing that his friend was close to having a meltdown, put a hand on his shoulder and gently gave it a squeeze. "He'll be long gone by then. I'll make sure of it."

Chapter 5

1ˢᵗ Round Qualifier (Replay): Sporting Les Behans' v Newton Rangers

Sporting Les Behans' were huddled together outside their truck container dressing room. Baxter was trying in vain to open the lock using a large collection of keys which he'd somehow managed to accumulate over the years when Mick pulled up in his car and lowered the window.

"There's no need to panic, I'm here," Mick haughtily announced.

Baxter glanced up but held his tongue. Some of the lads threw their eyes skywards while others groaned.

"It's okay, not everyone gets the intellectual jokes," Mick said to his less than amused audience. "What's up?"

"Some scally's jammed the lock," Baxter said, fuming.

"Why don't you try picking it?" suggested Mick.

"Now there's somethin' we never considered," Charlie said.

"Probably due to our lack of intellect," Yoyo said, chipping in.

Mick said nothing. Baxter squinted at the backseat passenger, trying to make them out. "Is that Davey?" he asked, impatiently.

Fran leaned across from the front passenger seat towards the open window. "No Boss, it's a surprise."

"Where's Davey so? It's Baltic out here." Baxter said, disregarding Fran's comment. "We were banking on him to open it for us."

"Runnin' late, had to drop somethin' off first," explained Fran.

Baxter turned to the rest of the players and rubbed his hands briskly together. "Looks like you're togging off al fresco."

"Who's he?" Jigsaw asked, wondering had they been jammy enough to sign some Italian player. He then quickly put that thought to bed knowing that there was no way they would have been able to afford the transfer fee.

"Who?" said Charlie.

"Al Fresco? Is he yer man from the chipper?" Jigsaw innocently asked.

"He means outside, ye bleedin' dope," said Podge.

"Outside?" repeated Jigsaw, more than a little alarmed. "But the place is full of robbers and perverts."

Baxter rested a hand on his worried striker's shoulder. "And that's just your own teammates, soft lad."

As if to further emphasise the point Charlie grabbed hold of his crotch and began to sleazily rub himself while flicking his tongue back and forth at the same time.

A short while later Davey arrived at the pitch on his motorbike, parked up and hurried over to the side-line where the game was already in progress. Sporting Les Behans' were wearing their white, tattered Murray's Pub jerseys. Someone had drawn a large black cross through their former sponsor's name using a thick permanent marker.

"The X-Men," Davey said to Gonzales who was viewing the match from his modified electric wheelchair. A megaphone had been crudely attached to the arm of the chair with a hinge, allowing it to be moved back and forth with ease. Gonzales stared at Davey, a puzzled look on his face.

"Do I know you?" Gonzales eventually asked.

"It's me, Davey," said Davey.

The lad in the wheelchair wore a blank expression.

"Davey Byrne, the outstanding winger with the dazzlin' footwork and the killer good looks?" he tried again, flashing a cheesy grin.

Gonzales shook his head 'no' before driving away over the bockety surface and almost toppling over, all the while muttering a string of profanities to himself.

'He'd have been better off if he'd fuckin' died in that accident,' Davey thought.

"Man on!" roared Baxter, alerting Gitsy to the impending danger from the opposition player who was closing in fast.

"Ye can't say that anymore, Pa. FIFA have said it's now an offence to use discriminatory language like that," Davey said, walking towards the manager.

"Give over and don't be daft," Baxter replied but his player's expression remained serious. "So what am I supposed to shout?"

"Person non gender specific on."

"What?"

"It's a mouthful, I know."

"But by the time you'd spit that out the player would be upended."

"Unfortunately, that's the world we're livin' in nowadays," said Davey. He spotted Richie wearing a Phantom of the Opera type mask, terrorising the opposition with his silky skills and lightning pace. Richie ran the length of the pitch, dribbling the ball past several Newton Ranger's players and nutmegging another one before finally blasting the ball into the roof of the net. He was mobbed by his teammates as the dejected opposition players looked on. Davey shook his head admiringly. "Wha' a complete and utter waste of talent."

Baxter couldn't help himself from jumping up and down, his fists clenched in the air. "Did you see that? The la is a legend!" he shouted.

"Never lost it alrigh'. Wha' did the ref say about him wearin' the mask?" asked Davey.

"Told him he's protecting a fractured cheekbone. Seemed happy enough," said the gaffer

He took a packet of chewing gum from his coat pocket and popped the remaining stick into his mouth watched closely by Davey. "Sorry, it's me last one. You can have half though, if you want?" He began to remove the partly chewed stick of gum from his gob.

"Yer alrigh'," Davey quickly replied, lying. "Dentist said I shouldn't."

"Your loss."

Davey nodded.

The manager shoved the gum back in.

"It's a pity the way things panned out for Richie in England," said Baxter. "Rumour has it that he was just about to break into the first team."

"I know, and at sixteen," Davey said, recalling the story he'd heard at the time.

"What went wrong?"

"Never said, so I never asked."

"Shame all the same."

Baxter motioned towards the truck container where a gang of kids were sitting on top. "As soon as the game is over, open that lock for me, will you? One of those little bastards did something to it."

"Give them a break," Davey encouraged.

"Break? I'll snap their fecking necks. Waste of space the lot of them. Every week before training I have to spend nearly an hour cleaning up their shit."

"They shit on the pitch?" Davey said, joking.

"You know well what I mean. Don't try to wind me up, lad," Baxter warned.

"Hearts and minds," Davey said.

"What are you on about now?" asked the manager, his patience wearing thin.

"Somethin' I seen on the tele the other nigh', about soldiers in occupied territories," Davey explained.

Baxter furrowed his brow. "I know this might seem harsh, son, but you need to get out more often and goose some bird."

Davey smiled.

When the referee blew for full-time, Davey motioned for the manager to follow him over to the truck container. He removed a key from his pocket, slid it into the lock and opened it without any problems. He then pulled the container door open as Baxter watched with growing curiosity.

"What in the name of Christ have you gotten yourself into now?" the manager asked, genuinely concerned for his player.

The container was packed to the ceiling with the stolen office furniture from Lawson's.

"Storage problems," Davey replied.

"You can't keep it here."

"Won't be for long. Have a geezer lined up."

Baxter scratched his chin, a thoughtful look on his mug. "Do you know where my allotment is?"

"By the canal?"

"The very place. Call up to me during the week, I might have a solution for you. Now lock that back up before the rest of the lads see what's inside."

The Sporting lads were ecstatic coming off the field after their five-nil demolition of Newton Rangers. It was the team's first ever cup win as well as their biggest natural high in years.

"Davey managed to get the container open but it's out of bounds for the time being," Baxter told his players.

None of the lads seemed to be that bothered, probably due to the victory. As they were changing back into their normal clothes, eagerly looking forward to the upcoming session in Frank's, Charlie turned to Yoyo and said, "Ye'd wanna get that shop of yers up and runnin' like a good man."

"Relax, will ye," replied Yoyo, trying to balance an oversized first aid box under his arm. "I'm tryin' to get things sorted as fast as I can." He looked to Baxter for inspiration.

"What about using Power's van?" said the manager.

"Suppose it'll have to do," Yoyo said.

Paddy Power's van was empty apart from some old furniture he'd been paid to dump. This provided Yoyo with enough space for his pop-up shop. He sat cross-legged in the back and opened his modified first aid box which resembled a travelling salesman's case. "All righ', girls, shop's now open," he gleefully announced.

Inside the case hidden behind bandages and dressings was an assortment of drugs held in place by clear plastic pouches neatly arranged in alphabetical order.

Jigsaw was over like a shot. "Need somethin' to give me a good buzz. Nothin' too heavy though."

Yoyo let his hand hover over the top row before settling on a package containing several circular white disc-like tablets. "These should do the job but yer better off dissolvin' them in water first, gets into the aul bloodstream that bit quicker. Ye'll be on a mad one before ye know it."

"Deadly," said Jigsaw.

Yoyo smiled and said, "A tenner will do." Jigsaw was delighted with himself and paid up. No matter what the striker asked for, Yoyo always gave him a couple of Alka Seltzer, sometimes crushed up. The other lads knew the score but never let on. And unlike the rest of them after a hard session, Jigsaw never suffered from heartburn.

Mick was next in line. "The usual," he said.

Yoyo slipped his customer a plastic bag containing a gram of white powder. "Anythin' else?"

"Need a few E's as well," said Mick.

"Ah, the aul disco biscuits. Watch ye don't get dehydrated," Yoyo advised.

"Don't be such an ignoramus. They're hardly for me," Mick said.

"Oh, righ'. The drug of choice for the younger ladies." Mick didn't answer. "They're a fiver each or ten for forty," said Yoyo.

"I'll take ten."

"Sound. That's one forty in total."

Mick handed over three fifties not bothering to wait for his change nor a receipt that would never be issued.

"More money than sense," Yoyo said under his breath about his affluent client.

It was Huey's turn next. "Roach, please," he politely asked.

"Can't go too far wrong with the Benzos," the amateur chemist said, dispensing a clear pocket-sized plastic bag of tablets.

"Thanks," said Huey.

"Hurry up, seizure boy," slagged Podge from further down the line.

Huey was absolutely mortified. "I don't have seizures, they're for a nervous condition."

Trigger tapped Podge on the back. "This isn't the queue for the battered burgers, fatso."

Podge took the hint and immediately shut his cakehole. When everyone who needed medicating was sorted, Baxter sidled up to the amicable drug dealer.

"Repeat prescription?" Yoyo discreetly asked, already knowing the answer.

Baxter nodded.

Yoyo gave the boss a pack of four blue friends. Baxter slipped the Viagra into the inside pocket of his coat and paid for his tablets.

"Is the defibrillator charged?" asked Yoyo.

"What's that?" said Baxter. Not really listening.

"The defibrillator? Can't be too careful, all that ridin' at yer age."

"Cheeky beggar."

The prison visiting room was busy and extremely loud. Most of the women who were calling to see their partners were accompanied by crying children either hanging out of them or cowering behind them. The stress levels all around were heightened as a result. A well-dressed, tarty looking blonde who obviously had the time and money to pamper herself sat across from Mr. Quinn, bucking the trend. She looked as if she hadn't a care in the world as she leaned towards her man and began to smooch him.

"Give it a rest, lovebirds," ordered the prison warder who was patrolling that particular area.

The gang boss and the blonde broke free.

"When you're gone, love, we don't want him taking it out on some poor innocent lad," the smart arsed screw added.

"Fuck off," said Quinn, not caring who he threatened.

The screw grinned but was clever enough to move further along the rows of inmates and their visitors.

Mr. Quinn grabbed the blonde by her wrist, holding it in a vice-like grip. The woman winced and tried to pull back her arm, but her partner wasn't ready to let go just yet.

"I don't want Richie Reilly to walk again, let alone kick a bleedin' ball. Is that understood?" he said, his face twisting in an ugly snarl.

The blonde climbed into the back seat of the car that was waiting for her outside the prison. She detested these weekly visits, particularly the waiting room. She always feared catching something off the pathetic women and their snotty nosed brats. Low-lifes. That was how she classed them since managing to drag herself out of the stereotypical gutter. The driver tapped the steering wheel drum-like awaiting further instructions.

"Wha' did he say then?" he finally asked.

The blonde looked at him. He was dressed in a dark tailored suit with a matching six o'clock shadow. A broody type of bloke. Good-looking, apart from the fact that his name was Stevo and that he was paid to chauffer her back and forth to the prison she knew very little else about him. She removed a folded piece of paper from her mouth and held it aloft.

The Sporting players were seated around several tables that had been pulled together in Frank the Publican's back lounge. Every conceivable space was awash with gargle. Birdy appeared from around a corner with a glass of lemonade in his hand and was immediately spotted by Baxter. The manager got to his feet, a little unsteady and put an arm around his new goalkeeper's athletic shoulders.

"Ah, there you are, ar kid. Right, time to formally introduce you to the rest of the boys." The team members paused their various conversations and looked at Birdy. "Up front we have Jigsaw, goes to pieces in the box," the manager explained.

The team laughed. Jigsaw frowned.

"Next is Trigger. Armed robber..."

"Alleged," interrupted Trigger.

"Convicted," continued Baxter, "And a deadly finisher too. In midfield we have Huey, you've already seen him in action..." Baxter whispered into Birdy's ear, "The aul nerves can get the better of him." The manager addressed his players once again. "There's Podge..."

56

Podge, beaming smile, raised his pint.

"...Sharon's gimp."

The team cheered loudly, some banged their glasses on the tables.

"I'll tell her ye said that," Podge said, threatening the gaffer but with no real conviction. He slumped back in his seat, folding his arms in a huff.

"Who knitted your face and dropped a stitch?" the manager said to his sulking player but there was no reply. "We have Mick 'Lord of the Rings' Young."

Birdy looked puzzled.

"As in women's rings," Baxter explained. Birdy was still none the wiser. Charlie made a circle out of his thumb and index finger. He then proceeded to rapidly poke the hole that this created with his other finger. Birdy got the picture.

"People in glasshouses," Mick said, reminding the boss that he was also partial to the ladies.

"Quite true, Michael," noted the manager. "We have Yoyo, on that many chemicals he's up and down like a brasser's knickers at a packed race meet."

Yoyo didn't fully understand the analogy but still jumped up and down to emphasise the point.

"Sit down you divvy," said Baxter, jokingly scolding the jester.

"Then there's Charlie, wishes for a white Christmas every day of the year..." Baxter touched his nose, "...if you catch my drift. We've Davey 'Houdini' Byrne. Now you see it, now you don't and that's usually your wallet."

"That's libel!" Davey shouted, pretending to be hurt but not really giving a toss one way or the other.

"You mean slander," Baxter said, correcting his player, "Libel is defamation in the written word."

"Ye knew wha' I fuckin' meant all the same," Davey said, enjoying the banter.

Baxter continued undeterred. "There's Paddy Power, would bet on two flies having a wank."

Power made a wanking gesture to emphasise the point. "Pull the other one, Boss," he said dryly.

"Touching," said Baxter. "There's Al, aka the Assassin, a centre-half known to have taken out a few people in his time."

The Assassin made a gun out of his fingers, pointed it at the goalkeeper and fired before blowing away the imaginary smoke rising from his finger barrel.

"Then there's Split the Wind, Ireland's answer to Bruce Lee..." Split squinted, did a few rapid chop-chop moves with his hands, accidentally knocking over his pint in the process much to the delight of his gathered teammates. He fumbled about trying to clean up the mess taking care not to spill anymore drink. Baxter threw his eyes to heaven.

"And Gitsy..." Gitsy sneezed. "...the boy in the bubble. Allergic to life but with a better left foot than Christy Brown." Gitsy blew his nose loudly into his handkerchief using one hand while acknowledging Birdy with the other.

"And not forgetting poor Fran. Lovely chap but we think he's gone to the dark side."

"Can a bloke not just fly solo for a while," pleaded Fran.

"Not natural," Mick said.

"Are there any ladies in your circus, Birdy?" asked Baxter.

"Many. All very beautiful," Birdy answered in his Eastern European accent.

"Suppose they probably wear those figure hugging costumes?" prodded Baxter, licking his lips at the thought of it all.

"Beautiful costumes, yes, for sure," said Birdy.

"And they'd be, fit?" Baxter asked as he took a sip from his pint.

"Oh yes. And, don't know how you say, very bendy," Birdy honestly replied.

Baxter spat out some of his drink almost choking with the excitement. He wiped his chin clean with his sleeve. "You'll have to introduce me to these wonderful young women sometime..." he said.

Fran piped up. "Watch him! Pa Baxter has fathered enough kids to populate a small African country."

"Where is best player, Richie?" Birdy asked.

"Under a curfew of sorts," answered Baxter, not wanting to reveal too much to the newest member of the squad although with the few drinks on board he'd probably already said more than enough.

"Curfew?" questioned Birdy, not familiar with the word.

"Not allowed out late, can't go to pubs and all that," Fran explained.

"Maybe reason he score five goals today," Birdy bluntly replied.

"Suppose," the manager said, conceding the point.

Mick leaned in closer to Fran. "That motor show I was telling you about is on tomorrow."

"Sorry, Bud, can't go. Why don't ye ask one of the other lads, Yoyo or someone?" suggested Fran.

"Yoyo? Are you serious? That imbecile probably thinks Top Gear is a show about drugs. What have you got on that's so important that you're unable to make time for your best friend?"

"One of my many best friends," Fran said, grinning.

Mick pretended to be put out.

"Promised the Ma I'd drop around to Tracey Mallon's, her washin' machine is on the blink."

"Tracey Mallon… Tracey Mallon…" Mick pondered aloud. "I know that name from somewhere."

Fran gave him a huge smile, flashing his teeth, trying to jog Mick's memory but without much success.

"Tracey Tracks?" Fran then said, giving his pal a further hint.

"The curly little Umpa Lumpa with the braces?" Mick asked incredulously.

"That's a bit harsh."

"You reckon? So, what's she doing since Wonka shut the factory?"

"Workin' in Cadburys in Coolock."

"Are you serious?"

Fran smirked.

"Fucker," said Mick, disappointed that he'd fallen for that one. "Haven't seen her since primary school, where's she living?"

"One of the terraced houses just off King's Street."

"A most salubrious part of town with excellent resale values no less. Married?"

"Not anymore. She was with a bloke from the Southside, turned out to be a real arsehole, so the Ma says."

"Those mixed marriages never work out," Mick said, his face remaining deadpan. "Anyway," he continued, "You'd better watch yourself there, mate. Don't be tempted if she decides to show you her appreciation." He made blowjob gestures followed by chomping actions.

"Yer a sick man, d'ye know that?" said Fran.

Mick smiled. "So my therapist keeps on telling me."

Davey stood at the polished bar counter with a neatly folded sports top resting on it. Frank the Publican topped up pints for the thirsty customers who were glued to the big screen watching the closing stages of a very competitive Gaelic football match. The team in blue seemed to be the fittest side and were starting to get the upper hand.

"Are ye ready or wha'?" Davey asked, trying to hurry things along.

"Just a tick," Frank said, finishing his task. He noticed Davey looking up at the screen and said. "Are ye into the GAA yourself?"

"Fifteen keepers against fifteen keepers? Fuck that," answered Davey. "How come there's no yoke on my tele?"

"The pint symbol?" Frank asked, in reference to the Sports logo at the bottom of the screen.

"Yeah?"

"It's only for pubs and business premises. Ye don't get it with an ordinary viewin' card."

"How much does it set ye back?" quizzed Davey, his interest mounting.

"Too feckin' much. It's up for renewal next week. Although in fairness, with the way your gang are shiftin' the drink, it won't be long payin' for itself."

Davey chewed on a fingernail, a thoughtful look on his face. "Do me a favour and don't renew it just yet. Give me a few days, I've an idea developin'."

Frank lowered his voice. "I'm not into anythin' illegal," he said.

"Aren't ye a publican?"

"And what's that got to do with it?"

"Well, the prices ye charge are criminal."

"If you saw the rates I have to pay..."

"I'm only buzzin' with ye, buddy," Davey said. "It'll all be above board, kinda. D'ye know anyone else who migh' be interested?"

"I've a few cousins who have bars."

"Righ', get me the numbers and we'll talk hard cash next week," Davey said, using all of his experience to up sell.

Davey strolled to the back of the pub followed by the eager pub owner. "Lads. Lads," said Davey, trying to be heard above the racket being made by his teammates but failing miserably. He stuck two fingers in his mouth and gave a loud whistle. "A bit of order for a minute!" he shouted.

Mick turned to Fran. "What's he up to?"

"God only knows," his friend replied.

"Give the chance a chap," Split said, trying to be funny but everybody ignored him as per usual.

"As yis know we have cut our ties with our former sponsor, Mr. Murray," Davey announced.

"The hungry fuck!" Jigsaw shouted.

"A very apt description, lad," Baxter said, complementing his player's judge of character.

"With my entrepreneurial genius..." continued Davey.

"Your wha'?" Power called out.

"Get on with it," said Fran.

Davey smiled. "As I was tryin' to explain…"

Charlie cupped his hands and went, "Boooo."

"I've found us a new sponsor," Davey said as he slapped the beaming Frank the Publican on the back. The team clapped wildly in appreciation.

"Free gargle for everyone!" Yoyo shouted in jest.

Davey pointed a finger at his unruly teammate. "Show some respect, you." He turned his attention back to the rest of his gathered audience. "The new set of jerseys is ordered but we've already managed to get hold of the trainin' tops. It goes without sayin' that we've had to change our name…" He gave Frank the nod. "So I made an executive decision."

The publican took his cue and unfurled the new training top. The team looked on, confused expressions to a man.

"What the…" said Baxter, his face reddening.

Written on the top in bold black letters was the team's new name, SPORTING LES BEHANS.

Chapter 6

Holding his battered, metal toolbox in one hand, Fran pressed the doorbell with the other. A few seconds had passed when a tall, stunning looking woman wearing a modest, knee length summery dress appeared.

"Sorry about this," said Fran, blushing, "I must have been given the wrong address, was lookin' for a Tracey Mallon. D'ye happen to know if she lives around here?"

The woman smiled warmly, displaying a perfectly aligned set of teeth. "You've got the right place, Fran Reilly."

Fran was momentarily at a loss until it clicked. He was staring at Tracey 'Tracks' and boy hadn't she changed.

Crouched on his hunkers, Fran watched the clothes almost trance-like as they slowly went around and around inside the washing machine. He eventually checked over his shoulder to where Tracey was sitting on the edge of the kitchen countertop, one of her high heeled shoes dangling seductively from her foot. Suddenly realising that he was staring at his customer far longer than was politely acceptable he sprung to his feet, more than a little embarrassed. Although Tracey remained quiet, the edges of her mouth curled upwards into a bold smile. Fran wiped his oily spanner clean with the bottom of his white t-shirt, shoved it back into his toolbox and headed for the sink to wash up. Adjusting her shoe first, Tracey slid gently off the counter and smoothed her dress. She handed Fran a clean towel once he'd finished rinsing his hands.

"Cheers," he said, not trusting himself to say much more.

The washing machine began to speed up, its hypnotic spinning drawing both sets of eyes towards it. It then started to vibrate, nice and easy at first before growing louder and shaking more violently.

Tracey turned to Fran. "Don't suppose you want to give it a try?" Fran's eyes opened wide, his cheeks flushing. Tracey did her best to stifle a laugh. She pointed at Fran's dirty white t-shirt indicating that it could do with a good wash.

"Oh, I'm alrigh', thanks," said Fran, feeling like a bigger tool than the one he'd thrown into his box moments earlier.

"What do I owe you?" asked Tracey, feeling a little guilty for teasing the poor workman.

Fran gathered up his equipment. "Yer grand, it was only missin' a bolt," he said, heading for the door to make a quick escape.

"Don't start. A man's got to be paid for his work," Tracey insisted.

Fran opened the front door and stepped out onto the street. "I was only doin' it as a favour for the Ma."

"That's lovely," Tracey said, pretending to be offended.

"Ah, ye know wha' I mean."

Tracey smiled. "There's a saying that if you work for nothing, you'll never be idle."

"I've heard it," Fran said.

"Look, if you won't take money, I'll have to pay you in kind, I suppose."

Visions of Mick's sexual innuendoes back in the pub the previous night came flooding back to Fran despite his best efforts to blank them out.

"What are you doing next Friday?" Tracey asked.

"Eh, eh," stammered Fran.

"Pick me up at eight. You're taking me out to dinner, my treat," Tracey ordered.

"I can't promise anythin'," he said. "I'll have to try and find a babysitter first."

"I'm sure that won't be a problem. See you Friday."

Fran opened his mouth to protest but Tracey nodded and closed the door before he could say another word. Inside the house, Tracey stood with her back to the door and exhaled a long, calming breath. She then took a bolt from a pocket in her dress and rolled it about in her fingers, smiling to herself. She'd always had a crush on Fran when they were in school and he was even cuter now, if that was possible.

Out on the street Fran stared at the closed front door not knowing how he should feel. He strolled away, unable to stop his mind from wandering, picturing him and Tracey having dinner together in some fancy restaurant.

Fran pushed Laura, who was out for the count in her buggy, through his mother's front door, closing it gently after him.

"Howya, Ma, it's only me," he half called out, not wanting to wake his daughter.

There was no reply.

"Ma?" he tried again, a sense of urgency growing in his voice but there was still no response. He made his way apprehensively along the narrow hallway, dreading what he might find. He was relieved however to discover his wheelchair-bound mother in her kitchenette, shrouded in cigarette smoke. At least he knew the human steam engine was still alive. She was parked next to the handy sized table with the hinged extensions in case of extra company and also within easy reach of an ashtray that was already full to the brim with spent butts. A heavy, thick woollen blanket covered her lap.

"Did ye not hear me, Ma?" Fran asked, unable to mask his concern.

"Where's Laura?" his mother said, ignoring her son's question.

"In the hall, havin' a kip."

"Bring her in, she'll catch her death."

"I've her well wrapped up. She's fine."

Mrs. Reilly stubbed out her fag. "You and yer anti-bleedin' smokin'," she complained.

"Be no harm if you'da took heed, migh' still have two legs," Fran pointed out but immediately regretted it.

His Ma gave him that withering look that only mothers can do. "Change the record, son, it's wearin' thin."

"Sorry. Are ye alrigh'?"

"Get me the scissors and cut them patches into three for me," Mrs. Reilly said. She was referring to the pain patches sitting on the table which she'd been prescribed for nerve damage following the amputation of her leg.

Fran did as he was told and got the scissors from a drawer.

"There's been talk on the radio that they're pullin' the patches from the medical card," his Ma said with some trepidation, "and I only have a few left."

"Why? I thought they worked," said Fran.

"They do. The only thing that's ever worked, in fact. Hopefully someone will see sense."

"I'm sure they will," Fran said but he doubted it. 'More cost cutting so the inner circle could hang onto their massive pensions,' he thought but he didn't want to upset his mother any further, so he let it rest. He'd have a word with Yoyo later on and if there were spare patches to be found anywhere in Dublin, he was the man to get them.

Mrs. Reilly gave a rasping cough, feeling as if she'd swallowed a strip of sandpaper and it had rubbed roughly against her windpipe. "I've had a visit from the law," she managed to say.

"Oh yeah?" her son replied, playing dumb.

"That bleedin' eejit of a brother of yers is only after doin' a leggin' job from the prison."

Fran topped up the electric kettle. "Wanna cuppa?"

Mrs. Reilly nodded 'yes'.

"He'll be alrigh', our Richie. Can look after himself," her favourite son said.

"D'ye reckon?" Mrs. Reilly answered spitefully.

Fran said nothing.

"By the way, how did things go with Tracey?" she asked.

"Was nothin' serious, I'm sure she could have fixed the machine herself if she'd wanted to."

"Did ye bring the baby with ye?"

"Nah, Davey watched her for me."

"Davey!" Mrs. Reilly exclaimed, almost falling out of her wheelchair. "That boy can't even mind himself, for Jaysus sake."

"Well not him, exactly. I meant his Ma of course," Fran lied. Davey had kept an eye on Laura while he'd gone to fix the washing machine, spoiling her with ice-cream and chocolate. It was just as well Fran was only gone for an hour, otherwise he'd be up all night facing the consequences.

"She's a lovely woman that Mrs. Byrne. I've a lot of time for her. Hope she's alrigh'?"

Fran looked at his Ma with a puzzled expression.

"Thought she'd lost a lot of weight the last time I saw her," Mrs. Reilly added.

"Ye know wha' she's like, runnin' around, mindin' all those little aul wans," said Fran.

"Still, she'd want to cop on at her age and mind herself for a change, that's all I know. Tracey's changed?" Fran's Ma said, switching the conversation as she fished for info.

"She's a bleedin' ri..."

"Language." Fran smiled. He poured the boiling water from the kettle into the teapot, swirled it around a few times before throwing it down the sink. Satisfied that the pot was sufficiently warmed, he put three spoonfuls of tealeaves into it, added more boiling water and gave it a gentle stir, leaving it to stew for a few minutes. The Japanese might have had their tea making rituals but so too had the old stock from the inner city. Too weak and it'd give ye lice, too strong and it was pure porter.

"I'm lookin' for a babysitter for next Friday. D'ye know anyone reliable who..."

"I'll do it," his Ma said before he could even finish his sentence.

"You? Wha' about yer bingo? Ye've never missed a day in yer life, except for Da's funeral."

"Shoulda gave that a wide berth too as it turned out," said Mrs. Reilly, reminiscing about the day she buried her husband. "The lads really smashed that pub up."

"I remember. Da would've enjoyed it. A good honest diggin' match," Fran admitted.

"And the face on yer man when yer Auntie Mags reefed his hair piece off," his Ma said, laughing at the memory.

"I'd forgotten about him," Fran said, a broad smile spreading across his youthful face. He fondly recalled the poor little baldy aul fella scarpering from the boozer leaving his bewildered aunt holding the clump of hair in her outstretched hand, screaming like a banshee.

Mrs. Reilly stopped laughing. "Friday'll be grand. The bingo's not on."

"How come?"

"Nancy down the street was tellin' me that they're decoratin' the hall or somethin' to that effect."

Fran poured the freshly brewed tea through a blackened metal strainer into two mugs. "Hadn't heard," he said, carefully placing one of the cups down in front of his mother.

Mrs. Reilly stared him straight in the eyes and warned, "If ye happen to bump into that waster of a brother of yers, tell him to do us all a favour and hand himself in."

Fran gave a compliant nod but once he was out of his mother's sight he began to massage his temple. All this secrecy was only going to lead to more grief.

Davey rode his motorbike carefully along the pockmarked tarmac pathway that ran parallel to the canal until he came upon the gap in the fenced off area surrounding the numerous, neatly kept allotments. He spotted an older lady dressed in kaki coloured pants and a matching baggy top, on her knees tending to a raised bed of what looked like a load of weeds to him. He spun over to her and politely asked for directions to Baxter's patch. The woman slowly got to her feet, putting her hands behind the base of her spine and giving the area a rub as she straightened herself.

"Old age, I'm afraid," she apologised.

"Don't worry about it, missus. Sure, I'm in me late twenties and am only short of needin' a forklift to get me outta bed in the mornin's."

The elderly lady laughed. The age of chivalry might not be dead after all.

"I'm lookin' for Pa Baxter's plot?"

"It's the one with the well-trodden pathway," she said with a glint in her eye, pointing Davey towards a large timber shed sitting on the only raised piece of land on the site.

"Thanks." He was about to go but curiosity got the better of him. "Can I ask why yer growing a bed full of piss in the beds?"

The woman laughed at Davey's innocence. "The dandelions?" she said, "or Taraxicum officinale, if we want to use the botanical name."

'This one's definitely smokin' the whacky tobaccy,' thought Davey.

"I use the leaves in salads and the flowers make a wonderful wine."

Davey was impressed. "Well, ye learn somethin' new every day." He thanked her again before making the short distance up to the hut just as a voluptuous woman with a very happy expression exited, almost skipping away. Baxter appeared at the doorway buttoning up his lumberjack shirt.

"Bosom buddy?" asked Davey, cheekily nodding towards the departing woman.

"Wanted to know about cucumbers," Baxter replied, standing aside and inviting his player into the shed.

Davey looked on as Baxter fixed the tossed sheets on the double bed positioned next to the rustic timber wall. The host pointed to an armchair next to a widescreen T.V. "Take the weight off your feet," he instructed.

Davey sat down and surveyed his surroundings. The place resembled a luxurious Alpine log cabin, not that he'd ever been in one, but he'd seen enough travel programmes to know. The centre of the living-room had a large rug with a shag pile high enough to have hidden an endangered Amazonian tribe in. A glass-fronted pot belly stove was strategically placed in a corner completing the look. "Like the bleedin' Tardis in here," Davey said, genuinely impressed.

Baxter removed a bottle of whiskey and two shot glasses from a press and poured.

"The what?" he asked.

"The Tardis. Dr. Who's police yoke – looks like a telephone box?" said

Davey but Baxter still wore a blank expression. "Ye know, looks small from the outside..." Davey further explained.

The manager shrugged his shoulders then gave Davey a whiskey. "Right. More of a Star Wars man myself, lad. That Princess Leia one, I'd have given her a lash of my life saver..."

"Ye mean light sabre," said Davey, correcting the common mistake.

Baxter looked at him questioningly before ordering him to drink up.

"I shouldn't. I have the bike," his guest said, politely declining the generous offer.

"Think of it as product sampling," Baxter encouraged, swallowing his drink in one go.

Davey followed suit but immediately suffered a fit of coughing.

"Put hairs on your balls that," said Baxter, laughing. He set his glass on a coffee table and crouched down, rolling back the rug. Davey watched with mounting curiosity as a trapdoor was revealed.

The secret compartment underneath the shed floor was more akin to Aladdin's cave. The two men were surrounded by neatly stacked boxes of whiskey covered in a generous layer of dust.

"At present I have a distribution problem, i.e. several hundred boxes of seasoned whiskey while you are experiencing some storage difficulties," Baxter said. "If you help me shift the gargle you can use some of the space. And I'll give you a percentage of the sales of course."

Davey was flabbergasted. "Where did it all come from and how the fuck did ye build this place?" he asked.

"Long story."

"I've got all day."

Baxter loudly exhaled. "About ten years ago I got wind that the council were going to give a field to the local community to use as allotments."

"Great idea," said Davey. He liked hearing positive stories.

"I'd also heard about this truckload of spirits being transported to a bonded warehouse out by the airport. So, one night while the truck driver was being kept busy..."

"Wha' d'ye mean by busy?"

"He was fond of the aul Roger Moore's..."

"The wha'?" said Davey.

"The Roger Moore's? Whores," Baxter explained. "I lined up a bit of company for him then stole his truck. Mary, that was the brasser's name, told me later that at one stage the driver thought he'd heard something. They were in a car parked next to the truck but couldn't see out 'cause the windows were all steamed up. Like the true professional that Mary was, she pulled the punter's head deep into her ample bosom and told him he was hearing things. Took me about half an hour to drive to the field where I had an excavator waiting. The hole was already dug so it was only a matter of lifting off the container, lowering it into place and covering it back over with soil."

Davey was back sitting in the armchair in Baxter's log cabin, holding another glass of the excellent tasting whiskey, the secret trapdoor once again hidden with the rug. Baxter was sat on the edge of the bed looking at his young accomplice.

"Ye've held onto the stuff for a while?" Davey finally said.

"The bizzies were all over the place. I mean, we were talking about nearly a quarter of a million quids worth of booze back then. I decided to leave the whiskey hidden away to keep it as a little nest egg for when I got older. I made a few modifications to the bunker, the trapdoor, stairs, ventilation shaft and I've had a little tipple over the years but other than that..."

"How'd ye keep it a secret?" Davey asked, very eager to discover the finer details. In his experience pulling off a stroke was usually a lot easier than keeping fellas quiet about it afterwards. Somebody always liked to boast.

"Nobody knew I did the job apart from Mary and the digger driver. And only myself and the digger lad knew where the container was buried."

"Wha' about the truck driver, did he not finger the prostitute?"

Baxter raised an eyebrow.

"No pun intended," Davey said, realising what he'd just said.

"He was married and made up some cock and bull story about being

71

hijacked by two masked men, so the law never looked for Mary. And fair play, she kept her lips sealed, a rarity in her profession."

Davey absently swirled the honey coloured whiskey around in his glass.

"The drink killed the digger driver shortly afterwards. God be good to him," the manager said, blessing himself.

"Was it his aul liver or pancreas?" asked Davey, knowledgably, having watched various medical shows about it on the box over the years.

"Nothing of the sorts, the man was as strong as an ox. He'd brought a case of the whiskey onto the building site where he was grafting at the time, to try and sell it like. Unfortunately, while driving around in his machine, one of the bottles rolled out of the box and got stuck under his brake pedal. Apparently, he'd bent down to retrieve it and didn't see the fuel tanker until it was too late. The whole place went up like a fucking bomb," said Baxter, recalling the incident as if it had only been yesterday.

"Holy shit!"

"I know. Sure they thought it was some sort of terrorist attack at first, it was all over the news. Suppose there was one consolation though…"

Davey found himself leaning forward. "Wha' was that?" he asked, curiosity once again getting the better of him.

The manager looked his player squarely in the eye. "He'd always wanted to be cremated."

The younger man tried to read Baxter's face, but his expression remained neutral, giving absolutely nothing away. 'It was no wonder the man almost always came out on top whenever the team had a poker night,' thought Davey.

The men emerged from the shed and Baxter looked up at the sky. The weather was holding nicely despite the poor forecast.

Davey straddled his bike. "I'll get movin' on this asap," he promised, fixing the strap on his helmet.

"Do. I've a bit of a cash flow problem," said the manager. Without warning he picked up a rock and smashed it against a snail that was glued to the side of the shed. Davey scrunched his face then nodded towards the splattered mollusc.

"I'm into the organic gardening nowadays," Baxter said, matter of fact.
After the horrible way in which Fran had spoken to his mother about her
smoking addiction and the possibility of still having both her legs, he was
determined to make amends. He'd rang Yoyo as soon as he'd left his Ma's flat
and arranged to meet up at a day-care centre of all places. On arriving at the
building, Fran was pleasantly surprised at how nice the centre looked from
the outside. It was freshly painted in bright and welcoming colours. Inside
was much the same, clean and airy and the furniture looked both expensive
and comfortable, particularly the four tanned leather recliners which were
all occupied. There was even a state-of-the-art flat screen television covering
almost an entire wall where a half dozen elderly people were glued to an old
black and white movie. Fran immediately recognised the film as the multiple
Oscar winning On the Waterfront. He'd watched it as a kid with his Da
loads of times. His aul fella loved Marlon Brando and would always repeat
the famous line 'I could've been a contender. I could've been somebody'
from that movie.

"Can I help ye, love," asked the friendly faced carer on seeing Fran enter
the building.

"I hope so," said Fran, giving his best smile. "I'm looking for me pal,
Yoyo, he's expectin' me."

The carer returned his smile. "Hold on and I'll get him for ye. What's
your own name, chicken?"

"Fran Reilly."

"Just a sec," the helpful woman said. She headed towards a closed door
at the far end of the room and gave it a peculiar sort of coded knock.

Moments later the door opened, and Yoyo appeared. The carer pointed
to Fran.

"Ah, me auld flower," Yoyo said loudly, waving his buddy over. "Thanks,
Linda." The carer returned to her clients and Fran thanked her as she went
past.

"What's the story?" Yoyo asked, giving Fran a man hug.

"It's the Ma, she needs these pain patches," Fran said, showing Yoyo a
box.

"Lidocaine. Harder to get than heroin at the minute," Yoyo said.

"Shit," said Fran, feeling deflated. His teammate had been his only real hope.

Yoyo grinned. "But lucky for you my friend I started to import them from the States a few weeks ago. Well, similar stuff, that ye can get over the counter."

"That's brilliant, the Ma'll be delighted," Fran said. "Are ye havin' to fly over yourself?"

"Would ye ever stop outta that. I have these trolley dollies on the books who love to powder their noses. They bring me back a case full of patches every time they do a trans-Atlantic hop and in return, I get them enough quality product to get them higher than the Spire."

Fran was only too familiar with the importance of getting clean stuff having seen first-hand the devastation that impure gear could bring. He was also well aware that he was being hypocritical having anything to do with a guy who dealt drugs when he abhorred pushers and the misery they caused. As crazy as it seemed though, he saw Yoyo as more of a facilitator, providing an excellent service for people, who, for whatever reasons, needed a fix and who would risk everything to get it. And of course there were no shortages of merciless scumbags queuing up to supply the addicts and better still, get them hooked on worse shit. Yoyo never went looking for business and only supplied a limited number of clients.

"Sounds like they're gettin' a bargain," Fran said in relation to the air hostesses.

"Believe you me, I'm gettin' the better end of the deal," said his teammate.

Fran didn't doubt it. Yoyo might've been a user himself but he was also an astute businessman. As Fran was musing over his good fortune in getting the pain patches and imagining how relieved his Ma was going to be, an elderly woman using a mobility scooter zoomed out of nowhere almost taking his foot clean off. The errant driver came to an abrupt halt and leaned forward, unzipping the cover on the basket at the front of her scooter, exposing an assortment of tablets.

"Fifty euro buys the lot," she said in a wheezy voice.

Yoyo grabbed the handlebars. "If ye don't fuck off, Bridie, I'm gonna throw ye under the number twenty-two bus, I'm warnin' ye."

Bridie glared at Yoyo for a moment then said, "Arsewipe." She did a u-turn and sped off almost taking Fran out of it again.

"That's an awful thing to say to someone that age," said Fran, thinking how he'd feel if his mother had been spoken to in that manner.

"Don't mind that wagon. Sold me a load of counterfeit pills last month that she'd bought on the internet and I'm still dealin' with the fuckin' fallout." He beckoned Fran inside his 'office', bolting the door after them. He then removed a key from his pocket and proceeded to open a lock on one of the press doors in what appeared to be a run-of-the-mill fitted kitchen.

"I never knew ye worked here," Fran said, pleasantly surprised.

"I don't. Happened upon the place durin' a spell of community service and spotted an opportunity. I have an arrangement which allows me to use this space."

"Well I have to say it's not the kinda place ye hear about on the news," Fran said, referring to the recent horror stories that he'd seen exposed by undercover reporters, "I thought it'd be basic and ye know, old and smelly if I'm bein' honest."

"That's because of the drug money," replied Yoyo without batting an eyelid.

"The wha'?"

"The geriatrics pass on their excess meds to me as well as pretendin' to have other ailments and I sell the tablets on. Some of the money from the sales is reinvested in the place and we also give the pensioners a percentage."

"Wha' about the carer and the other staff?"

"Everyone gets a cut so there's no need for anyone to be talkin' outta school. Ye'd be surprised how much stuff old people are prescribed and nobody seems to take any notice. What's your Ma on a day?" Yoyo asked, reaching inside the press which was filled to the brim with the pain patches.

"Usually the one but sometimes she has to use two," Fran said, "She'd be sparin' them these last few weeks, cuttin' them into narrow strips."

"Ye wouldn't believe how many times I've heard that recently. It's absolutely shockin'." Fran nodded in agreement. "Righ', here's four boxes to begin with but make sure ye let me know when your Ma's down to one."

"Good man. What's the damage?" Fran asked, rummaging in his jeans for the cash.

Yoyo shook his head. "I don't want money."

"Don't start, I know that stuff's not cheap."

Yoyo smiled. "Call it a free sample and we'll sort somethin' out with the next batch."

"Are ye sure?"

"I've that much cash comin' in that I'm runnin' outta places to stash it."

Fran didn't know whether his mate was joking or not, but it was still a lovely gesture. "Well, thanks again, I really appreciate it."

"No prob." Yoyo pointed to the boxes in Fran's hand, "Ye have to adjust the dosage to suit."

"Is there not a righ' amount?"

"They're a slight bit weaker that wha' yer Ma's used to and besides, we've all got different pain thresholds. The sufferer will know when they get things bang on," Yoyo said, trying to allay Fran's understandable concerns.

The reality of being part of a criminal gang was a far cry from how it was portrayed in the media or on film. The majority of the time was spent either running trivial errands or hanging around waiting for something to happen just so you could overreact to it. Stevo was well used to the mundane lifestyle having spent his entire adult life being a member of one faction or another. He sat behind the wheel of the flash car watching his associate, Scully, a weedy looking thug, emerge from a newsagent's carrying a folded newspaper under his arm. Scully hopped into the passenger seat, unfolded the paper and tossed two packets of cigarettes to Stevo.

"D'ye ever pay for anythin'?" asked Stevo.

"Up to them to have better security, isn't it," Scully said with a shrug, dismissing any wrongdoing on his part. It was a mind-set that was widely accepted in the criminal community. He searched through the sports section of the newspaper while Stevo unwrapped the plastic from one of his newly acquired cigarette packs, retrieved a smoke and lit up. He was contemplating what the packet would look like if the proposed explicit pictures featuring shams with missing toes or rotting lungs was plastered across it when a leggy Eastern European blonde caught his eye as she strolled towards him. She was accompanied by her muscled bound, shaven headed partner who appeared to have no neck. Scully looked up from the paper and watched as the couple passed by.

"I can never understand that. The women are absolute rides while the blokes all look like battered bouncers," he said.

"The fixture?" demanded Stevo, not giving a toss what the little sap beside him thought.

Scully rechecked the paper. "Yeah, found them. They're playin' this Sunday at two. How does he know this Reilly fella will be there?" he asked.

"Some mouthpiece in the local bookies was jabberin' on about it," Stevo reluctantly answered. "Time to get the crew together and tell them to tool up."

Scully look agitated and said, "Why don't we just do it ourselves without the gang, on a motorbike or somethin'?"

"Maybe because they're a football team and the Boss wants to show them that we've plenty of muscle behind us just in case they get ideas and come lookin' for payback."

Chapter 7

A sizeable queue had formed behind Mick at the ATM machine, impatiently waiting for him to finish his transaction. He had checked and rechecked his bank balance several times, but the bottom line remained the same. The latest top-up from his parents simply wasn't there. For the life of him he couldn't understand it, the monies had always been transferred into his account on time. Until now that was.

"Hurry the fuck up, will ye," said a male voice from behind. "We haven't got all day."

Mick glanced over his shoulder and was about to tell the loudmouth where to go, when he noticed at least a dozen other annoyed faces glaring back at him. He hit several buttons on the bank machine, ejected his card and mumbled, "Seems to be some sort of malfunction," before retreating into the anonymity of the numerous passing shoppers. After being carried aimlessly along the street by the river of people he eventually found himself deposited in a dead corner where one building jutted out several feet further than its neighbour. He retrieved his mobile, searched through his contacts and tapped the call button. Moments later the phone was answered.

"Of course it's me," Mick replied to the stupid question being asked by his father on the other end of the line. "Well I couldn't return your calls any sooner, I'm a very busy man you know," he said, brushing his parent off. He listened to the stifled conversation coming from his father.

"You're what?" Mick asked, refusing to believe his ears. Mr. Young repeated himself so that the news could sink in. "Don't you dare go anywhere, I'll be straight over," Mick said, ending the call.

The atmosphere in the Young household was tense to say the least. Mick was finding the news that his parents had been declared bankrupt and that the vast majority of their assets had been seized almost impossible to digest.

"How could you be so fucking stupid?" he swore, demanding an answer. His father sat dejectedly across from him, his head lowered in hands that had never seen a hard day's graft in their life.

"We were only following professional advice," Mr. Young said, trying to justify the unfortunate sequence of events which had led to his financial downfall.

"Great advice that turned out to be," his son smartly answered.

Mrs. Young appeared, carrying a tray of biscuits and tea.

His father looked up and said, "You'll have to vacate the townhouse by the end of the month."

Mick's mother stumbled slightly almost dropping the tray but managed to correct herself just in time. "Sorry, did I miss something?" she asked, pretending to be in the dark but failing miserably. She wasn't going to be winning an Oscar anytime soon.

"We no longer own that property, it's been put up for sale," Mr. Young continued.

"I'll just get a cloth, wipe up that mess," Mick's mother said, making a hasty retreat.

"They can't just do that, they have to give adequate notice," Mick said.

"They did and if you'd been bothered enough to return my calls you would have learned that a lot sooner."

Mick rose to his feet and began to pace slowly around the room, his father following him with his eyes. "This is unbelievable. I suppose I'll have to stay here, in the guest wing until you can sort this mess out," Mick finally said.

Mr. Young gave a slight cough, clearing his throat. "I'm afraid that won't be possible."

Mick swung around to face his father. "You'd have your own flesh and blood living on the streets?"

"Of course not and the amateur dramatics aren't helping," Mr. Young said. "It's just that they've repossessed this place as well. Myself and your mother are having to downsize to a one-bedroom apartment not too far from here."

Mick ran a hand through his hair. "This is like a bad dream. How much have we left?"

"Not sure yet. My people have promised to try and sort things out as soon as possible but in the meantime we'll all have to do some readjusting."

"And what does that mean, exactly?" Mick asked.

Mr. Young knew that his son meant 'what did that exactly mean for him'. He always knew that Mick was self-centred but anytime he'd tried to do something about it in the past his wife would plead with him to let it go and he had, for a quiet life. And now, although it pained him to see his son upset, he was also taking a small bit of pleasure from it too. "As well as finding yourself a place to live, there'll be no more allowances for the foreseeable future, if ever again."

"But the salary I currently earn wouldn't even cover the cost of my socialising."

"Your whoring and touring more like," Mick's father said, unable to help himself.

"Not everyone marries the first woman who spreads their legs," Mick retorted.

"Watch your mouth," Mr. Young threatened in a low but stern voice, "That's your mother you're talking about."

Mick knew it was a low blow, but he was royally pissed off. "I was happy where we lived as a boy, surrounded by my friends but no, that wasn't good enough for you and your newfound cronies. And where are those bastards now, in your hour of need? I don't see them queuing around the block to give you a dig out."

"Oh woe is me. You have an honours degree in computers, paid for by us in case you've conveniently forgotten."

Mrs. Young returned to the room at the tail-end of the conversation. "Oh that's a great idea, Michael, get yourself a nice job with the computers, you were always very good with them. And please God you'll be back on your feet in no time."

Mick glowered at his mother but held his tongue.

Darkness had fallen so suddenly it was as if someone had flicked a switch. Mick sat in his car, the contents from the envelope which his boss, Mr.

Watts, had given him earlier, resting on his lap. Although his father had informed him of the sale of the townhouse it was still shocking to see his home on the market, knowing that there was very little that he could do about it. He'd always presumed that homeless people were uneducated wasters, addicted to alcohol or drugs or both and yet here he was, a college graduate, a pillar of the community, in his own mind anyhow, facing the prospect of having no roof over his head in a little over a fortnight's time. It was so unfair.

Moping around wasn't going to solve anything. Mick evaluated his current status and came to the inevitable conclusion that he was up shit creek without a paddle. He needed cash, lots of it and fast but hadn't the foggiest idea where to turn to. He looked around his fancy pad, already grieving for the things he was going to lose when he caught site of his laptop. 'If in doubt, Google it,' he thought, reaching for his computer and tapping the on button. As the hard drive reawakened from its digital sleep Mick flexed and stretched his fingers as if they were mini-athletes limbering up for a big race. He cracked his knuckles and typed in the magical words 'Ten ways to get rich quick' and waited. The answers were predictable. Investing in the stock market was one of the top tips but unfortunately for Mick you needed money to begin with! There were various other ways, some criminal, although he wasn't yet ruling out that prospect. There was the possibility of renting out your property or properties. "Hello," he said aloud, getting more frustrated by the minute. Being left money by rich relatives; another non-starter since the only two wealthy relations he had were now bankrupt, the fucking idiots. He disregarded suggestion after suggestion. An idea that did catch his eye however was to upload a video onto YouTube hoping that it would go viral, in which event he could earn a whopping two dollars per one thousand views. Not a bad idea but not quick enough and besides, he hadn't a clue what he would post.

He flexed his fingers once again, looked pensively towards the ceiling before typing in 'Ten alternative ways to get rich quick' instead. Do the lottery. "Yeah, yeah, so original," he said, pretending to yawn. Donating sperm was there and he was in no doubt that people would pay a premium for his champion swimmers. On the negative side he had concerns that continuously going to the well, so to speak, would cause irreparable damage to his manhood and if that happened then what would be the point in living. And although signing up for drug trials where they pumped dodgy new chemical concoctions into your bloodstream was quite lucrative, he didn't fancy the risks. After all, he could end up like Yoyo or some of his other teammates. He shuddered at the thought. Marry someone wealthy. Now there was a suggestion that piqued his interest and was worthy of further consideration. Lady Wallace was the obvious candidate. She'd been made a very rich widow when her husband had drawn his terminal breath, not entirely surprising as the man was only a year shy of eighty.

Mick was almost done with his research after what felt like hours of looking when he accidentally came across 'camming'. He wasn't overly familiar with the term but was nonetheless intrigued. He decided to investigate further and discovered that people were willing to pay money to watch webcam performances. Most of the performers also had wish lists with one of the leading online retail companies where their clients or 'friends' as they preferred to call them, could select gifts to buy for them.

With his eviction looming ever closer, Mick set up a 'camming' account and dived straight into the murky waters of this unfamiliar world where he felt sure he'd be raking in the big bucks in no time. For some reason known only to himself he had presumed that his webcam performances would be for hot women, and most likely from the professional classes, aged in their early thirties. Bored cougars also came to mind. So he was definitely taken aback when he learned that the vast majority of his customers were male, were over fifty and overweight and apparently straight. Figure that one out. It was also a huge dent to Mick's ego to discover that there wasn't a queue of people lining up to see his talents and that the only thing he'd spent most of his day twiddling were his thumbs. Undeterred, he did a bit more investigating into this subculture and learned that a more lucrative fetish on the camming scene was to dress up as a lady while interfering with one's self. Although reluctant to go down this particular pathway he had very little choice. It was time to go dress shopping.

The sign above the door of the quaint looking shop read 'Inside Out You're Turning Me'. An older woman with large breasts spilling out of her low-cut top, dyed blonde hair and far too much make-up, sat behind the counter. She was sipping tea from a mug big enough to house a couple of goldfish, with a half-finished Sudoku puzzle laid out before her. Mick popped his head around the door.

"Come in, son," the woman said, beckoning him with a manicured hand. "We don't bite, that's extra," she added, giving him a saucy wink.

Mick shuffled inside, had a quick look over his shoulder before hurriedly closing the door.

The woman had kind eyes and a jolly disposition. "First time?" she asked. Mick nodded a cautious 'yes'.

"Well yer more than welcome, love. Me name's Mary, by the way."

Mary led Mick into a back room where rows of lockers lined one side with a long timber bench running down the middle.

"We sell a full range of clothes and shoes, specialising in the larger sizes of course," Mary helpfully explained. She pointed at the lockers and said, "Yer day to day clothes go in here and yer special garments and accessories are kept over there." She waved her hand across at the far wall where an assortment of colourful dresses, high heel shoes, thigh high boots, handbags etc. were set out in large, glass fronted wardrobes. Various names including Red, Dorothy and plain old Billy were printed above some of the units. "At least this way ye have peace of mind. Nobody will ever discover yer little secret unless ye want them to of course."

Mick frowned. "What if I want to take my new clothes home?" he asked.

"That's not a problem, love. Some partners like to play dress-up together."

"I live alone."

"That's grand as well. When yer ready just head through that door, some of the lads are in there already, havin' a chat."

Several cross-dressers sat inside at a table sipping tea. One was Red, who was six foot two with long curly ginger hair and a big bushy red beard. Another was Dorothy, sporting pigtails with blue ribbons, a blue dress and ruby red slippers. Mick, feeling absolutely ridiculous, tottered into the tea-room dressed in high heels and an emerald coloured cocktail dress. Both lads looked up at the same time, wearing warm, reassuring smiles.

Mick sat on the long bench in the changing room. He had switched back into his regular clothes and was lacing up his shoes when Red, who had also changed back into his civvies, walked past with a canvas bag slung over his shoulder. There was a rugby motif printed on the bag but Mick couldn't quite make it out.

"Might see you next week?" Red suggested in an upbeat tone.

"Maybe," Mick grunted.

Red exited the room just as the large breasted hostess entered.

"Take care, Johnny," she said.

"See you, Hun," Johnny replied, having left his alter ego hanging in a closet next door. He gave Mary an affectionate peck on the cheek and left.

Mary sat down next to Mick, a sympathetic smile embedded in an aged face which make-up couldn't fully disguise.

"Wasn't yer cup of tea, was it?" she asked, already knowing the answer.

"You could say that. Was half expecting to see Toto at any minute," Mick half joked in reference to Dorothy.

The woman laughed kindly. "I've been around the block a few times, literally. Was a lady of the night in a past life, seen all sorts of things," she said, reminiscing about her streetwalking days. "Anyway, wha' yer into is nothin' to be ashamed of, most people are just not comfortable with it yet, that's all."

"I'm not gay," Mick earnestly announced.

"Wha'ever floats yer boat but I'm glad to hear that. Be an awful waste of a strappin' young chap."

Mick's cheeks reddened at the compliment. "I just need to find out what clothes suit me, what's my size, how to put make-up on properly. Can't exactly walk into a shop for that, can I?"

"Ye'd be surprised. People in the retail sector have also seen their fair share of unusual things," Mary said, consoling her newest client. "Anyhow, ye don't need to worry about it. That's my job." She nodded towards the tearoom, "They're alrigh', them boys. A lot of them have wives and kids, that's just the way they're made." Mick and the woman both got to their feet.

"Give yer Auntie Mary a hug," she said, holding her arms open wide. Mick reluctantly allowed the woman to embrace him. After a few moments he tried to gently break free, but the over friendly hostess held on like a limpet.

"I better head," he said, trying to hurry things along as politely as possible.

Mary looked into his eyes and batted her lashes. "How are ye fixed to make an old gal happy?" she asked in an American accent before placing her hand on Mick's belt buckle.

Mick looked at her slightly taken aback before his eyes were inevitably drawn towards her heaving breasts despite his best efforts. Mary saw where his gaze had fallen. "Ye can squeeze me diddies if ye want. They're me own," she further enticed.

Jigsaw was standing at a bus stop directly across the busy road from 'Inside Out You're Turning Me', listening to music pumping through his earphones. He was oblivious to the other people waiting for the bus and who were also maintaining a safe distance from him.

"When, will I, will I be famous. When, will I, see my picture in the papers," Jigsaw sang the Bros song in his own unique voice, half Lady Gaga, half strangled cat. He spotted Mick leaving the specialist outfitters. "Mick, Mick!" he shouted.

Mick checked across the road and saw Jigsaw and everyone else at the bus stop for that matter, staring back at him.

"Shit," he said, immediately dropping his head and walking away at speed.

Jigsaw pulled out his earphones and began to stride along the pavement, parallel to Mick. "Buddy!" he called out.

His friend didn't seem to hear him, so he decided to jog across the road where he narrowly avoided being hit by a people carrier. The angry male motorist gave a prolonged beep.

"Keep that horn for yer wife," Jigsaw jeered before returning his attention to his fleeing teammate. "Stall the ball!" he shouted.

Mick reluctantly pulled up. "All right, Jigsaw. I didn't see you there," he lied.

"Wha' were ye doin' comin' outta that place?" asked Jigsaw.

"Where?" answered Mick, pretending that he'd absolutely no idea what his teammate was blabbering on about.

"The shop back there?" Jigsaw said, nodding towards 'Inside Out You're Turning Me', "Transformers, homos in disguise," he sang.

"I beg your pardon?" Mick said, keeping up the pretence.

"The gaff for the cross-dresser lads?"

"Well I wasn't aware that it was that kind of place, not that it would bother me in the slightest. And if I'm being completely honest with you, I find that type of language and your attitude towards the LGBT community quite offensive," Mick said, giving his teammate his best indignant stare.

"Jaysus, I'm sorry, bud. I didn't mean anythin' by it, I was just, ye know, havin' a laugh," Jigsaw apologised.

"Well, you need to educate yourself and stop being a Neanderthal," Mick chastised in an attempt to further deflect suspicion, "And for the record I was led to believe that the place was a plastic surgeons."

"Righ'," replied Jigsaw but he was far from convinced. "Wha' were ye thinkin' of gettin' done?"

Mick gave a swift look around then returned his attention back to the pest in front of him. He caught Jigsaw roughly by the arm. "A penile reduction," he said in a hushed tone. Keep it to yourself though, I don't want the lads giving me grief."

"Yer secret's safe with me," Jigsaw said, pretending to pull a zip across his gob. "Can't wait for our next game, have a good feelin' I migh' get on the score sheet," he added enthusiastically, already changing the subject.

His teammate gave a derisive snort.

"Ye look knackered, Mick, are ye doin' extra trainin' or somethin'?" Jigsaw asked all of a sudden, his powers of observation second to none.

Mick's smirk quickly disappeared, replaced instead with a sheepish expression as a montage of him banging the granny every which way inside the shop moments earlier came flooding back.

Mick already felt like a complete tit sitting on the edge of the bed with the wafer-thin mattress in his shabby rented accommodation, wearing a dress that could have come straight out of a Dickens' novel. But when the forty-something year old, quadriplegic American on the other end of the webcam practically went into convulsions from the laughter he knew that his life had reached an all-time low.

"And I thought my life was fucked up!" said the brash Yank, beaming through the screen from the other side of the world.

Mick sat there unable to say or do a single thing, his whole thought process paralyzed.

The American began to shout at someone out of view. "Hey, Victor! Victor!" Moments later a strapping young shirtless lad with a glowing tan appeared.

"What's the problem, sir?" the Costa Rican asked, making a fuss.

"The problem, Victor? The problem is that the Goddamn server has frozen again," said the irate American.

"Are you sure, Mr. Taylor?" the beefcake assistant asked, checking out the computer settings just to make sure. He looked at Mick onscreen and tutted. "What you watching this freak show for anyways, Mr. Taylor?"

"I mean, they have perfect Wi-Fi in warzones in the Middle East and here we are less than what, forty miles from Silicon Valley and what do we got, goddammit?" Taylor said, ignoring his partner's genuine concern.

"The connection looks ok to me," Victor said.

"Nada, that's what we got," continued Taylor.

Mick slowly got to his feet.

"Hey," said the Costa Rican, pointing to the screen, "The weirdo in dress is moving."

"What?" said Victor's sugar daddy.

The Costa Rican repeated himself. Mick had covered his face in his hands.

Mr. Taylor twisted his head vigorously trying to see the screen. "Well get your ass out of the way. Christ, do any of you foreigners understand plain English." Victor wasn't in the least bit offended by Taylor's insensitive remarks. He'd grown accustomed to them since the devastating traffic accident which had reduced the flamboyant playboy's movements to just his head and shoulders. Victor did as he was told and got his toned ass out of Mr. Taylor's way. He longed for their carefree days, travelling up and down the west coast in Taylor's convertible, with the soft top down allowing the sun's rays to warm their bronzed bodies.

Mick was just about to switch off his computer when the American yelled, "Hey, don't do that."

Mick stopped and looked at the screen. Mr. Taylor could immediately tell that all was not well with the 'Camming' guy.

"I didn't mean to laugh," said the American, "But if I'm being brutally honest here, pal, the dress does nothing for you."

Victor stuck his face next to his partners, scrutinizing Mick. "I'd sack the stylist for sure."

Mick disconnected the link.

2nd Round Qualifier: Sporting Les Behans' v St. Marks

Baxter trudged towards the truck container carrying a bagful of rubbish in one hand and a litter picker in the other. Glancing up at the gang of kids loitering on top of the steel structure, watching his every move, he was reminded of the old cowboy films where the vultures waited patiently, biding their time.

"Any chance of a hand there, lads?" he called out in as friendly a manner as he could muster but without expecting anything positive in return.

One of the taller kids, a lad named Derek, stood up. "Are ye for real?" he answered smartly, trying to sound a lot older than his thirteen years of age. "And put the council workers out of a job."

The rest of Derek's pals laughed, each trying to laugh harder than the other in order to impress their leader. Baxter forced a smile while cursing under his breath at the same time. He tied a knot tightly in the rubbish bag, imagining for a fleeting moment that it was this upstarts' neck. He threw the bag of rubbish to the ground before tearing off another one from the role and went back onto the pitch, absolutely fuming.

Sporting Les Behans' were kitted out in their new yellow training tops. They were doing their warmup drills, knocking footballs about, dribbling and taking shots on goal. A loose ball went whizzing past the gaffer's head almost lifting it clean off of his shoulders.

"Who the fu..." Baxter began to give out but stopped himself short when he spotted Fran with his arm raised by way of an apology.

"It's the new boots," Fran said as he jogged past Baxter to retrieve the ball.

"And that, lad, is why you're a defender," the manager replied with a smile as his player returned with the football. "You wouldn't believe what I witnessed a few minutes ago."

Fran paused to catch his breath. "Yeah?"

"I went into the dressing room to collect some gear and there was Charlie with some floozy hanging out of the door frame straddling his shoulders and not a stitch on either of the pair of them."

"Was he givin' her a jockey back?"

"My arse. He had his face stuck that far up her hoohah, I think he was looking to be reborn."

Fran couldn't help but smile at the image. "Sure isn't he only after finishin' a first aid course."

"And what's that got to do with the price of bread?"

"He was probably practicin' the hi-lick manoeuvre."

"I'll end up being put in the madhouse if I 'ang about here too much longer," the manager replied, shaking his head.

Davey walloped the ball low towards one corner where it was expertly stopped by Birdy's strong, outstretched hand. He sauntered over to the keeper and patted him affectionately on the head.

"Great save," he said.

"It's okay," the goalie replied in his broken English before effortlessly springing back to his feet. He banged his padded gloves together knocking off the tiniest bits of grass and earth that had stuck to them and got set for the next shot.

"D'ye do much climbin' in that circus of yers?" Davey asked.

"For sure," Birdy proudly replied, puffing his chest out into the bargain. "Good stuff. I was lookin' for a few tips on usin' ropes and all that," said Davey, smiling innocently as if butter wouldn't melt in his mouth.

Mick was doing a few stretching exercises for his hamstrings, careful not to overextend them when Jigsaw shuffled past. The not so proficient striker was pulling down on his new top reading what was written on it. He looked up and noticed Mick watching him.

"Fair play to Davey all the same," Jigsaw remarked, "Was a lovely touch, rememberin' aul Les like that."

Mick shook his head. 'Where did they get this guy from,' he thought.

"Funny thing, though," Jigsaw said, rambling on a bit, "I can't picture the chap's face."

Mick exhaled loudly and said, "That's because there never was a Les Behan. Davey was only acting the maggot."

"G'wan outta that," said Jigsaw, expecting Mick to break into a smile at any moment but his teammate's serious expression didn't change. "Are ye sure?" the not so bright striker asked, scratching his head, unable to process what he'd just been told.

Mick was going to explain further but thought better of it. It would be ten precious minutes of his life that he would never get back.

"Yer yankin' me chain, I knew it," laughed Jigsaw, walking away. "And ye nearly got me too, ye bleedin' messer."

Mick was seriously beginning to doubt Darwin's Theory of Evolution whereby all living things were constantly evolving and improving to insure survival. He was rapidly coming to the conclusion that the existence of the human race was in actual fact just one big continuous fluke.

Stevo sat in the passenger seat of the stolen vehicle next to one of his gangster buddies who had his arms resting on the steering wheel, leaning forward. The newish Transit van had been acquired the previous day down near the docks for the job in hand. Stevo had switched the registration plates himself, copied from a van up north that he knew for a fact wouldn't be anywhere near this part of the country for the next few days. He was well aware that people thought he was neurotic when it came to things like that but it was doing things like that which had given longevity to his almost blemish free criminal career. There was no partition between the cab of the van and the storage area in the back where Scully and two more criminal associates lay in wait. All of the men were dressed in identical boiler suits with balaclavas rolled up on their heads.

"Which one is he?" asked the driver as he watched the football match that was going on in the near distance.

"The yellow Number Nine," Stevo replied.

"He's fuckin' brutal. Thought he was supposed to be handy?" the driver said, his years of lounging on the couch watching Sky Sports giving him a sense of authority when it came to judging talent.

Scully leaned forward, poking his weasel-like face between the front seats. "Their gear is bleedin' horrible."

"D'ye hear Johnny Styles," slagged Stevo.

All the men laughed except for Scully.

"I was just sayin'," he muttered.

"Well don't," Stevo said, "Everyone ready?"

The crime gang pulled their balaclavas down over their faces. The men in the back carrying the guns checked their weapons before giving Stevo the thumbs up.

The two soccer teams were battling hard for possession around the centre of the field when the criminal's powered their van onto the pitch crushing one of the corner flags beneath its wheels. Several players from both sides had to quickly jump out of the way to avoid been sent scattering like skittles while one player kicked out in a futile attempt to hit the van as it sped past. The yellow number nine had the ball in his possession when the match was disrupted. He skilfully chipped it up into his hands as soon as he heard the referee blowing the whistle to pause the game.

"This is an absolute disgrace," the referee barked, not one hundred percent sure what to do next. He knew that under the laws of the game the vehicle was classed as an outside agent and that the restart was probably a dropped ball but for the life of him he couldn't be sure. This wasn't something you encountered every day. The van slid to a halt next to the centre circle leaving two long skid marks in its wake. The official and the angry players gathered around the invaders. After a short stand-off, the side door slid open and Scully and his two associates appeared, aiming their various weapons at the assembled crowd. Stevo and the driver calmly climbed out. The gang leader stretched his arms high above his head trying to loosen the muscles in his cramped body after being holed up in the van for several hours. He finally walked over to number nine.

"Need a word, buddy," he casually said.

"I've heard of players bein' poached but this is a bit much isn't it?" the number nine answered smartly, trying to be Jack the lad.

Stifled laughter escaped from both teams.

"That's all I fuckin' need, another poxy comedian," Stevo said, acknowledging the retort. He then swiftly punched number nine square in the nose, grabbed him by the hair and dragged him towards the van. The stunned player still had the ball tucked under his arm when Scully bundled him into the back of the vehicle. Stevo looked at his driver and the two other gang members.

"Keep an eye on them," he instructed, motioning towards the terrified players and referee. "Anyone attempts to leave the circle of life you have my permission to drop them," he added, his voice low but still full of menace. He then hopped into the back of the van followed by Scully who promptly slid the door shut behind him.

Number nine was tied up with leather straps, which Stevo had personally fixed to the inside of the van, in a spread-eagled fashion with a gag stuffed into his mouth. The gang leader rolled up his sleeves. "Goggles and drill," he demanded.

Scully duly obliged. Stevo put on the protective glasses and pressed the trigger on the drill. The metal bit rotated slowly before whining to a complete halt. Stevo lifted the goggles and glared at his sidekick.

"Fuck, forgot to recharge it," said Scully, meekly offering some form of apology in the slim hope of averting the inevitable bollocking he was bound to receive.

Number nine looked relieved. Stevo bit down on his fist. "Fail to prepare, prepare to fail," he said, barely audible to the other men present.

"Janice was wreckin' me head about puttin' up shelves in the kitchen last nigh' and wouldn't shut the fuck up until I did it," Scully said, whinging.

Stevo glanced to the heavens. "Give me strength." He returned his attention back to the fuckwit. "The toolbox," he ordered, "Get me the hammer and chisel, gonna have to do this the old-fashioned way."

On hearing this change of plan the number nine duly fainted, leaving him dangling like some sort of abandoned marionette.

The rest of the crime gang were outside smoking and having a yap while still covering the players with their loaded weapons.

"And youse are from Malahide and not town?" one of the gangsters asked, incredulously. The team in yellow nodded a collective 'yes'. The gangster looked at his associates for advice, but they just shrugged their shoulders unwilling to commit one way or the other. It wasn't their fault if there was a case of mistaken identity. They were only getting paid from the neck down after all. Inside the van, Stevo held the chisel against number nine's kneecap while Scully pressed a heavy piece of timber against the back of the joint. Stevo raised the hammer and was about to strike when the door slid open and the concerned gang member appeared.

"Bit of a problem, Boss," he said with some trepidation, "Looks like we've got the wrong Murray's."

Stevo and the rest of his men joined the two teams and the referee out on the pitch. The gang had no need to worry about supporters as nobody in their right mind would bother wasting their time watching this crowd of useless whores. Number nine was sat on the grass, his head in his hands, shaking with the shock of his near miss.

"The Murray's we want changed their name recently to..." the gangster coughed into his hand clearing his throat, "...to Sporting Lesbians."

"Wha'?" asked Stevo.

"Sporting Lesbians," the gangster reluctantly repeated.

"Queer name that," interrupted Scully, choosing the wrong time to begin his career as a stand-up comedian.

Stevo pointed menacingly at his associate. "You, get the fuck back into that van."

"But..." Scully said, trying to save face.

"Now!" roared Stevo. He'd had it up to his tonsils with the muppet.

The crime gang had returned to their vehicle having finished interrogating the two terrified teams and were now seated in their original positions. The van was still parked in the centre of the football pitch with the players and match official standing outside unsure of what to do next but petrified to move.

"Wha' are we gonna..." Scully began before being cut off mid-sentence when Stevo put a finger to his lips.

The referee knocked timidly on the passenger window after being unanimously elected spokesperson by the players despite not even offering himself forward as a candidate. Stevo cracked his knuckles before deciding to lower the glass.

"Sorry for disturbin' ye but could we please have our ball back?" the referee politely asked.

Stevo gave him a puzzled look.

The man in black rubbed his chin. "It seems to have accidentally ended up in the back of yer van when ye were, eh, havin' yer chat with the player," he explained. "And sure if we had a spare ball I wouldn't even think of botherin' ye."

The gang boss remained silent as the referee shifted uneasily in the soft mud not sure if he should open his mouth again. He bit the bullet. "I've another game to do and I hate bein' late..."

Stevo pressed a switch and held it down until the van window closed fully, shutting out the anxious official. The referee turned around to the expectant players and pulled a face. None of them were forthcoming with any suggestions or possible solutions so he decided to keep his gob shut and to just wait it out.

After what felt like an eternity Stevo finally turned to one of his subordinates in the back and gave the go-ahead. The side door was slid open and one of the gangsters appeared, holding the football in his outstretched hand. The referee smiled, glad that sense had prevailed but just as he was about to reclaim the ball the gangster kicked it high into the air, aimed his shotgun and fired. Everyone on the pitch hit the ground, taking cover as the deflated piece of imitation leather plummeted back to earth. The van then sped off with the crazed gangster half hanging out, roaring with laughter. He managed to duck back in and close the door a split second before the vehicle squeezed under the crossbar of one of the goals sending sparks flying. Under normal circumstances the roof of the van would have bounced back off the metal post but because the goalmouth had sunken a few inches from all the use the gangsters had just about gotten away with minimum damage. The same could not be said for the net which ended up in a sorry heap with a large hole ripped through the middle.

Sporting Les Behans' 6 St. Marks 0

The whistle blew three times signalling the end of the match. Some of the Sporting Les Behans' players jumped about, hugging one another while others shook the hands of the dejected opposition team. Trigger and Jigsaw strolled off the pitch side by side where they were greeted by their delighted manager.

"Nice hat-trick, Trigger," Baxter said, congratulating his star striker. He turned to a sorrowful looking Jigsaw, "Better luck next time, ar kid."

Sporting Les Behans' were milling about in their truck container dressing room in various stages of undress. Some of the lads were drying themselves after showering in the newly installed electric showers courtesy of a dodgy electrician come plumber who was a friend of a friend. He had illegally tapped into a nearby lamppost giving the lads unlimited free electricity for the price of a few pints. A reckless action by anyone's standards but free leccy was free leccy after all.

Mick caught Jigsaw staring at his groin. "Have you got some sort of an issue?" he asked.

"Ah, don't mind me, bud. Didn't realise ye had yer aul job done already, that's all," Jigsaw said.

"What are you on about?" asked Mick.

"The reduction operation?" Jigsaw said, pointing to Mick's penis. His hand was immediately slapped away by his less than impressed teammate. Jigsaw was somewhat taken aback but felt the need to further explain. "Remember ye were tellin' me about it after I saw ye comin' outta that place. What's it called again?" He raised his hand about to tap Davey on the back to see if he knew the name of the shop but it was instantly grabbed by Mick.

"Laser. All over in a flash," Mick lied. His cheeks were flushed with a combination of anger and embarrassment as he hurriedly pulled on his boxers.

"A little too much for my likin'," Jigsaw mumbled under his breath. He didn't mean anything bad by it, it was just that none of the other players even came close to measuring up to his unusually long standard.

"What was that?" Mick challenged, leaning aggressively towards his teammate.

"Nothin'. Wonder could they do somethin' for Charlie?" Jigsaw asked, attempting to deflect Mick's anger. The two men scanned the room, spotted Charlie and were unable to stop themselves from checking out his genitals. Charlie noticed the attention he was getting so he put his hands on his hips and thrust back and forth a few times, a dirty grin plastered across his face.

"D'ye like chicken?" Charlie asked aloud.

Jigsaw gave a small shrug.

"Cause this thing's foul," laughed Charlie, once again gyrating his pelvis. Mick and Jigsaw turned away in a unified show of disgust.

"There's not a hope anyone could do a thing with that. Looks more like a melted lion bar," Mick remarked.

"I'm a grower not a shower," Charlie said, having absolutely no shame.

"Wha' are yis on about?" asked Huey, his curiosity getting the better of him.

"The lads were just talkin' about wha' age they were when their third ball grew," said Fran, giving Mick a secret wink.

"Clowns," Huey replied.

Birdy, who was drying himself next to the lads, stopped what he was doing and glared at his teammate.

"No offence," gulped Huey.

Birdy rung his towel tightly in his vice-like hands while continuing to give Huey the death stare. The misfortunate player sensibly decided to retreat further down the truck container making sure to avoid all eye contact with the deranged goalie. It was a well-known fact that keepers were touched, and as for clown goalies, well that was a different ball game altogether.

"How old were ye, Davey?" asked Fran.

"How old?" repeated Davey, unsure of the question not having been paying much attention to the earlier banter. He'd been too busy going through the pros and cons in his head of his latest get rich quick scheme.

"Ye know, when ye grew yer third ball?" Fran said, prompting his pal.

"Ah... I was a late bloomer meself, I was about six..."

Fran quickly shook his head behind Huey's back.

"...teen," added Davey.

"Would yis ever fuck off. Pack of wind up merchants," said Huey.

"I find it almost incomprehensible to perceive that a man of your age could still only have two balls," Mick said, pretending to be shocked.

"D'ye think I came down in the last shower?" said Huey, dismissing his teammate's attempts to trick him.

Davey let his damp towel from around his waist drop to the floor, bent over and showed his scrawny pale arse off to Huey.

"Yer more than welcome to count mine," he offered.

"I think I'll pass," Huey replied, turning away from Davey and trying his best not to be sick.

At that very moment Baxter came rushing into the changing room with all the joys of spring and said, "That was terrific stuff, lads, absolute magic." He playfully patted Paddy Power on the back then noticed Davey bent over with his legs spread exposing his bare buttocks while the rest of the lads looked on.

"We used to celebrate a win a lot differently in my day," said the manager. The lads smiled before resuming their drying and dressing regimes with Jigsaw spending a considerable amount of time repeatedly patting his groin area, quietly counting his testicles but afraid to say anything.

"If this keeps up, we might get a shot at the big boys," Baxter said loud enough for everyone to hear, "Oh and by the way, I want you all to cop on and go easy on the ale." He looked at Charlie and Yoyo, "...and the chemicals," then pointed at Charlie, "...and the sexual acrobatics."

Charlie swivelled his hips some more and said, "Can't keep a good man down."

Baxter shook his head before singling Podge out. "And you, fatso, with the grub."

The pudgy player's jaw dropped. "Ye can't say things like that anymore, I have rights and feelin's."

"I'm sick to me back teeth listening to people whining, you can't say this and you can't say that. In my day you said what needed to be said, end of," the manager scolded. He was old school and didn't like change.

"I've a genetic problem," moaned Podge, trying to defend his ballooning weight.

"Yeah, ye married a mutant," Davey quipped and with that the entire place erupted in laughter.

Stevo and Scully watched the van from the botched hit at the football match earlier in the day, blaze violently away on the deserted waste-ground. It's scorching, colourful flames did little to offer even the tiniest sliver of comfort to Stevo. He was furious with himself for not doing his homework properly on his intended target. Sure, he could blame Scully for getting the wrong fixture from the newspaper but his paymaster, Mr. big bollox Quinn, would be having none of it. He'd been given the job and he'd failed in dramatic style and now he'd have to listen to all the noise that came with it.

"Me uncle won't be happy," Scully warned, stating the obvious.

Stevo grabbed him roughly by the collars, lifting him completely off his feet. "If ye weren't related to Mr. Quinn I'd have stabbed ye in the heart and burnt ye with the fuckin' van," he threatened through gritted teeth leaving his accomplice in absolutely no doubt as to his true feelings.

Chapter 8

Davey carried a reinforced cardboard box containing the stolen whiskey from Baxter's secret lair through the almost deserted pub and set it down on the counter. Alarmed, Frank the Publican immediately removed the contraband and hid it underneath, away from prying eyes. Nobody needed to know his business.

"Had a taste the other nigh' and me head nearly exploded," he said. "Where the hell did ye get the stuff, it's the best whiskey I've ever tasted?"

"Can't tell ye that but there's no need to worry, I've a plentiful supply," Davey said, reassuring his newest best friend and customer. "So, wha' d'ye think, six nil? The other crowd didn't get a look in," Davey said in reference to their demolition of St. Marks.

"Fair play. Did Jigsaw score?" asked the publican.

"Nah. Coupla great chances though. And one was an absolute sitter."

"Pity, he's a harmless aul sort but at least he tries."

"Ye know as well as I do that missed chances are a lot easier to forgive when ye hammer yer opponents."

The publican nodded in agreement, picked up a rag and gave the countertop a wipe, more out of habit than necessity. He looked at Davey. "Yer on a roll now, migh' get yer faces into one of the local papers or somethin'. Be a good plug for the bar."

Davey's ears pricked up. "And if we did, for arguments sake, would there be anythin' in it for someone?" he asked. Sensing an earner came second nature to him.

"Goes without sayin'," Frank replied. "Ye didn't hear about the carry-on up in Finglas today at a match?"

Davey cocked his head to one side and said, "Nah, wha' was the jackanory?"

"A van full of heavies drove onto the pitch while there was a game on and threatened the players with guns. They even shot the match ball," Frank revealed.

"Bastards," said Davey.

"I know."

"I mean a new ball's not cheap."

Frank looked at the other man not entirely sure whether he was having his leg pulled.

Davey glanced around and noticed Larry and Mo, two elderly gents, sitting at a low table, studying a shared newspaper. Mo was in a wheelchair with both feet set in plaster of Paris. Larry suddenly grabbed Mo by the throat and began to choke him. With his face growing redder by the second, Mo just about managed to grasp the newspaper and began slapping his attacker across the head with it. Frank stuck two fingers into his mouth and gave a loud, well-practiced whistle. The elderly men, noting that the publican was less than impressed, ceased their tussle. Larry raised a hand in acknowledgement and sat back down.

"What's the story with Happy Feet and his sidekick?" Davey asked.

"They're brothers. I wouldn't mind but the one stranglin' the lad in the wheelchair is supposed to be his carer."

"That's gas."

"Every day it's the same," said Frank.

"Yeah?"

"Yep. They scour the newspapers for funerals then go and try scrounge a bit of grub and a few free pints. Could teach ye a thing or two about livin' on a budget."

"The mad yokes."

Frank nodded his agreement. "Although by the looks of it they mustn't be havin' much luck findin' today's victim."

"And wha' about yer man with the scaldy puss?" said Davey, motioning towards a man slouched at the bar, staring into a pint of stout whose frothy cream head was a distant memory.

"Tommo? Salt of the earth. Findin' it hard to make ends meet at the minute. He was tellin' me that a new crowd have moved into the area and are undercuttin' him," Frank explained.

"Wha' does he do for a crust?"

"Hard landscapin'."

"What's that?" asked Davey, not familiar with the term.

"Ye know, patios, driveways, that sort of thing."

"Ah, righ'," said Davey, pondering the situation. "Got a scissors?" he finally asked after one of his many Eureka moments.

Frank scratched his chin before cautiously answering, "Yes."

Davey turned to the downtrodden man. "Tommo!" he shouted.

Tommo looked up from his consoling drink but didn't recognise the bloke who was calling out to him.

"Get yer measurin' tape like a good man," Davey told him.

Frank the Publican rummaged through the drawer of an old walnut dresser, a remnant from a past tenant, in the backroom of the pub and found a blackened scissors. When he returned to the bar with the scissors, Tommo was reluctantly handing over his long builder's measuring tape to Davey.

"How much d'ye charge for layin' the aul slabs?" Davey asked, taking the scissors from Frank.

"Averages out at about a hundred euro per square metre supplied and laid. That's for natural stone," Tommo replied, somewhat wary, "I can give ye a better deal on the concrete products."

"And yer competitor?"

"He's doin' it for ninety-five a square metre."

"Sound. Me fee for the followin'..." said Davey, scanning the boozer as he subconsciously narrowed his eyes. He then fixed his sights on the two elderly brothers, "Put a few quid behind the counter for the boys."

"Okay?" agreed Tommo, still puzzled.

Davey unravelled a section of the tape, paused, then pulled out a small bit more. He took the scissors to it and promptly snipped off a piece.

"Wha' are ye bleedin' doin'?" Tommo said but there was no point in protesting any further as the deed had already been done.

"Savin' yer livelihood, buddy," replied Davey, handing Tommo back his modified tape.

"Reduce yer costs to ninety a square metre. Yer tape now starts at two metres so yer up over three hundred and fifty smackerooneys before ye do a thing. It's a win-win situation," he said.

Frank fiddled with his ear while Tommo was still trying to do the maths on his fingers. Davey could see that the two geniuses were struggling with the calculations.

"As in two metres by two metres, i.e. four-square metres times ninety euro," he helpfully explained, "Three hundred and sixty cash dollar money if ye want to be exact."

Both men just nodded and accepted the numbers.

"There ye are now, ye robbin' pox!" shouted Podge from the far end of the pub. His hand was heavily bandaged and held up in a sling. Tommo took a fifty euro note from his pocket and shoved it into Frank's hand.

"For the aul lads," he told the publican. He gently squeezed Davey's shoulder and made a brisk drinking motion with an imaginary pint.

"Yer alrigh'," said Davey, politely declining the offer. "Another time."

"Thanks again," Tommo said, already scarpering for the door, not having the stomach for a row.

Podge squared up to Davey. "Knew ye'd be in here, hidin'," he snarled.

"Take a chill pill. Wha' seems to be the problem?" Davey asked, trying to get a read on the situation.

"Don't start with that shite. I could've bled to death and all ye could think about was makin' a few poxy quid at my expense," Podge said as spittle flew from his mouth.

Davey was going to be smart and tell his teammate that he didn't want to know the weather forecast but refrained. "Wha' are ye on about?" he asked instead, feigning ignorance.

Podge held up his bandaged hand. "Me weddin' ring."

"Oh, righ'," Davey said, conveniently remembering.

"Oh, righ', me hole," continued the pot-bellied aggressor.

Davey had enough. "So, d'ye want to have a straightner or wha'?" he asked, loosening up his shoulders in anticipation. He'd done a bit of boxing in his youth, even winning an amateur national title at fifty-two kilos, roughly the equivalent of super flyweight in the professional game before deciding to jack it all in to concentrate on the football and the robbing.

Podge knew Davey was handy with his fists but he couldn't let it go. Whatever he was in for now was nothing compared to the hammering that Sharon was gonna dish out if he came home from the hospital without his ring.

Frank butted in between the two men. "Here it is, Podge," he said, taking the twisted gold band from his shirt pocket and handing it back to the reserve keeper. "Davey gave it to me for ye the other day, for safe keepin'. Isn't that right?" Frank said, encouraging the other man.

"Yeah, that's righ'. Nearly forgot about it meself," Davey lied.

All three men looked at one another in silence, resembling a spaghetti western stand-off.

"Sorry, pal," Podge finally said, "But ye know wha' yer like."

"That's a fair enough comment. A bit of miscommunication is all," Davey said.

"Wha' d'ye want to drink?" Podge asked, by way of a peace offering.

"A bud, bud. How's the finger by the way?"

"Sore as fuck to be honest but they gave me tablets. Could be worse though, I've banged in for the disability. Please God, I'll never have to work again."

"Ye've never worked a day in yer bleedin' life," Davey said, messing.

"I resemble that accusation," said Podge. "By the way, how's yer Ma doin'?" he asked, genuinely interested.

"What's that?"

"Yer Ma? I saw her at the hospital."

"Nah, ye must have been mistaken. She's gone on her holliers with her mate, Vera," Davey said.

Podge gently bit down on his lip, a perplexed look on his face. "It was definitely her, or else she has a double," he said after a short pause, "In anyway, have to go to the jacks, am burstin' for a slash."

"Need a hand?" asked Davey.

"I'm alrigh'..." Podge replied then noticed that Davey and Frank were both smirking, "Ask me bollox," he said before heading for the gents.

"Don't know wha' gear that hospital has him on but he's losin' it," Davey said, "The Ma's in Santa Ponsa, soakin' up the rays by the pool and probably sippin' a few rocket fuelled cocktails with the sparkly thingamajigs into the bargain."

"It's well for some. Any news on that T.V. sports thing for me?" Frank enquired.

"Would I ever let ye down? Lower that screen," said the wheeler dealer. Del Boy would never be dead as long as Davey was around.

The envelope which Davey retrieved from inside his coat pocket contained a sticker that had a pint symbol printed on it. He peeled off the backing then carefully applied the symbol to the bottom of the T.V. screen, smoothing it into place. He stood back and examined his handiwork. Frank looked on, having second thoughts about the whole thing.

"Nobody will be any the wiser," Davey said, reassuring his nervous client.

"I'm not sure..." said the publican.

"Ye worry too much."

"Wha' do I owe ye?"

"Nothin'. Call it quits for Podge's ring but for anyone else it's a ton and there'll be a score for ye, for the commission."

Podge came out of the toilet still pulling up his fly.

"Are ye stayin' for a pint yerself?" asked Davey.

"Won't bother. Sharon will have the dinner on," Podge replied, "And I don't want to be late." He didn't need to elaborate any further. Everyone knew he'd married a psycho.

"Have a quick one and I'll give ye a lift home," his teammate insisted.

Davey brought his motorbike to a gradual stop in the weed infested lane that ran behind several small backyards, one of which included Podge's. The sub keeper, who was riding pillion, reefed his helmet off.

"For fuck's sake," he swore.

"What's wrong with ye now?" asked Davey.

"She's only after doin' the fuckin' washin'," Podge blurted out, tears welling up in his eyes. He struggled to dismount the bike and forcefully shoved the helmet into his teammate's hands.

"Wha' washin'?" Davey asked, not having a clue what the nut job was on about.

Podge pointed to a clothesline laden down with bed sheets.

"So?" said Davey, still absolutely clueless.

"There'll be no chance of gettin' the ride for at least a week now," Podge angrily explained.

Davey looked questioningly at his upset pal still unable to follow what was happening.

"Sharon doesn't like me dirtyin' the clean sheets with me jizz," said Podge, his two hands balled into fists.

"Way too much information there for my likin'," Davey said, holding up a hand, trying his best not to picture his fat friend and his mutant missus doing the bold thing.

"I'm only short of carryin' me balls around in a wheelbarrow as it is," Podge complained. He grabbed hold of his testicles reminiscent of Mickey Jackson's dancing to further demonstrate the point. "The fuckin' weight of them."

"Thought ye were walkin' a bit funny all righ'," said Davey, trying to make light of the situation but once he realised that Podge was having none of it he tried a different angle.

"Why don't ye use a few friendlies, contain the payload?" he suggested.

"Johnnies?" asked Podge. Davey gave him an affirmative nod.

"Never thought of it to be honest," his teammate admitted.

Davey took a pack of three condoms from his leather jacket pocket and handed the box over. "There's two left, should keep ye goin' for an hour or three, wha'?" he said before coming to his senses and shuddering at the thought.

Podge caught his teammate by surprise by giving him an affectionate hug. "Thanks, bud, this really means a lot to me. Ye might've just saved me marriage."

Davey felt sorry for the poor bloke for a split second. 'Fuck it, it could be a lot worse – it could be me,' he thought.

After leaving his teammate to face Jabba the Hutt's ugly sister, Davey continued on with his journey home. He meandered his way through the busy city traffic, careful not to scratch his bike or to be unseated as he went over a series of speed bumps. A red light momentarily halted his progress giving him time to think. No matter how hard he tried to rid his mind of Podge's nonsensical comment about seeing his Ma in the hospital the other day he just couldn't. Shaking his head he did a u-turn and travelled a short distance until he came to a row of neatly kept terraced houses. He shut the engine down and waited for a few moments then dismounted and knocked on the door with the lion's head knocker. A woman in her late fifties, her hair held up with foam rollers and covered with a net, opened up.

"Vera?" said Davey, somewhat dumbfounded.

Vera gently placed her hand on the young man's shoulder. "Come in, love and I'll stick us on a nice pot of tea."

It was feeding time at the zoo back at Podge's gaff. He sat at the table warily watching Sharon, who was built like a former Soviet hammer thrower who'd been pumped with a shitload of steroids, slap up the meal. She planted a plate full of something vaguely resembling food, swimming in grease down in front of him. He looked at it for a second too long.

"Problem?" Sharon growled.

"No, not at all, love," answered Podge as quickly as he could manage in as much of a non-confrontational manner as humanly possible.

"Wouldn't want to be," his better half declared. Sharon turned back to the counter to sort out her own grub.

Podge rested an elbow on the table while quietly pushing the food around the plate with his fork. "I was thinkin'..." he began.

"That would be a first," Sharon said, her voice laced with sarcasm.

Podge feigned laughter. "Good one. Could we have a salad or somethin' like that for dinner one of the nights?"

Sharon swung around, a large carving knife held firmly in her man sized hand. "A salad? Are ye a fuckin' rabbit now or wha'?"

"No, no, of course not. Just tryin' to watch the aul weight," Podge blurted out as he grabbed his belly and forced a less than convincing smile.

"Ye better not have some trollop on the go," she said, "I'm fuckin' warnin' ye."

"Jaysus no," replied Podge, physically squirming in his seat, "Sure wha' eejit would put up with the likes of me?"

Sharon raised an eyebrow.

"Present company excluded of course," he immediately added after realising what had just escaped from his big fat gob. Sharon's eyebrows always reminded him of Hairy Molly caterpillars but of course he was never brave enough to mention this.

His wife pointed the knife menacingly at him and said, "Eat."

With the toilet door bolted behind him, Podge listened carefully for what felt like an eternity before deciding that the coast was clear. He then proceeded to take handfuls of the fatty food from his pockets, threw it down the toilet and flushed. The water in the bowl rose perilously high with the lumps of food swirling around and around threatening to jump back out. He held his breath. His legs went weak. How in the name of Jaysus would he explain this to Sharon? At the very last moment when all seemed lost the waters began to recede, sucking with it the stodgy grub. He blessed himself while at the same time cursing his manager and the new healthy regime that had been unfairly imposed on the players. And without any form of medical consultation either!

Just like with any team there was no shortage of banter in the Sporting Les Behans' dressing room. Most of what was said was complete and utter bullshit but now and again a nugget of truth would be unearthed. Huey could of course have put his mind at ease with regards to growing a third testicle if he'd only checked the internet. But this was Huey and he had an aversion to technology. The lads were constantly giving him stick about his outdated mobile and he would time and again reply by telling them that he only needed a phone to make a call and to take a call. However, try as he might he couldn't shake the idea that he was somehow deficient in the trouser department. So here he was, shifting uneasily in his seat watching the doctor remove his disposable latex gloves and dropping them into the stainless-steel bin. The doctor washed his hands thoroughly, carefully drying them with some paper towels before dumping the waste. During the whole process he never once looked over in the direction of his worried patient. Huey knew he was playing for time. The doctor finally pulled his chair out from under his desk and sat down, joining his bony fingers tightly together.

"And you brought no one with you today?" he asked.

"No, I'm here on me tod," Huey replied.

"Okay, let's not beat around the bush. I've found a lump," the doctor solemnly began but was immediately interrupted by his patient.

"Thank God for that. I was beginnin' to think I was abby normal."

"I'm afraid you may have misheard me," the doctor said, caught completely off guard by the man's more than unusual response.

"No, pal. I heard ye loud and clear. Me third ball's finally growin'," Huey said. After all the slagging the lads had given him in the dressing room he was barely able to contain his delight. In fact, he couldn't wait to show them.

Fran and Tracey sat across the candlelit table from one another, toying with elaborately concocted desserts in the fancy Italian restaurant.

"I can't believe it's been almost two years since you were out on a date," Tracey said, gently probing for more info.

"The Ma talks too much," said Fran but not in an unkind way. He knew only too well what his mother was like.

"What happened?" his date asked, pursuing the truth.

Fran got the waiter's attention. "The bill, please."

Tracey reached across and took Fran's hand. He looked into her eyes searching hard for a fault, any fault but was unable to find one. He let out a tired sigh before deciding to open up. "Vicky got involved with the wrong crowd and started doin' drugs. She managed to get her act together, we made plans, decided to start a family. Not long after that she got pregnant."

The waiter returned with the bill, placed it on the table and left but not without giving the gorgeous blonde the once over. Tracey pretended not to notice although she did find it amusing considering the fact that in her younger, brace-wearing days, boys wouldn't give her a second glance in a fit. Fran put his hand in his pocket.

"Don't you dare, I told you this was on me," Tracey said, chastising him.

The couple strolled along the cobbled street past the numerous restaurants all of which seemed to be doing a steady trade. Maybe the boom was back. Fran had enjoyed Tracey's company but still felt a little guilty if he was being honest, like he was cheating or something.

"We were all out, the family, at me daughter Laura's Christenin', havin' a really good time," he said, continuing on from the conversation inside the Italian restaurant, "Vicky had been a bit down, ye know, after havin' the baby and all that lark but she was gettin' back to her old self, she was in great form." Fran stopped walking and bit down on his lip. Tracey took his hand but remained silent. "We were havin' a singsong. Vicky's Da had just finished his party piece, Matt Monroe's Born Free when she decided she needed some air. I told her I'd go with her but she was havin' none of it. She was a bit tipsy but not drunk so I wasn't too concerned. Her Ma was hasslin' me to go outside but Vicky insisted that I go to the bar instead and get her a double rum and coke." Fran rubbed his eye, embarrassed that a tear might escape.

"It's okay," Tracey said, trying to comfort him but not wanting to appear to be overdoing it with the sympathy at the same time.

"Vicky was found dead a few hours later in a doss house. Bad gear," Fran revealed.

Tracey looked confused. "But I thought you said she'd stopped taking drugs?"

He shrugged his shoulders. "Her former dealer just happened to be passin' by, offered her a little pick me up. Turned out the scumbag had mixed all sorts of crap with it, including rat poison, to maximise his profits."

"That's murder. I hope justice was done."

Fran absentmindedly kicked a bottle-top belonging to one of those new craft beers which was lying discarded on the ground with the toe of his shoe. "Let's talk about somethin' else," he said.

Tracey felt she'd intruded enough and decided to let it go. They walked past the Bingo Hall just as a crowd of geriatrics came scrambling out. The blue rinse brigade were only short of tripping one another up as they descended on the adjoining Italian chipper, squeezing through the narrow glass door as if the Great Famine itself was due to recommence at any moment. Fran stopped dead in his tracks.

"What's wrong?" Tracey asked.

"The Ma said they were decoratin' the Bingo Hall," answered Fran. He turned to his date, "I've been set up, haven't I?" he said, trying to comprehend how easily he'd been duped.

Tracey tried to keep a straight face but was failing miserably. "Ok, you got me but it was all your mother's idea."

The affluent housing estate was calm and serene at this hour of the night, a far cry from the part of town where Fran hailed from. He walked Tracey to her front door but wasn't sure what to do next as he'd been that long out of the game. Tracey wasn't quite sure either having dedicated almost her entire adult life to one man who turned out to be a complete whoremaster. She searched through her handbag and retrieved her door key with the silly, miniature horseshoe attached, not that she was overly superstitious. She turned to her date and they both stood there looking at one another, an awkward silence filling the gap. Edging closer, she gave Fran a gentle peck on the lips. "I really enjoyed tonight," she admitted, "Send me a text if you fancy a repeat. Night." She opened the door, disappeared inside and was gone.

Fran stood there, kind of feeling like a teenager all over again. "Nigh'," he eventually said to no one but himself, turned on his heels and headed for home.

Podge wasn't the only player trying to come to terms with the various restrictions that the manager, Pa Baxter, had imposed for the supposed good of the team. Yoyo was in purgatory having suffered from a chemical imbalance for as long as he could remember. This was no surprise as he'd been born a heroin addict to a junky mother and had spent his first few weeks on this earth being weaned off the stuff. For anyone unfortunate enough to be exposed to that sort of horror it was a heart-breaking sight.

"For fuck's sake," Yoyo swore.

The manager couldn't expect him to stop self-medicating just like that. It would be a very dangerous and completely irresponsible thing to do. No, he really should consult with a doctor first. But who could he go to? He'd been banned from practically every medical practice within a ten-mile radius for allegedly stealing prescription books, prior to developing his day-care centre scam. "Ye need to get a grip," he said aloud. He jumped up off the couch and paced back and forth in his small flat, feeling like a caged animal trapped in some dingy lab. With a steady roll of cash now coming in he could afford to move into a more spacious place, but he liked the area. Nobody asked questions and once he didn't flash the spondoolicks he was able to keep his 'other' enterprise below the radar. He stopped suddenly and glared up at the stained ceiling. A headboard was banging rhythmically against a wall in the flat above. In his heightened state, noises which he never knew even existed were now driving him absolutely demented.

"For Jaysus sake!" he shouted up at the ceiling, shaking both his fists, "Give her a break will ye, ye poxy show off."

He stormed off to the bathroom, stared at his sweaty reflection in the medicine cabinet mirror then reefed open the door. The press appeared to be jam packed with every possible tablet to have ever hit the market, legal or otherwise. He snatched one of the brown cylindrical containers and with hands shaking madly unscrewed the cap, emptying out a handful of pills. The couple in the upstairs flat were still going at it hammer and thongs. He was about to pop the tablets but just about managed to restrain himself.

"Bollox!" he roared, flinging the pills into the sink, recapped the container and fired it back into the cabinet. "This bleedin' football team will be the death of me, I swear," he screamed.

The terraced house seemed to be alive as it pulsed with booming, vibrating music, loaded with extra bass. Boozed up partygoers danced their way around the lightweights who were staggering out through the front door having already had their fill. Charlie checked his watch before rambling across the road to join in the fun. As he was approaching the doorway of the gaff a bloke came storming out, effing and blinding, almost knocking him over. Charlie snapped his head around and watched the man disappear into the adjoining property, slamming the door after him. There was something very familiar about the geezer, but Charlie couldn't quite put his finger on it. He decided the matter wasn't worth dwelling on and made his way into the party to join in the craic instead. The hallway was that narrow you wouldn't have wanted to be claustrophobic or be in a hurry from a fire. Charlie stepped over a wasted teenage girl who was slumped against a wall.

"All righ', buddy?" shouted Anto above the racket from the far end of the passageway on seeing his friend.

Charlie greeted his old mate with a man hug. Anto was wired to the moon at the best of times but he seemed to be in really top form tonight.

"D'ye see the head on yer man?" Anto said, laughing.

"Who?" asked Charlie.

Anto pointed towards the door and said, "The arsehole who just left. Don't worry, I marked his card well and good for him."

"Didn't take much notice to be honest."

Anto ran a hand over his sweating, bald head, flicking the beads of sweat off. "Only moved in the other day and he comes bargin' in here, runnin' amok, tellin' me to turn down the tunes."

"Yeah?"

"Told him where to go, the posh fuck. I mean, if he's that uppity what's he doin' livin' in a kippy bedsit?"

It suddenly registered with Charlie that the man he'd seen leaving in a snot was his teammate, Mick Young. But what would he be doing around here? It didn't make any sense. He'd have to ask him at the next training session.

"Come on, there's a ton of snow inside," said Anto, "Although Vinny Vac's doin' his best to make it disappear." Charlie followed his enthusiastic pal into the kitchen. "Look who's here!" Anto shouted.

Vinny Vac was on all fours on top of the kitchen table, naked except for his customised superhero boxer shorts which identified him as 'Out Of It Man'. He turned around, a Vuvuzela gripped tightly in one hand. Anto, seeing Vinny Vac's vacant expression, put an arm around Charlie's shoulders.

"It's Charlie? Good time Charlie?" Anto explained, pulling his mate even closer, almost squeezing the life out of him.

"Ah yeah, Charlie baby," jabbered Vinny Vac, his pupils seeming to drift independently of one another around his yellowing eyes. He quickly lost interest and turned back to the table where a pile of cocaine sat. Snorting gear wasn't exactly a spectator event.

"I've found a use for these cunt'n things an all," he proudly boasted, jamming the Vuvuzela up one nostril and true to his name began to vacuum up everything in sight.

Anto turned to Charlie with a beaming head on him. "He's some animal, isn't he? Better get in there while there's still somethin' left," he said, giving his friend some encouragement.

"Not for a minute," said Charlie. Despite the generous offer he had a nagging feeling somewhere in the back of his mind. The football team.

"Are ye not well?" Anto asked, suddenly concerned for his friend.

Charlie laughed. "I'm grand, just pacin' meself," he lied.

"Not like you," Anto said, "Yer usually up to yer oxters given half the chance." He rapidly flicked his tongue back and forth along the entire surface of his gums, dropped to his hands and knees and crawled towards the table where some of Colombian's finest produce had fallen to the floor and began to lap it up.

Charlie watched, utterly dismayed. Is this the way he acted when he was on one? Anto looked over his shoulder, eyes bulging and madness written all over his face.

"Waste not, want not!" he shouted.

Charlie nodded. "Pigs at a trough," he said in a barely audible voice. Turning around, he retraced his steps back down the narrow hallway where the teenage girl was still slumped. She had vomited an almost luminescent substance down the front of her top as well as spraying the ends of her matted hair.

'Couldn't handle the aul alcopops,' thought Charlie, shaking his head and making his leave.

Fran tossed and turned restlessly in his bed, his regular nightmare having returned once again. "This is not righ'..." he called out in his sleep. Images of the flashing sirens of various types of emergency vehicles lighting up the dark night filled his head. He saw himself sat on the edge of the pavement, his head hidden in his hands. Paramedics forced their way through a gathered crowd that had surrounded the lifeless body of the well-known local drug pusher. Some of the onlookers were recording the demise of the much-hated pariah of the community on their phones despite the best efforts of the police to stop them. One lad had even managed to lie down next to the corpse to take a selfie until the long arm of the law reefed him to his feet and flung him back into the ghoulish spectators. Richie, hands behind his back and clasped in cuffs, was being led away by a Garda to a waiting squad car. He made no attempt to resist arrest. Fran looked up and caught Richie's eye. His brother smiled back at him for a fleeting moment and was then put into the squad car. Fran got to his feet and made his way, trance-like, towards Richie. The Garda shut the car door and held a hand up to Fran, holding him back. "This is not righ'..." Fran half-heartedly complained.

The squad car slowly pulled away with Richie looking forlornly out through the rear window.

"No!" shouted Fran. He woke with a start and realised that he'd been roaring in his sleep. He wiped the sweat from his forehead and looked over at Laura who was still fast asleep in her cot. Although he envied her peacefulness, he hoped that she would continue having far more pleasant dreams than the one he'd just escaped from.

Chapter 9

Detective Lyons was sitting behind her desk reviewing another pointless document on how to improve policing in the community when she was interrupted by a polite tap on her open office door. She looked up to discover Cartland standing in the doorway and could immediately tell from his demeanour that he was the bearer of good news.

He cleared his throat. "Sorry for disturbing you..."

"You're grand, come in. It's only some tripe about doing a better job," Lyons said, referring to the glossy brochure in her hand, "If we all lived in la-la land that is." She deftly tossed the worthless document, expertly landing it into a bin sitting in the corner of her office.

"Good shot," said her colleague.

"Unfortunately, I get a lot of material to practice with."

The young detective smiled.

"You look like the cat that got the cream. Don't tell me you've already corrupted one of our pretty new recruits?" Lyons said, teasing her subordinate.

Cartland's cheeks reddened slightly. He was so easy to play. "No, nothing like that," he said, managing to recover, "But I think I might just have found out where Davey Byrne is hiding the stolen furniture."

"Say that again," Lyons said, the revelation lifting her spirits.

"It would be a lot easier if I showed you on your computer," Cartland answered, already moving towards his superior's desk.

Lyons rolled back in her chair allowing Cartland to gain access to her PC. He quickly began to tap away at the keyboard. His boss was extremely impressed with his dexterity but said nothing. Her own amazing typing skills consisted of using the index finger on each hand and punching the keys with the tenderness of a heavyweight slugger.

"There!" Cartland proudly announced, stepping back so that Lyons could see.

She rolled her chair forward accidentally touching her manicured hand off of her colleague's. Their eyes met momentarily before Lyons snapped out of it.

"What am I supposed to be looking at?" she asked, breaking the silence.

"It's Google maps," said Cartland.

"I can see that," she said, her professional cap firmly back on.

"Sorry," the young detective apologised. "This is a map showing the row of houses where Byrne lives."

"Okay?"

"All the properties are the same except for his place."

Lyons leaned in closer to the screen and smiled. "Davey Byrne's back garden is a lot shorter than his neighbours," she said. "Whereas the one that backs onto his is much longer." In a male-dominated workplace, women generally had to be that bit smarter than their Counterparts. And Lyons was just that and some.

Cartland pointed at a building on screen. "This is the large shed behind the hedge which we saw on our previous visit and presumed it was part of the other garden."

"Great detective work, Detective," Lyons said, congratulating her colleague, "We better get a warrant this time. I've a feeling we're going to need it."

Cartland was chuffed with himself. "I'm on it," he said, already striding for the door.

"We'll need another one for the property backing onto Byrne's as well. And get backup just in case the idiot tries to flee," ordered Lyons.

Davey happened to be in his living-room listening to the album Science & Faith from Dublin band The Script when he spotted the two detectives through the net curtains pulling in. A squad car eased up behind them and two energetic young cops jumped out, hoping to make a name for themselves no doubt.

"Wha' the fuck are they doin' back?" Davey cursed.

A warrant was flashed in Davey's face and he was forcefully marched down the back garden by the detectives until they came to a secret opening in the laurel hedge.

"Very clever, even if it kills me to say so," Lyons said. She could tell by her victim's expression that he was trying to work out how they'd learned about the gap in the bushes. He'd be thinking that somebody had grassed him up.

"Google maps," she gleefully revealed, taking the scumbag out of his misery, "Now, shall we?"

Davey went through the opening in the shrubbery as instructed and was met by Eddie, his petrified elderly neighbour who was accompanied by two police officers.

"Does this building belong to you?" Cartland sternly asked the old man.

The neighbour glanced at Davey, not wanting to land him in it.

"It belongs to me," Davey admitted, not wishing to drag Eddie any deeper into his Shenanigans.

"Open it," ordered Lyons.

Davey paused for a moment then did as he was told. He held the heavy shed door wide open as the expectant detectives peered inside. It was completely empty. Lyons immediately turned away and stormed off, obediently followed by her colleague. She didn't need to hang about knowing too well that they wouldn't find a single shred of evidence. Although he knew he shouldn't, Davey couldn't resist giving Cartland a dainty little wave as the detective left. As the other policemen departed the scene of the failed bust, Davey couldn't help but notice the smirks on their faces but decided not to comment.

The detectives got back into their car, neither one saying a word. Lyons reefed the sun visor down and stared hard at her reflection in the small rectangular mirror. She dragged on the skin under her eyes with the thumb and index finger of one hand.

"How did I miss that fucking shed? I'm getting too old for this shit," she swore.

"We both missed it. Besides, you're only in your prime," said Cartland, trying to console his boss.

"Bollocks but thanks all the same. I know that's where the little pup had the stuff hidden." She shoved the sun visor back up. "I need sugar."

The detectives drove the short distance to a small cafe that Lyons knew only too well. She sat opposite Cartland and studied him as he methodically ate a fresh apple and sipped still water from a plastic bottle. She emptied two sachets of sugar into her cappuccino and took a drink before devouring a bun that oozed enough fresh cream and jam to cause a coronary.

"Look at you, your healthy eating, you're putting me to shame," she said after consuming her treat and most likely her total daily recommended calorie intake, "I'll have to go on a diet."

"Don't be silly, you look great just the way you are," Cartland said.

"What planet are you from?" Lyons asked, knowing quite well that it was a load of crap but still secretly pleased.

"Men love real women," he said.

"Fat birds."

"Curvaceous ladies."

Lyons ran her finger around her plate wiping up the remaining fresh cream watched closely by her younger colleague. She put her finger in her mouth and slowly sucked it clean. Cartland gulped his water, spilling some down his chin. He quickly dabbed it dry with a cheap serviette.

"Fancy another one?" he asked, trying to disguise his awkwardness.

"No, but I do fancy something else," replied Lyons, deciding to up the ante.

The detective's car was parked at the very back of the deserted underground car park. Lyons was slouched on the backseat with her legs in the air resting on Cartland's muscular shoulders as he knelt between the front two seats. The female detective's tights and knickers hung around her ankles as Cartland banged her hard.

"Give it to me, bad boy..." she demanded to which her colleague duly obliged.

In all the excitement Cartland's foot hit a button on the dash activating the cars flashing lights. Neither detective in their heightened state of passion noticed the faint clicking indicating that the lights were on. The CCTV camera that was mounted on the concrete ceiling of the building homed in on the rocking vehicle, zooming in on the unsuspecting occupants.

Davey plodded along the sterile hospital corridor unsure of where he was going. He was carrying a massive bunch of flowers which he'd acquired – his little euphemism for robbed, along with several helium balloons with 'Get Well' messages printed on them as well as a jumbo-sized box of milk chocolates. Unable to properly see ahead, he collided with a petite nurse knocking her onto her backside and dropping the chocolates in the process.

"Jaysus, I'm so sorry, are ye alrigh'?" Davey immediately apologised.

"Probably have a bruise the size of the Glenties on me arse but besides that, yeah," answered the nurse in her cheeky Donegal accent. She picked up the sweets and handed them back to Davey. "Who's the lucky lady, then?"

"Me Ma. She's got cancer," Davey replied.

"Oh," answered the nurse, caught off guard by the man's frankness, "I'm sorry to hear that."

"Yer grand. Ye don't know where St. Clare's ward is, do ye?" he asked.

The nurse pointed to a list of overhead signs that guided the way to the various wards within the building.

Davey looked up and paused. "Righ'..." he said.

The nurse, picking up on his hesitation, put her hand softly on his arm. "Sure, I'm going that way meself. And anyhow, the place is like a giant maze. I've worked here for several years and I get lost at least twice a day."

"That'd be great," said Davey, extremely thankful for the help.

Davey shuffled through the packed ward trying not to stare at the mostly elderly patients, with their sunken cheeks and yellowy grey skin. It was the one place he hated the most, hospitals. That distinctive disinfectant smell made he feel queasy and it seemed to have the ability to camp inside his nostrils long after he'd escaped from the place. He was filled with relief when he finally spotted his Ma, sitting upright in a bed next to a large double-glazed window which was allowing the sun's warm rays to brighten the place. He kissed her gently on the forehead while at the same time almost knocking her eye out with the stems of the floral bouquet he'd brought.

"Hope they're lookin' after ye?" he quizzed, oblivious to the fact that he'd nearly blinded his Ma.

"They're doin' their best. Are they for me?" she asked, nodding towards the various gifts that her son was laden down with.

"They are indeed," he said proudly. He handed her the flowers and chocolates then tied the balloons onto the metal bed rail.

"Thanks, son. Put them in that vase," she said.

Davey put the colourful flowers into a glass ornament sitting on the bedside locker as instructed. His Ma set the sweets down on her lap and slowly traced her thumb along the brand name. "Me favourites."

Her son humbly nodded in acknowledgement. "D'ye need money? I'll get ye the cash, get ye into one of those posh clinics," he said, rambling somewhat.

"Not my style. Besides, chemo is chemo no matter where ye get it," his Ma kindly replied.

"Wha' abou' cannabis?"

"Become a drug addict at my age? Not a chance."

Davey knew it was pointless trying to explain to her that she wasn't going to become a junkie on a bit of weed. "Why didn't ye tell me?" he asked instead, finding the bad news difficult to take.

"Wanted to see how I'd get on first," she said, giving very little away.

"And?" he asked, pushing for more information.

"Takin' everyday as it comes, son."

The hospital visit hadn't lasted long. Davey's mother was very tired and had ordered her son to go home and get something to eat, even if it meant one of those unhealthy takeaways he was so fond of. He duly obliged and as he was attempting to retrace his steps, trying to find his way out of the hospital labyrinth, he once again met the helpful young nurse that he'd bumped into earlier.

"How's the Mammy?" the nurse apprehensively asked.

"Great. She'll be home in a coupla days," Davey replied.

"That's fantastic news," she said, genuinely pleased to hear something good for a change. "Want to go for a drink? I'll be finished shortly."

"Can't, have the bike," he said, nodding to his leather jacket and trousers as proof.

"Coffee?" suggested the nurse, not willing to give up that easily.

"Can't stand the stuff."

"Alright. How about a cup of tea?"

"Okay."

She extended her hand and said, "Me name's Lily by the way."

"Davey. Please to meet ye," he said, shaking her tiny hand warmly. A dirty thought popped into his head. Something the lads used to say about dating women with small hands 'cause it made yer mickey look bigger! He quickly tried to block this out as he was guaranteed to say something inappropriate.

Davey followed his new friend into another ward, St. Michael's. The walls were brightly painted with colourful cartoon characters. Rows of cots lined both sides of the room, with bean bags, toys and miniature chairs gathered at the far end. A second nurse checked on the young patients who were fast asleep in the cots. Davey stood with his back pressed tightly against the door feeling overwhelmed.

"You're allowed to breath," whispered Lily, "Take a seat, I'll be back in a tick." She winked at him then went over to her colleague and exchanged greetings. They both looked back at Davey and giggled.

"Hi, I'm Millie. What's your name?" said a little voice from out of nowhere.

Davey looked down at the small, bald-headed girl with the almost translucent skin who had just taken hold of his hand. Her bright and cheery smile tried to mask the pain she was suffering but her weary, chestnut coloured eyes told another story.

"Me name's Davey, Davey Byrne," he cautiously replied.

"Please to meet you, Davey, Davey Byrne. Will you read me a story, please?"

A short while later when Lily had finished the last of her duties she made her way over to where Davey was sunken into a yellow bean bag, looking as if he was being eaten by Pac-Man. The little girl that had asked him earlier to read her a story was now sound asleep, cuddled into his chest, still clutching her favourite book.

"Ye have a way with the ladies, I see," said Lily, smiling.

"Wha', bore them to sleep?" replied Davey. Although he was kind of embarrassed at the situation he was also secretly chuffed to bits.

As Davey and Lily left the hospital, an ambulance, sirens muted but lights flashing frantically, pulled up. Two paramedics bailed from the vehicle and whipped out a stretcher, its wheels automatically dropping to the ground. There was a man strapped to it, his face mostly covered by an oxygen mask. He seemed to be tangled up with what strangely appeared to be a builder's measuring tape of all things. Davey watched in silence as the stretcher raced by.

"Are you alright?" Lily asked.

"I could've sworn that was Tommo from the pub..." he said then shook his head dismissively. "Ah don't mind me, I must be hallucinatin' with all that's bein' happenin' lately."

"Stress can do some pretty strange things to the system," Lily agreed.

The spare helmet was retrieved from the storage box on the back of the motorbike by Davey and handed it over to Lily. She put it on and adjusted the strap without any difficulty.

"There's no need to be nervous or anythin'," Davey said, reassuring his would-be passenger.

Lily held out her hand. "Give me a go."

"Wha'?"

"Come on, sure I used to have a Vespa."

"A fuckin' scooter, pardon me Italian."

Lily batted her long eyelashes. "Ye look like a good teacher, sure ye can show me what to do."

Lily rode the bike slowly down the road with Davey riding pillion.

"Ye can go a bit faster if ye like," he said, really impressed by how well the young nurse was doing, especially handling a yoke as big as this.

Lily suddenly increased the throttle and the powerful bike surged forward forcing Davey to grab tightly onto her tiny waist, trying not to be unseated as the machine took off.

"Wha' are ye bleedin' doin'?" he just about managed to scream. Not only did Lily ignore him but she then proceeded to pull a wheelie.

Davey sat ashen faced on the old couch in Lily's bedsit. His stomach felt sympathy with the chair, its foam insides doing their best not to completely burst out. Lily handed him a mug of tea and set two glasses and a bottle of brandy down on the varnished timber floor.

"For the shock," she advised.

She filled both glasses with the alcohol and knocked back the contents of one before refilling it again. Davey looked around the room. The walls were decorated with motorbike riders doing outrageous mid-air stunts.

"Ye could have told me ye were into bikes. Frightened the shite outta me," he said, complaining but not really complaining at the same time. He'd never met a bird like this before in his entire life and didn't know how he should feel.

"Aye, surely," said Lily, conceding the point.

"Where d'ye learn?" Davey asked, knocking back his brandy with a trembling hand. "Lived in the arsehole of nowhere and had six brothers," the young nurse explained as she topped up her guest's glass.

"When will she be able to go home?" he asked.

"Who, Millie?"

Davey nodded.

"Never. The wee lass is terminal."

"Righ'," he said, completely taken aback by the revelation. He knew the little girl was sick but he presumed she'd get better. She wasn't old or anythin'. "So why is she in the hospital and not one of those other places then?"

"A hospice?"

"Yeah."

"Lack of funds and all that crap yet they're pissing money away left right and centre on managers and the likes."

"Not righ' that," said Davey. It always seemed to be the ordinary person who suffered the most.

"That's just the way it is. Try not to think about it too much, it'll only drive ye mental."

Davey rubbed his chin. "Still."

"Drink up, I want to show ye some of me other riding skills," the nurse said, teasingly.

He looked at her. "Hope ye didn't have to rely on yer brothers for the experience?"

"Ye cheeky little shit," Lily said, playfully grabbing him into a headlock and lightly punching him in the midriff. He wrestled her off of him and they ended up on the floor gazing into one another's eyes. Davey seized the moment and lobbed the gob. He had a good feeling about this young wan from Donegal.

It wasn't quite morning yet as Davey carefully climbed out of Lily's bed doing his best not to disturb her. After gathering up his clothes which had been hastily discarded in a crumpled heap prior to sex, he quietly left. Outside in the street there wasn't a sinner to be seen. The shaded moon struggled to light up the pitch black, something that always made Davey's nocturnal excursions that little bit easier. He pushed his motorbike about fifty yards down the road, kick-started the engine into life and rode off.

Once he'd reached his destination, a short distance across the sleeping city, he didn't hang about. He hid his bike behind bushes before retrieving a canvas bag that he'd stashed there on an earlier visit, slinging it over his shoulder. Recognisance played a huge part in how he operated and there was a lot less chance of things going pear-shaped when you did adequate prep. Having said that he still enjoyed the more opportunistic occasions when they presented themselves. The clay brick perimeter wall posed no difficulties for him to scale as he took advantage of the toeholds that had formed in the stonework from years of weathering. He raced across the deserted car park using the shadows for cover, pausing next to the large warehouse. After listening carefully for a few long seconds but hearing nothing, he shimmied up a drainpipe that gave him access directly onto the roof of the building.

The reverse warning alarms of a delivery van began beeping from down below. Davey crawled along the roof of the building with the deftness of a ninja, in his own mind anyhow, and craned his head over the edge to suss things out. The van slowly backed up to the warehouse roller doors, stopping just shy of the entrance. The chap on duty inside the building monitored the vehicle on his security camera and pressed a button on his control panel to send the roller shutters whirring into action and opening up. A portly delivery man just about managed to squeeze his way out of the now stationary vehicle, armed with an electronic clipboard. Despite the ungodly hour the man on the night shift came out of the warehouse to receive the delivery, brimming with energy.

"Yer enthusiastic?" said the driver.

"As soon as this lot's shifted, I'm out of here," the warehouse lad explained. "It's an awful long nigh' hangin' around on yer own."

"Wha' about security?"

"Yer lookin' at it."

The driver grinned. "Better make sure ye lock up properly or ye'll never hear the end of it," he warned in a jovial manner.

"In fairness they've the place well secured. No chance of anyone gettin' in, bit like the missus' knickers, wha'?" Both men laughed.

Davey pulled back from the edge, lit up a cigarette, took a deep, satisfying drag and prepared for the wait, hoping it wouldn't be too long.

"Do you smell smoke?" the warehouse worker suddenly asked, the concern audible in his voice.

"Don't think so," answered the driver, not really giving a toss if the place burnt to the ground so long as he got a signature for his delivery first.

"I don't want to be botherin' ringin' it in if it's a false alarm, they'll only eat the fuckin' head off of me, again," the store worker said, all in a quandary.

Davey looked longingly at his cigarette for a couple of seconds then stubbed it out and flicked it away.

"It's probably some gurriers burnin' out a robbed car somewhere," the deliveryman continued from down below, anxious to finish the job and be on his way.

"Yeah, yer probably righ'," the warehouse lad finally relented. "I'll get the trolley."

After about an hour the light coming up through the skylight in the warehouse roof went out.

"Thank Jaysus for that," Davey said to himself, rubbing the cheeks of his numb backside in an attempt to get the blood flowing again. He thought the two blokes below would never leave, jabbering on like two aul wans. At one point he felt like shouting down to get a bleedin' room. He checked his watch. He had a little under two hours to get in, do the business and get back out again before the day staff came on.

The canvas bag that Davey had earlier retrieved from the bushes contained a strong rope, as recommended by his unsuspecting teacher, Birdy, and a handy sized pinch bar. He prised open the skylight with ease, secured one end of the rope to a steel mounting which he'd noted while flying his drone over the area the previous weekend and lowered down the other end. It was time to see how his abseiling skills had come along after several strenuous but enjoyable sessions under the guidance of his own personal circus performer.

After successfully descending the rope, Davey, his face hidden by a ski mask, now stood in the middle of the warehouse with his hands on his hips. He was surrounded by a scattering of cardboard boxes all of which he had already ripped open. He held aloft a brand-new Ireland soccer jersey in his gloved hands. A large number 9 was printed on the back of the shirt while the front had miniature flags of Ireland and Brazil embroidered into it. He could barely contain his delight at the result.

"Davey Byrne, one. The F A fuckin' I, nil," he proudly boasted.

Chapter 10

Several squad cars were left abandoned outside the warehouse where Davey had completed his latest heist. A young Garda on sentry duty stood slouched behind yellow crime scene tape, his eyes following the comings and goings of an industrious ant as it made its way over the rough tarmac drive. He happened to look up at just the right time to spot detectives Lyons and Cartland out of the corner of his eye arriving in their unmarked car. He immediately straightened up. Although relatively new to the force, Lyons' fearsome reputation had preceded her, and the young man didn't fancy any unwarranted attention.

"As if I don't have enough problems to deal with," Lyons complained as she climbed out of the car followed by her obedient colleague. Cartland furrowed his brow at the comment, but the astute Lyons immediately picked up on his reaction. "Present company excluded of course, darling. If only I had a few more good men like you to call upon when the need arose," she said before uncharacteristically blowing him a reassuring kiss. She was beginning to lose the run of herself now that she was back in the saddle so to speak after a lengthy absence.

Cartland and the young Garda glanced at one another for a split second. The lesser ranked man dropped his eyes to the ground not wishing to get involved. He'd love to tell the lads back at the station what he'd witnessed but there wasn't a hope in hell they'd believe him. He barely believed it himself.

Inside the warehouse the detectives had begun their investigation in earnest. Cartland jotted down the info which he'd obtained from questioning the manager into his leather-bound notebook. While this was going on Lyons was strolling around, carefully taking in every inch of her surroundings.

"The camera monitoring this area had its lens spray painted," the nervous manager explained.

"What about the exterior cameras?" Cartland asked.

The manager shifted uneasily. "There's just the one and that only covers the immediate entrance."

"Clever," the investigating detective couldn't resist pointing out.

This did very little to calm the manager's nerves. "None of the alarms were triggered and there's no sign of the actual break in," he further explained. At almost sixty years of age he could have done without the hassle. Getting the contract to distribute the new Irish gear had been a major coup for the head honchos who owned the company and now the shagging stuff was gone. 'How was he supposed to ask for a pay rise now?' he thought.

"I'll need a list of every employee and all of the key-holders," Cartland said, snapping the self-pitying manager from his thoughts, "Don't suppose there's anyone here by the name of Keith Barry?"

The manager was addled. He racked his brain for an employee with that name but came up short.

Cartland closed his eyes and exhaled loudly through his nostrils.

The penny dropped with the manager. "Oh, you mean the magician chap," he said, finally getting the joke.

"Yes, the magician chap. Now, that list of employees?" Cartland said, impatiently clicking his fingers.

"Of course, of course. I'll get Susie in accounts to print that off for you."

The young detective leaned forward. "You know, more often than not it's an inside job," he said.

The stressed manager was about to defend his loyal staff but was distracted by the antics of detective Lyons. She was staring up at the skylight, scrutinizing its every feature. After a few seconds she turned to the manager.

"Roof?" she said.

"There's no access," he answered. "It..."

Lyons raised a hand cutting him off mid-sentence. She turned to Cartland. "Get me a tower heist."

The detectives rose up to the rooftop by way of a cherry picker operated by an employee from the local tool hire firm where it had been sourced. As soon as they'd reached the desired height the operator threw open the gate on the safety cage sensing the female detective's urgency. He was bundled out of the way as Lyons strode from the platform onto the roof and went straight for the skylight. She poked the curved, translucent piece of plastic with her shoe, easily dislodging it. Scouting the rest of the rooftop with a well-trained eye her attention was immediately drawn towards a lonesome cigarette butt discarded on the asphalt shingle. Cartland instantly spotted what his boss was focusing on.

"Bag it," she demanded.

The shattered pieces of glass from the grubby mirror were scattered across the floor of Mick's bedsit. He stared at the numerous cuts on his knuckles, mesmerised by the droplets of blood which were slowly forming on the surface of his skin. As the droplets expanded, they touched their neighbour, gathered momentum and finally fell to the ground. The wounds on his flesh weren't nearly as deep as the ones he felt from Lady Wallace's betrayal. After his disastrous introduction into the world of 'Camming' and particularly the ridicule he'd received from the American playboy and his Latino boyfriend, Mick felt he'd no option but to make contact with Lady Wallace.

He'd asked her for a loan as well as jokingly suggesting that they elope. Lady Wallace had laughed off his marriage proposal but promised to consider his request to borrow money. Instead she had rang Mick's boss, Mr. Watts, to make a complaint. She had threatened to take her business elsewhere unless Mick was taken off the sale of her stately home. The outcome was a call from Mr. Watts where Mick was read the riot act. His boss informed him that he was a very lucky boy to still have a job and that he was being confined to desk duty with immediate effect and for the foreseeable future. Of course, none of this would have happened if Mick's parents hadn't mismanaged their business affairs and in turn his inheritance. They were definitely the ones to blame and he wasn't going to let them forget about it in a hurry.

Davey's motorbike was parked outside the safe house that Mick had begrudgingly allowed Richie to temporarily hide out in. In an upstairs room, Richie, dressed in a t-shirt and shorts, was running hard on a treadmill, keenly keeping an eye on a news report on the wall-mounted television. On screen, Johnny Carter was swaying perilously on top of a tall construction crane waving about a half empty bottle of whiskey. A caption that read 'England Captain Johnny Carter Arrested For Public Disorder' streamed along the crawler at the bottom of the screen. Other images of Johnny Carter looking drunk and dishevelled and being escorted from a police van were also shown. Reporters and photographers frantically jostled with one another outside the courthouse trying to record the talented footballer's meteoric fall from grace.

Davey waltzed into the bedroom. "All righ', buddy," he cheerfully greeted his pal.

"What's the story?" replied Richie, reducing his running speed gradually before coming to a complete stop.

While Richie was towelling himself dry, Davey nodded towards the T.V. "Wha' a complete tosser. All that money and fame and he's still not fuckin' happy."

His teammate forced a smile. Davey threw him a plastic bag which he caught handy enough.

"A present," Davey half explained.

Richie opened the bag and retrieved one of the stolen Ireland jerseys. He held it up, a huge grin on his face.

"I knew it was you, ye mad bastard when I heard it on the radio. Wha' did Fran say?"

Davey winced and said, "Haven't exactly told him yet."

The three lads, Davey, Fran and Richie sat side by side on the leather couch wearing bold boy expressions. The stolen Ireland jerseys were heaped in a pile on the coffee table in front of them. Mick paced back and forth, a folded newspaper in his hand. He stopped suddenly and held the paper up, angrily jabbing at the headline with his finger: FAI GO NUTS OVER MISSING BRAZILIAN GEAR. He then lunged forward and grabbed one of the jerseys, throwing it at Davey.

"Did you not think for one nanosecond that they'd be missed?" he shouted, "And then to bring them back here. Are you trying to get me locked up as well as sacked?"

"What's a nanosecond?" Davey asked, genuinely having no idea.

Mick flung the paper away, sending pages fluttering into the air.

"I told him it'd be alrigh' if he left them here for a day or two, especially with his own gaff only after bein' raided," Richie said, trying to explain the situation. He felt that Mick was blowing things out of all proportion.

"Well, it's all fucking sorted so," replied Mick, unable to disguise his contempt.

Fran was slightly taken aback. He'd known Mick all his life and his friend could be argumentative at the best of times but there was something different about him these past few days. He seemed to be unusually stressed out about something or other.

Richie rose slowly from the couch and squared up to Mick. "There's no need to be rude," he calmly warned.

Mick wisely took a step back knowing just how explosive Richie could be when he got going. He looked at Fran and said, "Outside," then stormed from the room.

Richie and Davey exchanged glances. "Oooh," they both said at once trying their best not to laugh.

Fran stared at the pair of them, shaking his head disapprovingly. "Not helpful, lads, not helpful at all." He then hurried outside to catch up with his friend.

Davey turned to Richie. "D'ye believe that shite Mick gave us about his car bein' robbed?"

"Not a chance," said Richie, "The Porsche is worth over two hundred thousand and his insurance company gives him a car fit for the scrap yard as a replacement? Don't think so."

Davey nodded in agreement. "There's somethin' goin' on there, big time. He must think we were only born yesterday."

Mick leant against the jalopy that he was now forced to drive, his arms folded defensively across his chest. He couldn't risk leaving his sports car parked outside the kippy bedsit as it would have stuck out like a sore thumb.

Instead he'd agreed with the mechanic who'd previously fixed his car to store it in his garage until circumstances improved, if ever. The downside to the arrangement was that the mechanic could only lend Mick this heap of shit he was standing next to but at least his prized possession was safely tucked away.

"He has to go," Mick said to Fran as soon as he saw him coming out of the house. He was completely frustrated at the blatant abuse of his hospitality and the risks that he was taking especially after recent events. He actually looked as if he might cry at the drop of a hat.

Fran gave him a comforting smile. "I know, bud, I know. In fairness though, Richie was only tryin' to get Davey out of a hole, hidin' the nicked jerseys. And besides, if Richie's forced to move out now, he'll more than likely end up back in prison and our cup run would be over." It wasn't subtle Fran knew. He had no way of knowing what was going on in his friend's world, he was just hoping to tap into Mick's inner winner mentality or something along those lines. The catchphrase was some ballsology Fran had heard recently and he hoped for the love of Jaysus that it worked.

A group of prison inmates looked on as two fellow cons, both stripped to the waist and bathed in sweat, battled against one another in a frantic game of handball in the concrete alley. Mr. Quinn waded through the onlookers at the rear of the court, receiving fearful nods which he mistook for respect, from anyone stupid enough to make eye contact.

"And the bleedin' dopes were about to kneecap the wrong geezer," said one of the inmates to his acquaintance unaware of Quinn's presence.

"Would ye ever fuck off," the other lag replied, not believing a single word out of the mouth of a man serving five years for fraud and embezzlement.

"I'm tellin' ye. Sure they had the wrong football team and all," the first inmate insisted, "I heard yer man shit himself."

The prisoners laughed at the botched punishment shooting. It was stories like these that helped relieve the boredom of being locked up all day and went some way to shortening a man's sentence. Mr. Quinn pushed his way aggressively through the men. It had surprised him how quickly news travelled, even in here.

"Watch where yer..." began the inmate who was telling the story.

The crime boss spun around and caught the lag by the throat, squeezing him tighter and tighter while his terrified pal looked on. A warder, noticing the potential flashpoint, strode towards the men to nip the situation in the bud. Quinn reluctantly released his grip allowing the prisoner to catch his breath.

"Sorry, Mr. Quinn. He didn't realise it was you," the pal apologised.

Quinn glared at the two cons then spat on the ground before walking away.

"The bloke's a bleedin' psycho," said the inmate as he massaged his throat.

His friend nodded in agreement. "God help the poor fucker who messed up the shootin' if Quinn has anythin' to do with it."

Chapter 11

The Sporting lads were milling about in the container dressing room getting ready for training. Charlie was the one exception as he sauntered about in just a towel.

"Heore, Jigsaw!" he called out.

His teammate looked up from adjusting the Velcro straps on his boots.

"D'ye like jellies?" Charlie asked.

Jigsaw hesitated for a split second then nodded his head vigorously and said, "I do."

Charlie dropped his towel. "Well, wine yer gums around that." A few of the lads shook their heads.

"I give up," said Davey. He then suddenly grabbed hold of Yoyo's wrist, "Is that nail varnish?" he asked.

The embarrassed player immediately tried to pull his hand away but Davey held on tight.

"That's a lovely shade of pink all the same," said Trigger, getting in on the act.

Yoyo was resigned to the fact that he'd been caught red handed so to speak, having forgotten to remove the nail varnish before he'd left his house that evening. "Look, I was stuck in the gaff all day and without the few pills I had time to think about me life and got a bit lonely and I, I decided to jazz things up a bit. Ye know the score."

"Ye dirtbird," slagged Al, knowing exactly what Yoyo had been up to.

"Is that wha' they mean by jazz hands then?" Jigsaw innocently asked.

"More like jizz hands," joked Trigger.

Fran shook his head and said, "I weep for the future."

"Ye should get yerself an aul dog, for the company," Trigger said but immediately changed his mind, "On second thoughts, don't."

Paddy Power sat forward. "I know this bloke who was thinkin' of settin' up a brothel with dogs."

"That's sick," Split said.

"Is that sick as in disgustin' or in a cool sort of way?" Jigsaw asked. He'd heard his nephew and his young mates talk like that but hadn't a clue what they were on about most of the time.

Mick gave his teammate a withering look that needed no words.

"There's a name for that sort of carry on," Davey said, trying to remember the term. Most of the lads looked equally puzzled.

"Bestiality," said Lenny, coming to their rescue.

"How well you knew that," Charlie said, pointing at Lenny, "Told yis, lads, it's the quiet ones ye have to watch." A few of the players laughed.

Lenny went puce. "I'm not into that... it's, that's horrible..." he stammered.

Fran put an arm around Lenny's shoulder. "He's only windin' ye up, take no notice."

"As I was sayin' before bein' rudely interrupted," Power said, pretending to be offended. "This bloke I know had this idea that he'd keep a few bitches in fancy kennels where ye could bring yer mutt along so he could do his business instead of humpin' the leg off of everyone who called around to yer gaff. Think he was gonna call it 'Give the Dog a Bone.'"

Al was suitably impressed. "That's a good fuckin' name that," he said.

"I've a better one," Trigger said, "The Lady is a Tramp, like the cartoon."

"Wha' about Bow, Wow," Gitsy suggested, emphasising the word Wow.

Podge was mad to get in on the act. "Wha' about The Doghouse?" he suggested.

"You'd know all about that," said Yoyo.

"I don't think the people who invented brainstormin' had this quite in mind," Fran said drolly.

Charlie jumped up all excited. "Lads, lads, I even have the theme song."

The rest of the players eagerly awaited the revelation.

Charlie cleared his throat. "How much is that doggie in the window, woof, woof," he sang before most of his teammates decided to join in. "The one with the waggly tail..." they sang.

Baxter stood outside the truck container dressing room, mobile phone held tightly to his ear, trying to drown out the singing coming from inside, while he listened to the voice on the other end. "Alright, lad, you take care," he said. He hung up and began to gently tap his phone against the palm of his hand, contemplating his next move. A trip to the alehouse didn't seem like a bad idea at a time like this. Instead, he went back into the truck container to deliver the bad news. He rubbed his hands slowly together, stalling for time. The lads rightly sensed that something was amiss and began to take their places on the bench, their singing and chatter dying out.

"That was Huey on the phone," Baxter said, when the lads had settled. He took off his cap and gently smoothed out creases that didn't exist.

"What's up, Boss?" Fran asked, cutting to the chase.

The manager looked at his players, taking in their concerned expressions. "Huey's sick."

"He's always fuckin' sick," Charlie said, slagging off his absent teammate but not in a bad way.

"No, lads, this time he's really ill," Baxter added. The team waited for more information. "Testicular cancer," the manager further explained.

"That's a balls," joked Podge. Everyone glared at the reserve keeper. "I was only tryin' to break the ice," Podge quickly apologised.

"How's he doin'?" asked Davey.

Baxter shrugged his shoulders. "He's hoping to call over. Said he'd fill us in on what's happening. In the meantime, let's get going. I want to work on a few set-pieces."

The lads collected the footballs and cones and filed out of the dressing room as instructed. They might have acted like hard men most of the time, but they still had feelings.

Charlie caught hold of Mick's arm. "Can I have a word, pal." Mick paused, curious to learn what his teammate wanted. "Ye wouldn't want to be messin' with yer new neighbour," Charlie told him, "Anto's alrigh', so long as he gets his meds."

Although Mick was caught on the hop, he didn't show it. "What on earth are you rabbiting on about?" he asked, dismissing his teammate's advice.

"Temple Road?" said Charlie, not going to be brushed off that easily. Mick shook his head, trying to keep his newly impoverished situation private. "I saw ye the other nigh', after ye'd gave out about the noise at the house party," Charlie added.

Denying that it was him complaining wasn't going to wash with his teammate so Mick decided to try another angle. "To be honest," he said, giving a quick look around, "And I'm more than a little embarrassed by this, but I've been kind of slumming it of late. I'm knocking off a slapper who lives there. She's as common as muck but a gymnast in the sack if you know what I mean."

"And there's me thinkin' ye were only interested in the posh totty," Charlie said, "Sure yer just like the rest of us." He slapped his teammate on the back. "Wonder would she be up for an aul four-ball?"

Mick smiled, trying to project a carefree attitude but in truth was deeply troubled inside. "I'll ask," he said, repulsed by the idea. He'd never had a problem in the past indulging in threesomes so long as they involved two women but he didn't think he could stomach getting a slap in the face with another man's wedding tackle when things really got going.

Training had passed without incident even though it was the most intense session to date. Nobody said it but the lads were glad of the distraction after hearing about Huey's diagnosis. It was the manager's job now to try and keep them focused on their upcoming game as heartless as it sounded. Up until this evening they'd been relishing the challenge of unchartered waters, i.e. the first proper round against local side, Glasnevin Celtic. Baxter knew he would need all of his of experience to keep everything on track.

Things seemed to be going from bad to worse for Mick though. No matter how many times he turned the key in the ignition he just couldn't get the jalopy to fire. The Assassin was still in the car park having had to take an urgent call from a client who he did the occasional piece of protection work for. Having put the anxious client at ease Al ended the call and looked out through his windscreen. He spotted Mick a few yards away inside the banger, furiously bouncing his fists off of the steering wheel. Al observed the tantrum but did nothing until Mick eventually slumped forward, resting his head on the steering wheel having run out of steam. The big man then climbed out of his taxi and strolled over to Mick, tapping the window on the driver's side. The unexpected noise startled his teammate. Al motioned for Mick to lower the glass, but nothing happened when he pressed the button, trying to comply. He reluctantly opened the door.

"How the mighty have fallen," Al remarked, taking in his teammate's scruffy appearance.

"Don't start, Al, please. I've had a really bad day," Mick said.

The Assassin gave him a free pass. He'd never seen the lad so stressed out. "C'mon and I'll give ye a lift home."

"What?" Mick asked, panicking.

"It'll be grand, nobody's goin' to rob this heap of shite," Al said, thinking that his teammate was worried about the banger being stolen. "I'll make a call and get my man to tow it."

Mick frowned. The lies were piling up and he knew that sooner or later he was bound to be caught out. Mick spent the entire journey back to his former upmarket pad working out what he was going to do once Al had dropped him off. He'd decided that when he got out of the taxi he would pretend to tie his shoelaces while waving Al off. And then once his friend was gone he would slide away unnoticed, crawling back to his dingy bedsit. However, like the best laid plans of mice and men, Mick's went awry. They pulled up outside the fancy pad and there, for all to see, was a brightly coloured 'For Sale' sign fixed to a post.

The Assassin spotted it immediately. "Goin' somewhere?" he asked. Mick didn't know what to say and remained silent. "Am I talkin' to meself here?" the Assassin said, not used to being ignored.

"The bastards have gone and put my house up for sale," Mick finally said, tears rolling down his unshaven face. Al looked at his passenger and started laughing, a real hearty laugh that only comes from deep down. Mick glared at him, violent thoughts swirling around his head.

"They sound like a gas crowd of fuckers yer workin' with, stickin' up a sign like that outside yer gaff, pretendin' it was up for sale." Al said, staring at the long streak of misery sitting next to him, "Ye'd want to lighten up and take a joke."

Mick steadied himself, regaining some semblance of composure. Al had just given him the excuse he needed. Maybe there was light at the end of the tunnel. Or it could just be a train hurtling towards him! No, he cleared his mind of the negativities and pretended to see the humorous side of the prank which his colleagues had supposedly played.

"You're right, Al, sure I'm always doing stuff like that to them," he laughed. He got out of the taxi said thanks then pretended to tie his shoelace as Al drove off. He needed to get his act together, big time.

1ˢᵗ Round: Sporting Les Behans' v Glasnevin Celtic

Frank the Publican chatted away to Davey and the flamboyant male photographer while Baxter and most of the Sporting Les Behans' players got into place for the official team photo. Split stood next to Mick who was tying the laces on his boots.

Mick looked over at the photographer. "Who's the guy with Frank?"

"He's a photographer," said Split.

"No shit, Sherlock. What's he up to?"

"Takin' pictures."

Mick looked at the imbecile next to him and decided that he lacked the intelligence to be winding him up so he tried again, almost spelling it out this time. "Have you any idea why he's taking our photo?"

"It's a publicity stunt for the pub," Split explained, "Davey said it's all part of the sponsorship deal."

Mick finished tying his boots. "No doubt our boyo's going to do well out of it," he said, referring to Davey.

"Suppose. He definitely knows how to sniff out an earner, that's for sure," Split said, agreeing with Mick, "I tell ye, ye never know where this could lead to. I could end up gettin' a walk-on part in one of them soaps or somethin'."

"Or maybe even a role in a martial arts film?" Mick suggested but the sarcasm was lost on Split.

"That'd be bleedin' deadly, yeah," said the karate enthusiast. He hurried off to take his place with the rest of the team just in case he missed out on his fifteen seconds of fame.

Mick shook his head. "Sap." He noticed Gonzales parked up in his wheelchair watching the proceedings. "Are you not going over to have your picture taken, then?"

"With those brain-dead fucks? Are ye for real?" replied Gonzales, laughing like a maniac.

'Ten out of ten for observation,' thought Mick.

Trigger brought a clean-cut lad, who was dressed in a nice fitting but inexpensive suit and sensible brown brogues, over to Baxter.

"Howya Boss. This is Leonard, the chap I was tellin' ye about the other day," he said.

Leonard and Baxter shook hands.

"You must be Pa Baxter. Trigger's been telling me all about you," Leonard politely said.

Baxter shot Trigger a look. His player quickly shook his head 'no' behind Leonard's back. "Nice to meet you, son," the manager said, welcoming the new man aboard. "Head over to the dressing room, there's a spare kit inside but hurry, apparently we have to get our photo taken while the light's still good."

"Will do, thanks," Leonard said before disappearing towards the truck container as instructed.

Baxter's smiling face changed abruptly as he gave Trigger the evil eye.

"I didn't tell him any of yer business, I swear," the player said, making sure Leonard was out of earshot. "I know ye like yer privacy."

Baxter popped a stick of gum into his mouth, looking pensive. "All right, lad," he finally accepted, "How do you know him by the way?"

"He's me financial advisor," Trigger replied.

"Used to have one of them meself back in the day," Baxter revealed, "Divorced the wagon in the end."

"Didn't know ye were married?" said the surprised striker.

"Yeah, unhappiest ten..." the manager rooted inside his ear with his finger, "...weeks of my life. He better be handy?"

"Who, Leonard? He's had trials, Boss," Trigger said, enthusiastically.

"Son," Baxter said softly, "the whole shagging team's had trials."

"Not them sort of..." the player began but stopped mid-sentence when he copped on that the gaffer was only pulling his leg.

Jigsaw stood in line for the team photo next to Huey. He turned to his sick teammate, worried.

"So will all yer hair fall out?" he asked.

"The doctor said it probably will, yeah," Huey replied.

"Righ'," said Jigsaw, "Suppose on the plus side ye'll save a fortune with the barbers."

Huey smiled, knowing well that there wasn't a malicious bone in his friend's body. "I'll tell ye wha'," Huey said, "I'll put the money I save in a jar for the celebrations once I beat the fuckin' thing."

"Fair play," commended Jigsaw, "And I'll be lookin' forward to that party."

"Good man. Can't play for a while though, am only really here for the photo."

"Does it hurt, the chemo and all that?" Jigsaw asked.

"It's not too bad. Yer jaded most of the time though."

"I see."

"Burns the bollox outta ye as well."

The Sporting Les Behans' were finally in position for their picture to be taken. The photographer was making a fuss, shaping this way and that, trying to get the best angle and light for the shot.

"Can ye do us a flavour, petal, and pull yer helmet off for me?" he cheekily asked Davey, "I can give it a little tug if ye'd like?" Davey cocked his head to one side. The photographer turned to Frank the Publican half afraid he'd offended the player with his risqué comments, particularly in this day and age where everyone was hyper sensitive about every fucking thing.

"Take no notice of him, he has issues," Frank said, reassuring the photographer, "Just work away and do the best ye can."

Banging noises could be heard coming from the boot of the taxi that was parked beside the pitch. Everyone looked towards it, puzzled.

"For fuck's sake," swore the Assassin. He jogged over to his car and popped the boot open before reigning down several blows on the victim inside.

Frank the Publican noticed that the photographer had started to move his camera in the Assassin's direction. "Don't think that's a good idea," he whispered into the cameraman's ear.

The photographer immediately lowered his lens. "Ah Jaysus no, love, I wasn't goin' to do, do anythin'," he stuttered.

The Assassin slammed the boot closed then jogged back to his teammates and got in line once again. Baxter looked at him questioningly. "The bollox tried to do a runner," explained the Assassin.

Baxter nodded sagely. Just when everything seemed to be under control a mobile phone with a Hitler ranting speech went off. The entire team looked at Podge who was wearing an impish-like grin. "It's me new ringtone for Sharon. Got it off the History channel," he said, giggling.

Trigger reached across and snatched his teammate's phone and said, "Give me that," before hitting the decline button and handing it back.

Davey turned to Mick. "His mot's gonna bash him when she finds out about that ringtone," he predicted but Mick was too preoccupied to even notice.

"Righ'. On the count of three, say knob cheese. One, two, three," counted the photographer. The camera flashed, "Just a sec and I get a few more..."

Sporting Les Behans' had already dispersed, kicking balls around the pitch. The photographer looked with pleading eyes from Frank the Publican to Baxter.

"They're camera shy, what can I say," said Baxter. Frank nodded in agreement.

Baxter was on the sideline chomping hard on his chewing gum with Podge standing that close that he was almost hanging off the gaffer's lip. Split and Huey were standing on the other side of the manager, glued to the game. Glasnevin Celtic were proving to be no pushovers. With his back to the opposition goal, Gitsy had the ball at his feet looking for options. An opponent raced towards the Sporting player on his blindside. The manager spat out his gum and was about to shout 'Man on!' but remembered Davey telling him that the phrase had been outlawed.

"Person non gender... What the fuck is it again?" he roared instead but before he could remember the exact term Gitsy had been dispossessed and left sitting on his arse.

Split, Huey and Podge looked at the boss as if he'd two heads while Davey was grinning from ear to ear. It was only then that it dawned on Baxter that his player had been winding him up, the little bastard. The opposition number ten who had stolen the ball from Gitsy led the counterattack. He pushed the ball through the Assassin's tree trunk legs and as the bulky defender tried to spin around, he ended up falling over causing Baxter to throw his hands into the air in utter despair.

"What in Christ's name was that?" he complained, "A flipping juggernaut would have turned quicker." His face suddenly grew contorted as he sniffed the air.

"Ah for fuck's sake," Split complained, frantically waving his hand about in front of his face, "Who's the rotten pox?"

Huey piped up and said, "A dog smells his own dirt first."

"It wasn't me," Split protested.

Podge gave a sheepish smile. "Sharon was tryin' out a new curry recipe last nigh'," he apologised.

Baxter, Split and Huey moved further down the sideline away from the human stink bomb.

Despite the inhumane smell emanating from Podge's cakehole, the manager was doing his best to concentrate on the match. "Split, the Assassin's being skinned, you're going on," he ordered, having seen enough.

"But I haven't even warmed up," Split moaned.

The manager leaned in closer to his player. "It doesn't matter, you won't be on for too long, lad. I want you to take out their number ten."

"Take him out?" Split asked, alarmed, "But how?"

"You're the chop-chop merchant, you decide."

"But I'm not supposed to use me special gift against the ordinary, unsuspectin' public. I could lose me license. After all, these hands are lethal weapons." Split did a few karate chops to demonstrate just how deadly his martial arts skills were.

Baxter narrowed his eyes. "Right," he said, dismissing Split's delusional notions. He whistled loudly at the referee, "Ref! Ref. Substitution!"

Split lay stretched out cold on the muddy ground in the middle of the pitch with blood trickling from one nostril. He was surrounded by Charlie, Yoyo, Fran and Mick.

Fran furiously beckoned to the sideline. "Water!" he shouted.

"Bit of aggro here," observed Gonzales from his sideline position. "No, wait. It's only handbags. Let's hope the Les Behans' don't decide to kiss and make up or we could be here all nigh'."

In the background the referee held a red card up to the Glasnevin number ten while his teammates were doing their best to drag him from the field kicking and screaming. Baxter and Podge jogged onto the pitch with the dumpy player carrying a freshly filled water bottle. He handed the container to Mick who in turn took a big drink before wetting his hand and rubbing his fingers through his hair, trying to copy the way the professionals styled it, when he had money. The rest of the gathered players looked at him.

"What?" he asked, petulantly.

The players glanced down at Split. Mick eventually realised that on this occasion it wasn't all about him. He unceremoniously squirted water into Split's bloody face but to no effect.

"Has anyone got any smellin' salts or somethin'?" asked Charlie.

Podge grinned. He shuffled over to Split and squatted above his face, letting a loud one rip. Split started to come around. Mick and Charlie furiously waved their hands about while Fran and Yoyo held their noses trying to prevent the nasty toxins from entering their systems.

"That's not natural," Charlie spluttered through his jersey which was now covering the lower half of his face.

Gitsy waved his handkerchief in the air. "I surrender."

"A big Barry White would sort that out," Yoyo suggested.

"Castor oil's yer only man to shift the backlog," said Charlie.

"Literally," Mick said.

Glasnevin Celtic had finally gotten their number ten off the pitch but he was still furiously complaining. "I never laid a finger on the cheat!" he roared.

The referee ignored the dismissed player having heard it all before and walked over to Split and his teammates instead.

"Is he all righ'..." the man in black began but was overcome by the foul smell, "Who opened their lunchbox?" he demanded, retreating backwards.

Everyone looked at Podge. The referee pulled out a red card and showed it to the player.

"What's that for?" asked the sub keeper, thinking it was some kind of bad joke.

"Unsportin' behaviour. Now get off the pitch," the official ordered.

"But I wasn't even playin'," said Podge.

"Yer on the match card, aren't ye?" the referee asked.

"Yeah, but surely it should only be a yellow," said Podge.

"Okay, here's a second one for dissent. Happy now?" replied the official, "On yer bike."

Podge wasn't in the least bit impressed about getting his marching orders but Baxter persuaded him to accept his punishment and to help Fran carry Split off the field.

"The ref was bang out of order there," Podge whined, "I'm gonna lodge an appeal."

"You'll do no such thing," said Baxter, "I'll make sure the ref puts it down as two yellows so you don't get suspended." He then looked at Split who was still dazed, "Well done, ar kid." The lads helped the bewildered karate chump into a sitting position on the sideline.

"I didn't even see yer man touch Split," Fran said about the carded opposition player.

"He didn't," laughed Baxter. He looked down at his wounded player, "The divvy kicked himself in the face."

Sporting Les Behans', with the exception of the Assassin and Richie, were sitting around tables laden down with drink in the back lounge of Frank the Publican's bar.

Davey turned to Leonard. "Super game today, Lenny, took yer goal well."

"Thank you, Davey. I know it's a small thing but I prefer to be called Leonard," said Leonard, almost apologetically.

"Like the movie star?" Davey asked.

The newest member to the team hesitated for a moment. "Do you mean as in Leonardo?" he offered politely.

Davey stared at him.

"Di Caprio?" said Leonard in a non-condescending way.

"Not that bleedin' sham although he was deadly in The Departed. I meant Leonard as in Nimoy, as in Doctor Spock," said Davey.

"Are you out of your Vulcan mind?" Leonard joked but quickly switched his smiley head to a more serious expression once he noticed that his companion wasn't laughing. "You're a bit of a Trekkie then?"

Davey didn't reply immediately. Instead he massaged his chin, never once taking his eyes off his teammate. Leonard wished he'd kept his trap shut and left the comedy to the professionals.

"A trackie Trekkie, that's me," Davey finally said with a smile.

Leonard left out an audible sigh of relief.

"Am into sci-fi in general, especially the Star Wars' films," Davey admitted, "But they're startin' to tear the arse out of it."

"I completely agree. I'm a huge science fiction fan myself," said Leonard, happy to have something in common with at least one of his new teammates.

"Did ye ever see a film called Enemy Mine?" Davey asked.

"I don't recall the name," Leonard said, racking his memory but still coming up short.

"Don't worry about it, it was ages ago, ye woulda been still in nappies. Anyway, this fighter pilot in the future like, shoots down an alien and they both end up crashlanding on this deserted, hostile planet. They can't stand the sight of one another and they're both doin' their best to kill each other. But eventually they realise that they'll have to work together if they've any hope of survivin'."

"A symbiotic relationship of sorts," Leonard said.

"I suppose. Ye'll never believe wha' happened next," Davey said, taking a sip of his drink.

Leonard politely waited for him to continue.

"Unless of course yer gonna watch it and I don't want to spoil it for ye?" Davey said.

"It's okay, work away."

Davey gleefully rubbed his hands together, eager to continue his story. "So Gerry the alien, that's wha' yer fighter pilot man called it, only goes and has a poxy baby, a little ugly fucker at that. Bit like one of the germs in the bleach ads and the bloke says 'Ah heore, Gerry, that had nothin' to do with me. I wouldn't ride yer mot let alone you' or words to that effect."

Leonard wasn't sure if his teammate was making it all up but the chap did look sincere.

Davey suddenly shot forward in his seat. "I definitely know you from somewhere."

The statement caught Leonard completely by surprise. "One of those faces I suppose," he just about managed to say.

"Don't worry, it'll come to me," Davey said, rapidly clicking his fingers for inspiration.

Leonard was worried though. He dreaded the lads discovering his secret. "What happened at the end of the film?" he asked, trying desperately to disrupt Davey's train of thought.

"Ah, the alien popped his clogs and the geezer had to mind it's ugly sprog, tryin' to save it after it got kidnapped by space miners."

"The irony being that all his life the fighter pilot was trying to kill aliens but now here he was doing his best to keep one alive," Leonard said.

"Precisely. What's that yer drinkin'?" asked Davey.

"A shandy but I'm okay, thanks," his teammate courteously declined.

"Get up outta that. It's like this, Lenny, a team that gargles together, stays together. So if yer gonna be playin' ball with us, yer gonna have to sup pints with us too." Davey got to his feet. "Anyone else want one?" he called out.

None of the players took him up on his offer.

"Large Bulmers," slurred Gonzales.

Davey bent down close to the chap in the wheelchair not wanting to embarrass him in front of the other lads. "Think ye've had enough, buddy. Ye don't want to get bagged again for the aul drink drivin'."

"Are ye me fuckin' Ma now or wha'?" snapped Gonzales.

Davey shrugged his shoulders and straightened back up just as the Assassin appeared out of nowhere, carrying a full pint. "There ye are, Al, thought ye were lost."

"Some business needed seein' to," answered the Assassin, giving nothing away. The man mountain sat down across from Yoyo and Jigsaw and slowly ran his finger through the condensation which had formed on the outside of his cool glass. The two boys moved closer in a conspiratorial fashion.

"Go on, ask him," Yoyo said in a hushed voice.

"No way. You ask," said Jigsaw, trying to encourage his friend.

"You get on better with him," Yoyo replied.

The Assassin sank his pint in one go. As he planted the empty glass back on the table he caught Yoyo and Jigsaw watching him.

"Wha'?" he demanded in a thunderous tone.

Jigsaw and Yoyo both jumped. The Assassin peered at the pair of them as they shifted uneasily in their seats. "Well?" he pushed.

Yoyo elbowed Jigsaw. "We were wonderin'..." Jigsaw began.

"He was, more so," interrupted Yoyo.

"Spit it out, I haven't got all day," said the Assassin.

Jigsaw squirmed. "Wha' happened to the bloke ye had locked in the boot of yer car?"

"Which one?" Al asked. Jigsaw and Yoyo sat open-mouthed.

Davey returned with two pints and a large bottle of cider. "There ye go, Gonzales," he said with as much pleasantry as he could possibly muster while handing over the bottle.

"Were ye growin' the fuckin' apples or wha'?" Gonzales asked. He didn't wait for a response, instead he guzzled down a large sup of the thirst-quenching cider.

Davey thought about taking the bottle back and bouncing it off his head but reluctantly decided against it, for the time being anyhow. He sat back down next to Leonard and gave him one of the pints.

"Thank you," said Leonard.

"No prob."

"Has he Spanish heritage?" Leonard asked, the curiosity getting the better of him.

"Who?" said Davey, taking a slow sip of his fresh pint while savouring the chemical aftertaste.

Leonard discreetly nodded towards the lad in the wheelchair. "Gonzales."

Davey laughed. "That's not his real name ye big eejit."

"Oh," said Leonard, feeling like a big eejit.

"We call him Gonzales, as in Speedy Gonzales."

Leonard looked perplexed. He then leaned in closer to his teammate. "That's not very, you know, PC," he suggested in a low voice.

Split was passing by and heard Leonard. "If ye want PC get a computer," he said, delighted with his own cleverness.

"Stop ear-wiggin' or I'll give ye a kick up the hole," warned Davey. He turned back to Leonard, "Wha' are ye on about?"

"Politically correct," Leonard helpfully explained.

"I know wha' the letters bleedin' stand for."

"Sorry, of course you do. I mean calling someone with disabilities a name like that..."

"Wha', Speedy Gonzales?"

"Yes, that."

Davey sat forward. "He was always called Speedy Gonzales, long before he ended up in a wheelchair. He was a terror as a nipper for robbin' the aul cars and joyridin' around the local estates. That's how he had his accident. Hit a kerb doin' one-twenty and flipped the car over, took the brigade hours to cut the dope out."

"I see."

"The other young fella in the car was decapitated."

"That's tragic."

"No, that's just life. They chose to rob the car. The real tragedy was that they also killed an innocent granny and her nine-year-old granddaughter who just happened to be crossin' the road on their way back from the shops."

Leonard felt sick. It was as if someone had suddenly clenched the muscles inside his gut and began twisting them.

Davey picked at a jagged piece of his fingernail leaving what he'd just said time to sink in. He then looked Lenny in the eye and said, "So, if we'd changed Gonzales' name to somethin' else just because he ended up in a wheelchair would that not then have been discriminatory?"

Leonard was stumped. As mad as it seemed the man did have a valid point. And as much as he abhorred violence, he felt a strange urge to take the glass bottle from Gonzales and to batter him across the head with it.

"I'm only buzzin'," the Assassin told Yoyo and Jigsaw after they'd enquired about the fella who'd been held captive in his boot, "Brought him for a drive up the mountains. I know this deserted clearance in the woods..."

Yoyo was about to ask another question, but the Assassin put a finger to his lips. "When I got there, I opened the boot and told him to get out. He was a bit slow; legs were kinda jelly. I suppose they were a bit cramped after spendin' most of the day in the car," he said without any real remorse.

Jigsaw and Yoyo nodded.

"He was shieldin' his eyes from the brightness and all that so I had to help him out," laughed the Assassin as he recalled tearing the little bastard from the car by the scruff of the neck and dumping him unceremoniously onto the forest floor.

The rest of the team moved in closer to hear the story.

"I got me spade from the boot and handed it to him. He looked confused for a minute then started bawlin' like a big baby when he realised wha' I had in mind. Started beggin' for forgiveness and all that shite," Al revealed with contempt. He was a firm believer that if you were man enough to do the crime then you should be man enough to accept the consequences if you got caught.

"You carry a spade in your car?" Mick asked, surprised, even though he knew he shouldn't be with this nutter.

"A telescopic one, yeah. Keep it in a hidden compartment," said the Assassin as if it was the most natural thing in the world. "Where was I?" he asked, momentarily forgetting what part of the story he was at.

"Ye gave yer man the spade," Yoyo said.

"That's righ'. So I lit a smoke and rested against the car and told the runner to dig. But he gets a bit scorpy, says that if I'm gonna kill him I can dig the fuckin' hole meself."

"Some nerve," Fran offered in jest.

"Exactly wha' I thought," continued the Assassin, completely missing Fran's attempt at humour.

"Did he not try to hit ye with the yoke?" asked Jigsaw.

The Assassin smirked. "He thought about it alrigh'. Made this pathetic attempt to scare me with it but I just blew smoke in his face and told him straight out, that if he didn't dig the fuckin' hole I was gonna bite off his fingers one by one until he did. And in the highly unlikely event that he still refused, I was gonna tie wha' was left of his stumpy hands behind his back and bury him alive. He dropped to his knees and then started all that cryin' shite again."

"Good Jaysus," Yoyo said aloud, not really sure if this conversation was actually happening or if he had taken one pill too many in his short life.

"I let him dig away for half an hour then told him to piss off, that he better not even so much as think about doin' a legger again. I have it on me phone. It's a classic," the Assassin revealed with tremendous satisfaction.

"Gis a look?" Jigsaw couldn't help himself from asking.

"It's on me other phone," said the Assassin.

"Out of curiosity, Al, how much was the fare?" Fran asked.

"That's not the point. It was a matter of principal," explained the Assassin. He looked around at his teammates' expectant faces before deciding to answer, "Eight euro, ten cent."

The lads began to disperse after their day on the lash, celebrating another victory. Some were heading off to bed to get some badly needed shuteye with work, legitimate or otherwise, looming in the morning while others would go rambling, doing their best to keep the night alive. Outside the bar, Leonard was having trouble closing his jacket while waiting for a taxi. He couldn't quite figure out that he'd fastened the wrong button into the wrong hole to begin with. Davey helped him out and re-did his buttons.

"Thanks, Davey," Leonard said, trying to keep steady.

"No prob," said his teammate, giving him an affectionate pat on his upper arm.

"I know Al's a bit mad, but I presume that a lot of it is just for show," Leonard slurred.

Davey had taken a liking to the new lad and didn't want to see him come to any harm by underestimating the Assassin's capabilities for causing mayhem. He decided to give Leonard the heads up but without implicating Al too much in the process. "I'm gonna tell ye a little story but yer not to repeat a word of it to anyone, especially not Al, understood?"

"Of course," Leonard promised, but still half thinking it was all part of the pantomime.

"The first time we arrived at our new pitch the rest of the lads didn't want to leave their cars unattended in case they got vandalised, but Al had no such concerns. He stopped his taxi in the middle of the flats, got out and left the keys in the ignition and asked these young fellas hangin' about who was the toughest bloke they knew? Without hesitation every single one of them pointed to a flat on the top floor and said, "Hego". Al then removed his good tracksuit top, carefully folded it and left it on the driver's seat before disappearing into the building. He took the concrete stairs two at a time with the gang of curious kids almost trippin' over one another, followin' him every step of the way. A few minutes later and Al's kicked in Hego's front door with his size sixteen's. We could hear the commotion, furniture crashin', glass smashin', lots of shoutin' and then yer man Hego's hangin' over the balcony with Al holdin' him by his ankles."

"That's absolutely insane," said Leonard, laughing.

"I know, isn't that wha' I'm tryin' to tell ye. It gets worse. He then let go of one of yer man Hego's legs, holdin' him with only the one hand and the bloke must have weighed at least fifteen stone. I'm not spoofin'. I couldn't look if I'm bein' honest, I genuinely thought that this fella was headin' for a date with the concrete footpath a hundred plus feet below."

Leonard was growing paler by the second and looked as if he might throw up.

"Al eventually hauled the chap back in and they exchanged a few civil words and that was the end of it."

"Did nobody call the guards?"

"Are ye havin' a laugh?"

Leonard knew the question was rhetorical.

Davey edged forward. "And by the way, if Al ever asks ye to pick a number always say one and if that's gone say the next lowest number that's available."

"How come?"

"Hopefully ye'll never have to find out."

With that Leonard bent over and emptied every single drop of alcohol and every morsel of food that he'd consumed throughout the day.

Chapter 12

Stevo sat behind the wheel of the flash motor watching the tarty blonde as she exited through the prison gates heading towards him. 'Bambi on ice,' he thought as she balanced precariously on her extremely high heels. She climbed into the back of the car, lit a cigarette and took a deep drag then slowly exhaled.

"I think he's losin' it," she declared.

Stevo and the blonde looked at one another via the rear view mirror.

"Wants ye to help some footballer give up the smokes and the drink all in the one go, and permanently," she said, taking a top of the range mobile phone from her handbag and holding up the screen for Stevo to see, "Says this is wha' he looks like in case ye screw things up again."

Stevo rolled his tongue around the inside of his cheek trying his best not to say what he really felt.

"Speakin' of screwin'," the tarty blonde said, "Fancy comin' around to my place?" Stevo said nothing. "I know I shouldn't proposition the help but..." She ran her hand suggestively along her long, smooth thigh, "It's just that it's startin' to eat the side of me leg off."

Stevo gave a derisive laugh. "And end up with a bullet in the back of the head like the one Reilly's gonna get? Don't think so, love."

2nd Round: Transport United v Sporting Les Behans'

Paddy Power raced up the pitch, dribbling the ball past several of the Transport United players as Davey sprinted along the wing to join in the attack.

"I'm open!" shouted the winger.

On the sideline, Split, Yoyo, Huey and Baxter looked on with growing anxiety.

"Pass the bleedin' ball, ye big donkey!" Huey roared.

The manager stood with his hands on his hips, his face fit for murder.

"Plenty of fumblin' around the box but no real penetration," Gonzales giddily reported from his wheelchair vantage point.

"He'll be knackered by half-time if he keeps that up," Split said, highlighting the obvious.

"I know what the gobshite's up to," swore Baxter.

Trigger made a diagonal run across Paddy Power's path in order to collect the ball but Paddy shielded it from him. He chose instead to go it alone and take a shot even though he was still at least thirty yards out. Needless to say the ball missed the intended target and went high and wide.

"What's yer fuckin' game?" Davey said, squaring up to his wasteful teammate, "I was wide open, again."

"Power, get your arse over here, now!" Baxter shouted from the touchline.

Paddy Power, his head hung low in shame, reluctantly made his way over to the furious gaffer. Baxter caught hold of him by the ear, pulling him in close. "You're after doing a bet on the game, haven't you?" he said. Before Power could reply the boss walloped him across the back of the head. The player had guilt written all over his sorry face.

"I put a few quid on meself as first goal scorer," Paddy confessed.

"How much is a few quid?" asked Baxter, his tone softening slightly.

Fran and the Assassin watched the commotion that was going on over at the sideline between the manager and Power.

"The gaffer doesn't look very happy," Al said.

"Nope," Fran agreed.

"Pretend you're injured, lad, as soon as you can," Baxter told his player, giving him clear instructions. He then gave him a kick up the backside for good measure and sent him back onto the field of play.

The game had no sooner restarted when Paddy was rolling around on the mucky ground, moaning like some bit part actor in a cheap porn flick. He was surrounded by Baxter and the rest of his teammates although they were more interested in grabbing a drink of water than checking on the player's wellbeing.

"Get up, there's nothin' wrong with ye, ye bleedin' whinge-bag," said Charlie.

"'Ang on a mo'," ordered Baxter, "Jigsaw, your coming off and Power's going up front."

"Wha'? Sure he's injured," Trigger said. He'd never once questioned the manager's tactics but this was ludicrous.

"Don't interrupt," Baxter warned, pointing a finger at his star striker. He turned back to the rest of his players, "I want you to give the ball to Paddy, we need him to score first, there's a lot of money riding on this," he revealed.

Shot after shot went wide of the posts, over the crossbar or harmlessly into the Transport United keeper's hands as Paddy Power tried desperately to get that all important first goal. The rest of the Les Behans' team looked at one another with growing despair but Baxter urged them to keep on going. With the first half almost up the Transport keeper launched the ball up the field against a slight breeze, dropping it into the centre circle just inside the Sporting half. Yoyo was first onto it and lashed it back up the pitch on the half volley. The spinning ball soared high into the air, landing just in front of the opposition keeper and bouncing over his head into the empty net. The referee blew his whistle to signal a goal. Mick glared at Yoyo who nervously smiled back. The rest of the team looked towards their manager for guidance, but he was too busy choking on his chewing gum. Huey had to bang him hard across the back a couple of times to dislodge the gum from the gaffer's windpipe. Tears welled up in Baxter's eyes as he suffered a fit of coughing. He eventually managed to steady himself and catch his breath.

"Are ye alrigh', Boss?" asked Split.

"Offside, ref," Baxter screamed while shoving his concerned player out of the way. He waved his arms furiously, bird-like, trying to get the official's attention, "Offside," he tried again.

The referee glanced up from his notebook where he was recording the score and paused for a short moment before deciding to trot over to the sideline. Both teams watched with growing curiosity.

"He can't have been offside, he scored from inside his own half," the referee helpfully explained.

"Yeah, but it was active offside. The striker was putting the keeper off," the manager pleaded.

The referee bent his head closer to Baxter's. "Ye do know that it was yer team that scored, don't ye?" he said, not sure if the poor aul fella was having a senior moment or was just not up to speed with the rules.

"I do indeed. It's just that we're big into the whole fair play thing," Baxter lied.

"Are ye sure now, before I rule out yer goal?" the referee asked, emphasising the 'yer goal'.

"We are. Thank you."

The man in black shrugged his shoulders. "Fuck me, that's a new one," he muttered to himself. He then blew his whistle and raised his hand skywards indicating an indirect free kick. "Offside," he loudly announced.

Sporting Les Behans,' minus Podge and Richie, were in great form, singing with gusto as the gargle flowed that evening in Frank's pub.

"Here we go, here we go. You'll never stuff the Les Behans', you'll never stuff the Les Behans'," they heartily sang.

Davey took a black Burqa out of a plastic bag and held it aloft. "Me mate, Jacko, he's only after robbin' a truck full of these yokes. Hasn't a clue wha' to do with the bleedin' things."

"Which way is Mecca?" joked Leonard, who was more than a little tipsy. For a lad that didn't go out much in the past he was really making up for lost time.

"Funny," replied Davey, stuffing the garment back into the bag just as Podge appeared, sporting a fresh black eye.

The tubby sub keeper set a colourful, gift-wrapped box down on the table.

"There was no need," Fran said, winding up his teammate.

"It's not for you, it's for my Sharon," snapped Podge, rising to the bait.

"Ooh, someone's in their flowers," said Charlie, further taunting Podge.

Frank the Publican arrived with a tray laden down with an assortment of pints and rested it on the table.

"Relax ar kid and get one of these into you," Baxter said, handing his grumpy player a fresh pint of lager, "Double celebration. We beat Transport five-one and Power won us a few quid for the first goal scorer."

Sporting Les Behans' cheered loudly.

Frank turned to Podge. "What's the story with the shiner?"

The sub keeper gingerly rubbed the area immediately surrounding his black-eye, careful not to put too much pressure on it. "The other half gave it to me," he admitted, "But it was fully deserved," he quickly added.

"My aul man use to say that a woman who hit a man was no use," recalled Frank, his mind wandering to another place and time long gone. Everyone looked at the Publican but they remained silent.

"What did you do?" Frank asked, sympathetically, "Not that there's any excuse for violence."

"Remember me Hitler ringtone?" Podge reminded the lads. They all nodded a collective 'yes'. "Well, I lost me fuckin' phone in the gaff the other day and like an absolute dope I asked Sharon to ring it for me. She wasn't impressed when she found out that it was me special ringtone just for her."

Davey shook his head. "Yer a disaster."

"I know," said Podge, "She kept goin' on about it, is that wha' I thought of her? Truth is, sometimes she's worse than any dictator to have ever walked this earth." Everyone laughed. "But don't tell her I said that," Podge quickly added, already worrying that Sharon might somehow find out what he'd said.

"Did he say dick taker?" Yoyo asked.

The team laughed even louder.

"There's no need for that type of vulgarity here," said Baxter.

"Sorry Boss, that's wha' I genuinely thought he said," Yoyo apologised. Baxter raised an eyebrow. "Honestly," said Yoyo.

"She sounds like one tough woman," Frank said to Podge.

"Ye've no idea," admitted the downtrodden, sub-keeper. He rose to his feet and headed for the toilet.

Although Frank had never met this Sharon one, he was absolutely disgusted with her behaviour. "He should probably ring one of those help-lines, that's a form of abuse."

"Don't mind him, he loves it," replied Gitsy, disregarding the pub owner's genuine concerns.

"I know people who'd pay big bucks for that sort of attention," said Charlie.

"You included, ye sadomasochist," Trigger buzzed.

The publican nodded politely then headed back to check on his other customers, not satisfied that the lads fully understood their teammate's perilous domestic situation. Fran poked the gift box which Podge had unwisely left sitting on the table. He looked over at Davey and instinctively knew that his pal had read his mind when he spotted a mischievous grin lighting up his face.

Podge was delighted with himself as he watched Sharon, who was sitting down at the kitchen table directly across from him, unwrap the gift box that he had just presented her with.

"It's somethin' small to show ye wha' I really think of ye after our earlier misunder..." he began but immediately realised that something was wrong. Very wrong.

Sharon took the Burqa out of the box, got to her feet and held the garment up for further inspection. She smacked her lips together several times as she glowered at her squirming husband. "I'd love to," she said, her eyes appearing to double in size in an instant.

"There's been a mistake," grovelled Podge as he desperately checked inside the now empty box. He held it upside down in his two hands, shaking it vigorously, in the slim hope that the real gift would somehow reappear and fall out. 'Them bastards back in the pub have made a switch,' he thought.

Sharon dropped the Burqa onto the floor and balled her hands into fists. "Mistake? Ye got that righ'," she said, her top lip curling up into an ugly snarl.

Chapter 13

3rd Round: Sporting Les Behans' v Ballyer Boys

Baxter and Frank the Publican looked on as Sporting Les Behans' did their warm up, jogging up to the halfway line then turning and sprinting back in perfect harmony.

"They're looking good," Frank complimented.

"We're getting there," Baxter casually replied, secretly hiding the overwhelming pride he now had for his boys.

Frank absentmindedly picked up one of the oranges from the team's supplies, peeled the skin off and popped a segment into his mouth. He screwed up his face. "This tastes funny," he said, spitting out the offending piece of fruit.

"Yeah, the lads have stopped injecting them with alcohol," Baxter explained.

The match was ten minutes old and Gitsy was readying himself to take a corner with his trusted left boot.

"The Les Behans' could really do with a big lad bangin' away up front," Gonzales commented from his wheelchair to no one in particular.

Davey was in the box being tightly marked by Chicken Balls, a stocky Ballyer Boys player. Chicken Balls had intricate, oriental-type patterns tattooed onto his shaven head. Davey wondered was it in case he forgot his order at two in the morning while out of his bin in some local takeaway.

Trigger was jostling with his marker, a tough looking bloke with pronounced jawbones named Johnny Boy. 'The chap could have been the missin' link in man's evolution,' thought Trigger about his ape-like opponent.

Davey was loitering near the penalty spot. He called out to Johnny Boy, "D'ye have any DVD's of yer Ma shaggin' animals?"

"No," Johnny Boy replied defensively, if not a little confused.

"Wanna buy some?" taunted Davey.

Johnny Boy tried to grab hold of Davey's shirt, but Chicken Balls held him back.

"Ignore him. He's only tryin' to wind ye up," the experienced Ballyer Boys player said.

"It'd more like yer aul wan gettin' it up the arse in the videos," Johnny Boy said, counteracting Davey's slur.

Davey knew he had him. "My sincerest apologies," he said, "Sure I forgot, yer Ma's in bits and was only the fluffer on set." Johnny Boy had had enough. He lunged at Davey despite Chicken Balls' best efforts to restrain him.

At that precise moment Gitsy swung the ball in leaving Trigger to rise up unopposed and get a free header on the goal. The ball was met squarely by the striker's forehead and the onion sack rippled.

"Go on, my son," cheered Baxter, knowing only too well the tactics that Davey had just employed. It was the oldest trick in the book and the manager was still amazed when players fell for it.

Sporting were back in their container dressing room after the convincing four-one victory over their opponents. Johnny Boy had tried to get revenge for Davey's earlier disparaging remarks about his mother and her sexual preferences for all creatures great and small. Unfortunately, the opposition player had failed to heed the Assassin's friendly advice and to just let it go. And it now looked as if the poor fucker was facing the next three months at the very least eating his dinner through a straw after a sweet uppercut from Al had laid him out cold. Despite robust protests from the opposition team the experienced referee had decided that he'd seen nothing and hastily departed the scene, blowing the match up several minutes early if the truth be known. It was at times like this that he was grateful for the advice an older ref had given him when he'd first started out. 'Always insist on gettin' yer match fee before the game' was his number one rule, and the second little gem which had always served him well was, 'If it looks like shit and smells like shit, it usually is shit so step around it.'

The Sporting lads were in various stages of undress after showering and most were making an extra special effort this evening, putting on their smartest clobber and splashing on their most expensive cologne or knock-off smellies at the very least.

"Has anyone seen me First Aid kit?" Yoyo asked, beginning to panic a bit. A few of the lads shook their heads while others shrugged their shoulders.

"I saw it," said Jigsaw,

Yoyo was relieved. "Good man. Where is it?" he asked.

"The manager told me to give it to the lads next door when their man, Johnny Boy, got injured."

The words were barely out of Jigsaw's mouth when Yoyo went racing outside just in time to see the opposition minibus pulling away.

"Stop!" he shouted at the departing vehicle but to no avail. He watched in despair as a group of lads who were occupying the back seats in the bus, waved the assorted bags of tablets which they'd found in his First Aid box. The Ballyer Boys might have lost the game but they'd definitely gotten a result.

Yoyo trudged back into the dressing room, empty-handed, a deflated look on his face.

"Cheer up, ar kid," said Baxter.

"There was at least two grands worth in that box," the player said. He shot Jigsaw a dirty look. "Yer some dope."

"Hey," said Baxter, pointing a finger at Yoyo. "I warned you about the gear."

"The head on him," Davey said, laughing at Yoyo. "He looks like he's goin' to have a schizoid embolism."

"Ha, ha," his upset teammate sarcastically replied.

"Look lad, you win some, you lose some," Baxter said, "And there's to be no more drug dealing on site."

"Could've been a lot worse, bud," Charlie called out.

"How's that?" Yoyo asked.

Charlie retrieved a clear plastic packet containing colourful tablets and shook it in the air. "At least we got our rations first." There was a big cheer from most of the lads.

Yoyo bit down on his lower lip, trying to contain his anger. 'Fuck it,' he decided, he'd nip home and shoot a goofball before heading out.

"You're looking very dapper, Mr. Baxter," Leonard said, complimenting the manager's taste in clothes. The boss was decked out in a grey, double-breasted suit with a narrow charcoal pinstripe and a neatly folded, cerise coloured handkerchief strategically placed in the top pocket.

Baxter adjusted the lapels on his jacket and said, "These are me bezzies."

Leonard looked closer at the not so discreet label that had been sewn onto the cuff of the sleeve. "Saville Row, no less."

The manager put an arm around his naive player's shoulder. "'I'll let you in on a secret, Lenny, it's all jarg." His player gave a puzzled look. "Jarg? Fake," Baxter said, "Have this mate who has an enterprising sideline stitching designer labels onto clobber. Can hook you up if you like?"

"I'm okay for the moment but I appreciate the offer, thank you." Leonard looked around, "It's like a fashion show in here this evening," he noted.

Split overheard Leonard. "First Tuesday of the month, bud," he explained.

"I'm not quite sure of the significance?" Leonard politely said.

"Mickey money?" Charlie said, joining in the conversation.

"Sorry, I still don't follow," Leonard apologised.

"Children's allowance? All the single mother's gaggin' for the ride and ye don't even have to buy them a drink," said Charlie, "It's a win-win situation."

"Oh," said Leonard, feeling completely stupid.

Charlie looked over at Davey. "Ye comin'? Get ye fixed up with one of me exes."

"Have yer sloppy seconds, don't think so, pal," Davey replied.

"Wha' a man we have," Yoyo said, teasing his pal, having already gotten over his drug loss, "Sure only last week ye would've got up on the crack of dawn."

Charlie piped up. "What's yer sayin' again, Davey?"

"If it moves, fuck it. And if it doesn't, fuck it 'til it does," the whole team answered in unison having heard the saying a thousand times before.

Baxter ruffled Davey's hair playfully. "Leave ar kid alone. He's in love."

Podge emerged from the shower area towelling his extremely hairy body dry. He now had two matching black eyes after his latest bout with Sharon.

Gitsy pointed at him. "Look, it's Kung Fu Panda." The whole place erupted bar Leonard. He was seriously beginning to question his decision to join this group of lunatics.

Charlie, tears coming from his eyes with the laughter, pointed at Podge. "Imagine meetin' that thing at the beach. Ye wouldn't know whether to shake its hand or pat it on the head."

Pa Baxter sat alone at the counter in Frank's bar nursing a pint, watching the publican fill in the latest result from Sporting Les Behans' cup run on a chart that he'd hung on the wall behind the bar.

Frank turned to Baxter, worried. "Ye don't look too good, Pa. Are ye sure yer ok?"

"Was out with the young fellas last night, over did it a bit," Baxter replied, rubbing the side of his throbbing temple, "Got a capture though. Some auld mare, can't remember her name for the life of me though. We ended up back at her flat and I'd have probably been alright if I didn't pick up that bottle of vodka from the offie on the way to her place."

"Are ye not gettin' a bit long in the tooth for all that carry on?" asked Frank.

Baxter smiled. "Maybe, lad. But sure what else is there to life apart from birds, booze and football?"

Frank nodded in agreement, a trifle envious of the man's carefree attitude having been stuck with the same slob for several decades. His wife was more interested in spending his hard-earned cash on clothes that were never going to fit rather than having the ride.

"Do you ever have trouble getting the old soldier to stand to attention?" Baxter asked out of nowhere.

Frank wasn't sure he heard him right.

"In the trouser department?" Baxter added, noticing the look on Frank's face.

"Oh, righ'," Frank said, a little embarrassed to be speaking about the subject. Women, it seemed to him, were able to talk about anything and everything whereas fellas didn't, contrary to popular belief. He decided to open up a bit. "If I'm bein' honest, Pa, no. It's that seldom I get the chance to use me pistol that when the opportunity presents itself in all the excitement the gun nearly goes off in the holster before I even get to draw."

Baxter laughed but in a knowing way. "Speaking of draws, we're into the drum in a few days with the big boys," he said, referring to the upcoming cup draw.

"Righ'," said the publican, snapping out of his gloomy thoughts.

"Yeah. Being shown live on the box. Myself and Davey are heading over."

"I'll organise something for the two of ye to wear, a plug for the pub and all that," Frank said.

"Sound. Ar Davey will be made up," said Baxter.

The day of the cup draw wasn't long coming around and the excitement among the Les Behans' players was mounting even though the manager had forbidden them to talk about it in the run up. The hotel where the draw was taking place was a real hob-nob establishment. Just inside the entrance gates there was an ornate pond with a powerful fountain set into the middle of it. Water shot high into the sun-kissed sky and fell back to earth, fractured into thousands of droplets resembling sparkling diamonds. The hotel conference room was organised in a theatre style and was packed with animated managers and their assistants from the various other clubs still remaining in the competition. They were smartly dressed in their respective club blazers and slacks and were chatting boisterously to one another. The cup host stood at the top table flanked by two former international players who were obviously doing well on the after-dinner circuit if their waistlines were anything to go by. A large, clear glass bowl filled with plastic balls sat in front of the trio.

Some of the managers were sniggering as they looked at the bizarre official team photo of Sporting Les Behans' which was splashed across several of the tabloid newspapers. Baxter and Davey were seated at the back of the room trying to look inconspicuous but their yellow, shiny shellsuits emblazoned with Sporting Les Behans' didn't exactly help their cause.

A smug manager who was seated several rows in front of the lads turned around. He nudged the man beside him. "If it's not the Munch Bunch themselves," he said giving Baxter and Davey a condescending wink.

Baxter was livid. "You and your fecking lesbian name," he said to Davey, almost growling, "I'm telling you, if that Muppet utters another word, he's getting the slaps."

The draw host gave a polite cough into his microphone. "Settle down now, gentlemen..." he began.

"And ladies!" quipped the smug manager.

Laughter filled the room with all eyes firmly fixed on the two lads. Baxter's blood was boiling. He made an attempt to get to his feet but Davey caught him by the arm and discreetly held him back. The smug manager was too busy playing with a set of car keys dangling off his index finger to take much notice.

Apart from Davey, who was busy trying to keep Baxter from killing the smug manager at the cup draw, the Assassin and Richie were the only other players missing as the team gathered in Frank's pub. They were huddled around tables, watching the draw live on the big screen, dressed in matching t-shirts emblazoned with the official team photo and their individual nicknames printed underneath.

"There's the boys now!" shouted Frank, pointing at the screen, delighted with himself.

The team cheered loudly while some wolf whistled.

"Look at the state of the pair of them, like two down and outs," slagged Yoyo.

"Watch it, that stuff cost me a fortune," said Frank.

"Hope ye got a receipt?" Charlie said, goading the publican.

"Jaysus, Baxter looks fit to burst someone," Yoyo remarked.

"Talking about killing people, has anyone seen the Assassin?" Mick asked.

"Had to work, not a happy camper," Fran said.

"I thought he picked his own hours?" queried Mick.

"Only doin' the taxiin' part-time now," Fran said, "Got a bit of maintenance work in some hotel as well. No doubt he'll find somewhere to watch the draw." Mick almost asked Fran if he'd thought there'd be any more jobs going in the hotel but caught himself just in time. A combination of pride and embarrassment wouldn't allow him to ask for help even though Fran was his best mate. No, he'd have to find another solution to his enforced poverty.

Across town in a large budget hotel, the Assassin, toolbox in hand, hurried past the check-in desk. The receptionist, her face flushed and tears welling up in her distinctive, emerald green eyes, was on the phone.

"Right away, Sir, and again, my sincerest apologies," she said, her voice quivering slightly. She hung up. "Sorry, hello," she called out to the Assassin as he rushed by.

Al thought for a split second about pretending not to hear but it wasn't in his nature so he pulled up.

"You're the new maintenance guy?" she asked, politely.

He nodded 'yes' while sneaking a look at the time on his watch.

"I don't know your name, sorry," she said, pointing to where his name badge should have been.

"Al," he said, "I'm still waitin' on personnel to issue me with a dog tag."

"Right."

"Are ye okay? Ye look a bit upset."

"Demanding guest," she explained, "Goes with the territory I suppose. That was room six-o-five, they want you to sort out a tap in their bathroom for them."

"No prob. Will take a gander at it after me break," he politely replied and began to move away.

"Don't suppose there's any chance..."

The Assassin paused then said, "All righ'."

The fact that the receptionist had a nice smile, fabulous eyes and a terrific rack helped to make his decision a little easier. 'Ye never knew yer luck,' he thought, 'One good turn migh' deserve another.'

Rhythmically drumming the inside panel of the lift with his thick, calloused fingers, Al monitored the slowly changing numbered lights as the lift made its ascent. A loved up couple, oblivious to the world, were wearing the faces off of one another, their hands beginning to wander towards more intimate parts. The Assassin watched them, unable to avert his eyes.

"Have you taken yer pill today?" he asked, mimicking something he'd seen on the telly.

The amorous couple broke free and looked over at him. "Couldn't help it, ye know, the ad an all that," he explained with a smile he presumed was friendly but was in fact was quite unnerving.

The bewildered couple continued to stare. The Assassin rubbed his chin. He was going to explain further, not that he felt under any obligation to do so but decided against it. Neither of them looked as if they had a humorous bone in their bodies. The lift stopped on the fourth floor and the doors eased open revealing a middle-aged man and woman accompanied by their three kids. The entire family were togged out in their swimming gear with the children carrying large inflatable animal toys. One of them had a green alligator, the other a dolphin while the third kid had what looked like a pink unicorn all of which they were using to batter each other with.

"We're goin' up," the Assassin said, conscious that the time for the football draw was fast approaching. He hit the button to close the lift but the kids' father stuck his brown sandaled foot between the doors forcing them apart.

"That doesn't matter, kids, now does it? Let's all go along for the ride," the man said in a sickeningly sweet voice.

The Assassin glanced at the loved-up couple and smirked. "Isn't everyone?"

The young woman cowered behind her partner, genuinely scared. They were all cramped inside the lift as it slowly began to rise. The children continued to bash one another with the inflatable toys with the Assassin receiving several belts to the face for his troubles. He glared at their parents, but they just smiled back at him as if this sort of behaviour was acceptable.

"Youngsters, sure what can you do?" their mother offered in a voice almost as sickeningly sweet as her dose of a husband.

"A good kick up the hole would soon sort them out," replied the Assassin, not one for beating around the bush.

The parents were gobsmacked and just stood there open-mouthed while their children looked up at them for reassurance. The lift shuddered to a halt on the sixth floor and the doors parted with a nervous squeak. The Assassin gave all of the other occupants the once-over then casually exited but not before biting the head of the inflatable alligator and bursting it.

Al rapped on the recently painted door of room six-o-five then checked his watch for the eleventh time. The door was reefed open and a man named Murphy appeared. He was a heavy-set bloke of about sixty who had his thinning grey hair slicked back with gel and was shrouded in an invisible cloud of cologne.

"What fucking kept you?" he cursed loudly in a pompous tone as if he owned the entire gaff.

The Assassin swung around and surveyed the deserted corridor. He then turned back to Mr. Murphy and pushed past him without uttering a single word.

Cold water gushed from a tap into the already overflowing bathtub. The shelf surrounding the bath had scented candles strategically placed on it with most of them already burnt down to the last. The Assassin surveyed the scene closely watched by Murphy, his arms folded and a scowl on his sagging face. His breathing was loud and laboured, reminiscent of an overweight Labrador on a really hot day.

"Problem?" the Assassin asked.

"Is it not obvious, you big oaf?" said Murphy, "The tap is fucking jammed."

The Assassin rechecked his watch, turned and brushed past the grumpy guest, making his way towards the bedroom.

"Am I keeping you from something?" Mr. Murphy sarcastically called out after him.

The Assassin picked up the remote control, switched on the TV and plopped down on the end of the double bed. He glanced over his shoulder and noticed a pretty young woman sitting up in the bed holding the covers tightly to her chin.

"Alrigh' chicken?" he cheerfully asked.

Murphy stormed into the bedroom and attempted to grab the remote control from the Assassin's hand.

"I don't believe this!" he shouted.

Al caught the disgruntled guest's hand jerking it back at the wrist, knowing exactly how far to go before it snapped. He held it at an acute angle just shy of breaking point as the man howled with pain and collapsed to his knees like a sack of spuds. The Assassin gave him a swift bitch slap leaving the side of the guest's face smarting. The shock of being hit momentarily stunned Murphy into silence.

Al nodded at the man's wedding ring. "Happily married I see."

Still cowering behind the bed covers, the young woman started to cry. "I'm leaving."

"Shut it, tramp or you're sacked!" roared Murphy, recovering slightly.

The Assassin increased the pressure on the obnoxious guest's wrist which brought the soft jowled man to tears. Looking his victim squarely in the eyes, Al calmly said, "That type of language is totally unacceptable, but I'm prepared to give ye a chance. I want ye to pick a number between one and sixty."

The Assassin monitored his watch as he held Mr. Murphy's head under the bath water with his other hand.

"Twenty-eight, twenty-nine, thirty," Al counted aloud. He then tore Murphy back up by the scruff of the neck. "It's just as well ye didn't pick a higher number, buddy or ye mightn't have made it."

The guest greedily gulped in badly needed, life-saving air. It wasn't as good as waterboarding, but it was still effective none the less and had served Al well on a number of occasions in the past.

"And remember, I got yer name and contact details from the hotel's computer if ye want to take things any further," the Assassin warned before shoving Murphy's skull back under the water and resuming his timekeeping all over again. Although he was raging that he was missing the football draw he felt strongly about teaching bullies a lesson. And this bully was definitely going to remember this particular lesson.

Back in Frank's pub the team watched the big screen as the T.V. host unfurled a piece of paper with his two hands and held it up for the camera.

"And finally, Sporting Les Behans'," he very carefully announced, not wanting to make any mispronunciations, "Are away to Real Roscrea."

"Where the fuck is that?" asked Yoyo.

"Tipperary," Leonard explained.

"It's a long way…" said Split.

Mick shot him a condescending look.

"Wha'?" Split added. "That's one of me better ones."

"We're gonna need to hire a bus," Fran said.

Mr. Murphy stood shivering in the middle of the hotel bedroom, his greasy wet hair dripping onto the dull carpet. He opened his wallet and attempted to hand the Assassin a grubby ten euro note but Al shook his head disapprovingly and helped himself to a crispy fifty instead.

"Ye wouldn't want to appear cheap," Al whispered, "And don't worry, so long as ye keep schtum, yer missus has no need to find out about yer extracurricular activities." Even in the unlikely event that Murphy went running to the authorities Al still wouldn't squeal him up to his wife. He had his principles after all. No, in that case he would just have to break the fucker up, big time, the first chance he got. He turned to where the young woman was still hiding in the bed, clutching the duvet to her chest. "Cop on, love, he's only usin' ye. He'll never leave his other half no matter wha' he's promised," he advised, "And while we're bein' honest here, if ye were one of me own and ye carried on like that, I'd be after smotherin' ye by now."

The football managers and coaches chatted away noisily in the swanky hotel room about the various fixtures which the draw had thrown up. While this was happening the smug manager was frantically patting his pockets. He then got down onto the floor on all fours, desperately checking under seats.

"Has anyone seen my car keys?" he asked.

Outside the building, Davey and Baxter watched as the smug manager's flash motor went rolling down a hill towards the ornate fountain. Davey winked at his friend then threw the car keys into the neighbouring thorny bushes.

"Thanks, lad. He was doing me head in," said the grateful manager.

Chapter 14

Leonard slung his kitbag over his shoulder as he glanced back towards the closed truck container dressing room. He couldn't figure it out. There was no padlock on the metal doors yet they were still shut tight. Maybe training had been cancelled and he didn't get the text, these things happened. But there were cars belonging to some of the other players parked nearby so that was definitely peculiar. Hopefully nobody was hurt. He paused momentarily, took one last look then threw his leg over the crossbar of his racing bike, a gift from Trigger, and slowly pedalled away. Davey edged one of the container doors opened and peeked out through the tiniest of gaps watching Leonard depart.

"Is he gone?" whispered Charlie.

Davey turned around and faced the rest of the team who were all seated along the benches, wearing a combination of angry, perplexed and sombre expressions.

"Yeah," he replied.

Podge jumped to his feet. "Workin' for the social fuckin' welfare, how low can ye get," he cursed.

"Lenny of all people," Jigsaw muttered, "He seemed so, ye know, normal."

"I told ye. I never forget a face. There he was, the shyster, in the back of the dole office, doin' stuff on a computer," revealed Davey, barely able to disguise his contempt.

Charlie furiously kicked his kit bag across the floor. "He's got to go."

"Somebody's got to tell him," urged Paddy Power.

The Assassin stood up and slammed his powerful fist into the palm of his other hand. "I'll do it."

"No!" the entire team shouted at once. As serious as things appeared right now, they didn't want the man murdered. A few broken bones maybe but death, now that'd be a touch excessive especially with Leonard being an otherwise nice bloke.

"I think it should be Trigger," said Gitsy, pointing at the star striker,

"After all, he was the one who brought him here in the first place." Some of the players grumbled in agreement.

Trigger was horrified. "How the fuck was I supposed to know? He does a great job with my accounts."

"It's alrigh' for you, yer semi-legit. Wha' about the rest of us?" Podge moaned.

"We could all end up losin' out on our fiddles," Split said. He lowered his voice but still loud enough for the rest of the group to hear and said, "D'ye think he was wearin' a wire?"

"Fuck," said Podge, alarmed at the possibility.

"A wire, me hole," Fran said.

"Or planted a bug," Gitsy suggested, scanning the inside of the dressing room as if he knew what he was looking for.

"Lads, it's the labour we're talkin' about not the bleedin' FBI." There was murmured discontentment as each man desperately tried to recall what information they had inadvertently revealed to the welfare mole.

"I think it's the manager's job to tell him," Davey finally said. The players turned to Baxter.

"Thanks," replied the less than impressed manager.

"Pity, the lad's gifted," said Fran.

"Seemed like a good aul skin too," Yoyo added.

"Don't be fooled, lads," said Split. "That's all part of the social's undercover trainin'."

Fran was about to guzzle his teammate when Baxter caved in from the pressure, that and not wanting the Assassin to pay Lenny a visit in person. "Look, I'll call around to him tomorrow and get it sorted, ok?"

Baxter rang the doorbell of the modest but well-kept terraced house. Leonard's Ma answered immediately as if she'd been hiding behind the door expecting someone to call. She stepped past the manager, checking up and down the street.

"I'm..." he began.

"Pa Baxter, I know. Go on in."

"I haven't really got the time..."

Leonard's Ma forcefully shoved him inside almost causing him to lose his footing and quickly shut the door.

The manager sat on the edge of the brown and cream coloured armchair, awkwardly balancing a wafer-thin China cup, filled to the brim with tea, resting on an equally delicate saucer. The good tea set for guests Baxter deducted. Leonard's Ma and Da, beaming smiles, sat across from him, waiting patiently. Baxter sneaked a look at his watch.

"He'll be home soon," said Leonard's Ma. She turned to her husband, "What's he like? Always goin' on about the football team, the way the boys treat him like one of their own," she said, hoping for support.

"Says they're a super bunch all righ'. Some very talented lads as well," Leonard's Da enthusiastically added, taking his wife's hint.

Baxter removed his cap and scratched his head. "To be honest, there's a bit of a problem with the team. That's why I've called around."

The room fell deathly silent. Leonard's Da slowly leaned forward trying to formulate his words before he spoke. "They've found out where he works, haven't they?" he said, his earlier eagerness having completely vanished.

"I'm afraid so," Baxter admitted.

Leonard's Ma reached out, taking her husband's hand in her own and holding it tightly.

"We understand," Leonard's Da said with a heavy heart.

"He's always struggled to make friends he's that quiet, it's why his Da got him into the football in the first place," explained Leonard's Ma, almost in tears.

Her husband shifted uneasily in his seat. "Turned out to be very handy as well, so he was," he said but not in a boastful way. "We had scouts over regularly from England, checkin' on his progress and he went over there for a few trials as well. They were quein' up to sign him but in the end he decided to finish his studies, get his qualifications and all that lark."

"He was always a sensible boy," Leonard's Ma insisted.

"Or so we thought," said the disappointed father, "Ye can imagine how we felt the day he came home and told us that he'd got that job...," he took a deep breath, closed his eyes and shook his head. His wife rubbed his arm tenderly, "...that job with the social bloody welfare," he continued. "He's brilliant with numbers. He could have got work anywhere if he didn't fancy bein' a professional footballer."

Leonard's Ma looked Baxter straight in the eyes. "I had to give up goin' to the bingo, people would just stop and stare and whisper," she revealed, "And as for the neighbours..." she shook her head disappointedly. "There was nothin' bad like that ever happened before on either side of our families, apart from yer Uncle Danny murderin' that old woman..."

"Ah heore, Danny had his reasons in fairness," her husband said defensively.

"I suppose," Leonard's Ma agreed, "Anyway, we had to sell up and move in the end. The only thing I'll tell ye and God be me witness," she made an elaborate show of blessing herself, "he's never squealed on anyone in his entire life. Sure his own Da's been workin' on the QT for years."

"Everything okay?" asked Leonard, suddenly appearing out of nowhere. Everyone jumped. Leonard's parents stole a quick glance at Baxter.

The day of the fourth round tie away to Real Roscrea had arrived. Baxter was pacing back and forth like an expectant father in the car park next to Frank's pub when Davey popped his head out of the waiting team bus.

"No sign yet?" he anxiously asked.

"Not a dicky," Baxter answered. "Are the lads alright about what happened with Lenny?"

"Sure wha' else could ye do," Davey replied, trying to reassure the gaffer that he'd done the right thing.

Like some kind of modern-day interpretation of the Ben-Hur chariot race, Jigsaw came half sprinting, half scutting across the car park steering Gonzales in your common-or-garden type wheelchair.

Baxter turned to Davey. "Here comes trouble."

"Dumb and dumber," joked Davey.

"Sorry I'm late, Boss," Jigsaw said, panting heavily as he pulled up next to where Baxter and Davey stood waiting.

Getting straight to the point the manager turned to Jigsaw and said, "Where's Birdy?"

Jigsaw, exhausted, was bent over trying to catch his breath. "His uncle organised... a special show..." he answered between deep intakes, "...some bank knobs and their families... He's not goin' to make the game."

Baxter patted Jigsaw gently on the back. "All right, son, thanks," He turned to the nuisance in the wheelchair, "By the way, where's your own wheels?" he asked, pretending to be somewhat interested.

"Battery's fucked," said Gonzales, "But luckily I have this as a spare in me shed."

"Lucky, yeah," grunted Baxter.

Gonzales took a megaphone out of the plastic bag that was resting on his lap. "Look at the state of that bus!" he shouted through the speaker. "It's like somethin' outta the fuckin' Flintstones."

Baxter fiddled with his ear, almost deaf from the unexpected barrage.

"And where's the bleedin' lift?" Gonzales roared.

"Jigsaw, will you get some of the lads to give you a hand with Gonzales?" the manager reluctantly asked.

"No prob," Jigsaw said, already climbing onto the coach to fetch help.

Baxter and Davey moved a few steps away from Gonzales who kept giving them the evil eye while his head lolled from side to side. Gonzales had complete control over his neck muscles but he knew his actions freaked a lot of people out especially the manager so that's why he did it.

"If it wasn't for the disability grant, we get he could go and fu..." Baxter didn't bother finishing his sentence.

"I hear ye, Pa, but God help him all the same," said Davey, hoping that the manager didn't really mean anything by it and was just feeling the pressure of the upcoming match.

"We're going to have to stick Podge in goal," Baxter said.

"Gonna have to score a shit load of goals as well," said Davey, trying to inject some humour into the proceedings as he turned to get on the bus.

"You can say that again," Baxter agreed. He caught his player by the arm. "I'm after getting a phone call from the league, they're not happy with your Lesbian team name."

"It's Les Behans'," Davey said, correcting the gaffer.

"Anyway," Baxter said, waving his hand dimissively, "They never thought we'd get this far in the cup. They've received a number of complaints following the televised draw and are threatening to kick us out unless we change our name."

"Sure that's just prejudice, wha' about poor Les?"

Baxter gave Davey a look that said cut the bullshit.

"Leave it with me, I'll get it sorted," said Davey.

"You better, and don't say anything to the lads. I don't want them getting distracted."

The bus was making great time on its epic journey down the country, a drive of almost two and a half full hours. Some of the boys had been winding up Jigsaw, asking him where he'd changed his money and what rate did he get. The manager eventually had to tell them to lay off when Jigsaw came to him all in a dither, wondering could they turn the bus around cause he hadn't brought his passport. The joys of team bonding. Baxter decided to stop off about half ways to give the players a short break and to stretch the aul legs. He leaned in beside the coach driver who had crater-like skin and a big bulbous whiskey nose.

"There's an alehouse about a mile on your left..." he said.

"I know it well," the driver answered without missing a beat.

Baxter raised an eyebrow and was about to slag him off about being an alki but decided that he didn't look like the joking type and more than likely did have a drink problem.

"We'll give the lads a few minutes," he said instead. He then moved down the bus and took a seat next to Podge. "How's the hand?"

"Some days are better than others," answered Podge.

Baxter nodded sympathetically. "Know what you mean."

"Yoyo gave me a few tablets earlier on, purely medicinal," Podge explained, "Said they were the good ones, can't feel any pain. Can't really feel me hand either now that I come to think about it," He suddenly whacked his hand hard against the window, almost putting it through the glass, "Not a fuckin' thing."

The driver spun his head around on hearing the noise, but Baxter gave him a smile to let him know that things were still under control, for the time being anyhow.

"Calm the fuck down," Baxter told Podge. "We're putting you in goal, meself and the lads are one hundred percent behind you."

"Appreciate the vote of confidence, Boss."

The manager smiled. He got to his feet before he'd have to tell anymore lies and moved along the aisle. He gave the elderly brothers, Larry and Mo, who were busy milling cans of cheap cider a friendly nod. They raised their drinks returning the greeting.

"Are your feet better then?" Baxter asked, noticing that the plaster of Paris was gone from Mo's legs.

"Brand new," Mo replied, "Not that there was anythin' wrong with them in the first place. It was all an act for a claim I've banged in."

"We've banged in," corrected his brother Larry.

"We've banged in," Mo reluctantly agreed.

"Well, the best of luck with that," said Baxter, swiftly moving on. He passed Gonzales who was fast asleep and held upright with a seatbelt, his folded wheelchair stored neatly beside him. He then stopped next to where the Assassin and Leonard were sitting.

"Everything alright, lads?" he asked.

"Sound," replied the Assassin. The big man turned to Leonard, "Show him yer t-shirt, head."

Leonard did as he was told and unzipped his tracksuit top revealing a drawing of the three chimpanzees; Hear no evil, See no evil and Speak no evil. A fourth chimpanzee had been crudely drawn in thick black marker with a hatchet through its skull and the words written in what appeared to be blood underneath in large capital letters, OR ELSE! The Assassin playfully grabbed Leonard in a headlock and rubbed his thick knuckles against his noggin.

Baxter smiled. He was delighted that he'd been able to convince the players to allow Lenny to remain on the team. The fact that the Assassin had also warned Lenny that he'd hack his Ma and Da's heads off and shove them where the sun didn't shine undoubtedly helped to sway the vote too.

The Sporting players got off the coach and filed past Baxter towards the pub. He was like a hen with an egg watching them as they went by.

"No gargling, men, not til after the game. A slash and a lemonade, I warning you," he said, pretending to threaten them.

"Wha' about a small one?" said Davey.

"That's wha' yer bird said last nigh'," slagged Charlie.

"G'wed," said Baxter, enjoying the banter with the boys, "Order us a chip butty."

Davey gave the boss the thumbs up. The day's journey had gone a lot smoother than Baxter had imagined. He stuck his head inside the door of the coach. "Do you want me to get you something to eat?"

The driver shook his head no.

"Ok. Give us abar half an hour," said Baxter.

The mood was relaxed in the boozer as the players tucked into the soup of the day, delicious creamy vegetable with a hint of chilli. They also made light work of the freshly made sandwiches which were as big as doorstops. The pub grub was going down a treat and the Assassin had decided to continue his story about the dodgy patio man.

"So I'm at home havin' me tea," explained Al, "The Ma had done me a massive fry up, batch loaf, black and white puddin', the works. She told me that a lad named Tommo had called around to measure up for the new patio. I was only half listenin' if I'm bein' honest, the Ma has a tendency to rattle on at times. And in anyway, I was more interested in dippin' me bread into me runny egg."

"Did you know that the white part of an egg is called the albumen?" Leonard informed the lads. Al threw Leonard a look that didn't need an explanation. "Sorry for interrupting you, Al," Leonard immediately apologised before shrinking back into his seat.

"Anyways, I asked the Ma wha' the story was with this bloke Tommo and she handed me a fancy piece of paper he'd given her with his name and contact details at the top."

Davey slid further down in his seat, partially covering his face with his hand, remembering his earlier encounter with Tommo in the pub when he was only trying to help the poor chap out.

"The fucker was tryin' to do me aul wan," the Assassin said, his face turning crimson with anger.

"As in shaggin'?" asked Jigsaw, aghast at the notion.

The Assassin glared at him. He thought about thumping the head off of him but decided to give him a walkover, after all, it wasn't the lad's fault he was touched.

"I checked the measurements meself and yer man Tommo's were way off," Al said.

"Some right scallys out there, doing that to a defenceless elderly woman," said Baxter, sympathising with his highly strung player in the hope that things wouldn't escalate, at least not today and definitely not until after the game.

"I wasn't lettin' it go so I rang this Tommo bloke up and told him to drop by, see if we could do a deal," the Assassin said, grinning, "The greedy pox called around the followin' day, bang on time. I answered the door and there he was, holdin' his bogey measurin' tape in one hand and a clipboard in the other, all smiles as if I was the world's biggest fuckin' eejit. I tore the little bastard inside." Al took a big swig of his lemonade as the rest of the team hung onto his every word in trepidation, "I tell ye, he wasn't grinnin' when I tied and gagged him to a chair in the livin' room. Wrapped his measurin' tape around his skinny neck, was tempted to finish him off there and then but I decided that that would be far too humane. So I left him there to stew and went to get me hatchet. While I was gone the bleedin' Ma only went and snuck back in and untied him. He'd hopped out of the gaff before I knew wha' was goin' on."

There wasn't a sound in the pub. The players shot one another sneaky looks, all thinking the same thing but with nobody daring to utter a word. The Assassin was a bona fide psychopath.

Baxter coughed. "Sorry for cutting in, Al, but we better head, times shoving on."

The Assassin stretched his powerful arms above his head. "No problem Boss, fully understand. I'll finish the story off later for the boys," he promised.

The coach driver got off the bus and opened the luggage hold. He reached inside trying to get at a loose bag that had been knocking about but it was just out of reach and he was forced to climb inside. Seconds later, Jigsaw sauntered out of the pub and saw that the luggage hold was wide open with nobody in sight.

"The dope, leavin' that open," he gave out to no one in particular, "Any sham could have just walked up and robbed the kit."

He slammed the door down and there was a loud thud before it swung back up again. This time he put all of his weight into it and kept slamming the door until he eventually got it fully closed. He had no sooner finished the task when the rest of the team exited the boozer and began to climb back on board.

Baxter scratched his head. "Anyone see the driver?"

"He's probably inside throwin' the gargle down his throat," Trigger said, "Did ye see the size of the conk on him."

"No, I'm the last one out and I made sure there was no one left inside," replied Baxter, more than a little puzzled.

"We have to get goin'," Fran said, checking his watch.

"Can you drive a bus?" asked the manager not expecting a positive response.

Fran smiled. "Nope, but I know a man who can."

The team had searched high and low for the missing coach driver during the five minute period that the manager had allowed but came up short so an executive decision was made. Paddy Power had been elected, unopposed, to drive the bus. He now sat behind the steering wheel with a big happy head on him, absolutely buzzing.

Baxter leaned in close to Paddy. "Fran said you used to work on the buses?"

"It's been a fair few years but yeah," said Power, already concentrating on the task in hand.

"Like getting back on a horse, I'd imagine," Baxter said.

Paddy nodded his head in agreement as he started up the engine. "It was mostly city tours, for the aul tourists. Not that ye'd want to be dependin' on them for tips," he explained.

"I hear you," said Baxter.

"Although in fairness the Yanks were very generous for the most part. Wasn't a bad gig either for pickin' up the chicks, used to tell them I was a Zulu prince," Paddy said.

"I didn't realise you were from Africa. What part?" the manager asked.

"Africa! I'm from Blanch ye mad thing," Power said, laughing.

Baxter smiled. "Right, crack on, we've a game to get to." The manager left his substitute driver to it and made his way along the aisle to check on the rest of his troops. Larry and Mo were still guzzling cans of cider.

"Alright, boys?" he said.

"Couldn't be better," Larry replied.

Baxter moved further along and paused next to where Jigsaw and Split were seated.

"See that fly?" Split said to Jigsaw.

"Yeah," said his companion, his eyes following the lazy flight of a small fruit fly. Split made a rapid chopping action toward the unsuspecting insect. The fly continued its slow motion aerobatics, seemingly unaffected.

"Ye didn't kill it," said Jigsaw, unable to hide his disappointment, not that he was into animal cruelty or anything.

"No, but it won't be fatherin' any more kids," Split answered, winking at his teammate. He then blew along the edge of his hand, pretending to cool it down.

Jigsaw squinted at the airborne insect but couldn't see any difference, not that he knew how obvious a fly's flute should be. He presumed that it wasn't that big and was in proportion to the rest of its body or else it could just pogo from one fruit bowl to the next. Shrugging his shoulders he turned back to Split. "So wha' belt are ye now?"

"What's that?" Split said, only half listening. His vivid imagination had already transported him onto a film set in Chinatown where he was batterin' the bejaysus outta hundreds of Oriental lads with the help of his best friend, Bruce.

"The martial arts?" Jigsaw said, somewhat miffed at being ignored.

"Oh, eh... gold."

"Spoofer," coughed Baxter into his hand.

Split looked up at the gaffer.

"Don't mind me, lads..." said the manager, patting his chest lightly, "...a bit of a cold or maybe an allergy to nuts, that's all." He left the two bright sparks to it.

Jigsaw stared at Split and said, "Gold?"

"Can't get any higher than that, pal," boasted Split, puffing out his chest to emphasise his own self-importance.

"I thought black belts or Dans or somethin' along those lines were the best," his companion said.

Split moved in closer to his teammate. "I'm the seventh Dan of a seventh Dan," he revealed, "Which makes me a gold." He sat back, a smug grin on his face, knowingly tapping the side of his nose.

"But I thought ye only have the two brothers, Johnner and..." Jigsaw bit down on his lip trying hard to remember the other lad's name.

"Barry," said Split.

"Ah yes, Baldy Barry, sure how could I forget him."

"He's not baldy."

"He's got no hair and wears a wig."

"He's got alopecia."

"Well that's wha' everyone else calls him, no offence," said Jigsaw.

"Forget about it but don't ever let me Ma hear ye call him that or she'll burst ye," Split warned.

"Thanks for the heads up. So what's the story with the Dans?"

"It's complicated…"

"And doesn't yer Da only have the one leg?"

Split looked around then leaned forward, conspiratorially. "That was the result of a big scrap in Hong Kong but I can't say too much," he vaguely explained in an ultra-confidential tone.

Jigsaw wasn't entirely satisfied with Split's explanations and his teammate didn't seem to want to elaborate any further so he decided to let it go, for now.

Baxter joined the Assassin and Leonard who were sitting further down the bus. "How's the new job in the hotel going, Al?"

"Didn't work out."

"Sorry to hear that."

The Assassin shrugged his shoulders. "Some people can be very sensitive," he said, recalling his altercation with the hotel manager after the sappy family who were on their way to the swimming pool had complained and then the subsequent confrontation with the police and a small number of terrified guests including the loved up couple from the lift fleeing the premises.

"I know what you mean," Leonard said with empathy, "You wouldn't belief half the complaints I've to deal with on a daily basis."

"What's up with your regular job, Al, the taxiing?" Baxter asked.

"Too many at it," Al replied, the muscles in his jaw visibly tensing.

The manager immediately regretted asking the question, sensing a rant coming on.

"Them dopey fucks of politicians would let anyone drive a cab these days," the Assassin swore. "Deregulation me hole. They destroyed a perfectly good industry."

"I hear you, lad," Baxter said, nodding in agreement but realising too late that he had inadvertently lit the touch paper on one of Al's many issues even though he agreed one hundred percent with his player on this particular topic. He hoped that Al's pent up aggression could be used as an advantage later on. He then noticed that Trigger, who was sitting alone, was kind of jogging in his seat.

"Are you alright there, Trigger?" he asked.

Trigger made an okay signal with his index finger and thumb while staring straight ahead. The striker then checked his watch and began to jog faster, still in a sitting position. Baxter left him to it. He moved towards the back of the vehicle and sat in beside Fran who in his opinion was the most levelheaded player on the team.

"Story," said Fran.

"Trigger really seems up for this one," Baxter observed.

The two men studied Trigger as he continued his seated jogging. The striker rechecked his watch, ducked left, ducked right then pulled out an imaginary gun and took aim. Fran and Baxter looked at one another and shook their heads.

"Nah, plannin' a new job," said Fran.

The coach drove past a sign that read: Welcome to Tipperary. All the players on board, with the exception of Jigsaw who had never heard the ditty before, started singing, "It's a long way to Tipperary, it's a long way to go, without yer Granny. It's a long way to Tipperary, to the sweetest girl I know..."

Podge turned to Larry and Mo who were both wearing stony-faced expressions. "Are yis not joinin' in, lads," he asked.

Mo glared at him with undisguised contempt. "With that imperialistic jingoism?"

"My arse," agreed Larry.

Podge decided not to delve any further.

A Garda checkpoint had been set up just ahead with traffic cones, in dire need of a good power-hosing, spread out and a police car parked in the middle of the road. Several vehicles were backed up, dutifully waiting to be processed. A motorist at the head of the line handed one of the policemen his license for inspection.

"I hope they're not lookin' for ye, Trigger?" shouted Charlie, knowing that there were several warrants still outstanding for his teammate.

Everyone on board laughed and turned to look at their star striker but he was nowhere to be seen. It was as if he had vanished into thin air.

"Where the fuck has he gone?" asked Davey, genuinely impressed.

Paddy Power checked his rear view mirror. Everyone was seated except for Baxter who was standing in the middle of the aisle towards the rear of the bus talking to Fran. Paddy scratched his head, beads of sweat forming on his brow.

"Shit," he cursed under his breath. He suddenly slammed the bus into gear, pressing down fully on the accelerator and swerving around the other cars in the queue. Baxter was thrown forward but the Assassin managed to grab him in the nick of time before he lamped himself.

"What in the name of Christ?" shouted Baxter.

Traffic cones were scattered as the coach hurtled towards the checkpoint. One of the Gardai stood in the middle of the road, furiously waving his arms about in a futile attempt to stop the oncoming ten tonnes plus vehicle. Paddy Power ignored the instruction and drove on. The Garda wisely decided to dive out of the way just as the bus hit the corner of the squad car, shunting it to one side and smashing it against another parked car before speeding off. Stunned drivers hesitantly emerged from their motors, surveying a scene more reminiscent of an action movie, albeit a low budget one. One of the Gardai scrambled into the damaged squad car. "Get in, Mikey," he called out.

Mikey hobbled towards his colleague and followed him in. The patrol car roared to life, sirens flashing and wailing. As it gave pursuit the rear metal panelling dragged its arse along the ground sending a trail of metal sparks flying in its wake.

Despite the fact that the players were being thrown about like rag dolls inside the coach, Paddy Power wouldn't ease off on the gas. He swerved hard narrowly missing an oncoming tractor loaded with bales of silage tightly wrapped in black plastic.

"Slow down, ye bleedin' fruitcake!" Davey yelled.

Larry and Mo held tightly onto their cans, their faces lit up with the kind of excitement usually reserved for small kids on Christmas morning.

"This is like bein' back on manoeuvres, bro!" Larry screamed in delight.

The Assassin clawed his way to the front of the bus using the seats for assistance.

"Power, if ye don't pull over I'm gonna have to break yer hands, pal," he warned.

Paddy gave a quick glance over his shoulder at the approaching hulk. "I can't, Al, I'll get locked up."

Birdy sat at his cluttered dresser staring forlornly at his reflection in the mirror. The numerous lights framing the glass did little to brighten his demeanour. He was dressed as a clown with a multicoloured wig stuck onto his head and his face plastered in thick makeup. A pretty female assistant charged into the small room.

"Five minutes to show-time," she informed Birdy before quickly disappearing again.

He looked up at the wall clock and sighed. He was extremely disappointed to be missing the big game in Tipperary especially when today's circus performance was for a group of people who would shit on you if they could get away with it. He forced a smile but it soon slipped and was once again replaced with a frown as if his face was made of melting wax.

There was a huge gap in the hedgerow where the team coach had left the road and ploughed straight through it. The front wheels of the vehicle were wedged in a muddy field that still contained the remnants of an earlier season's crop. Inside the bus, the lads were scattered about the place, gradually getting to their feet, some feeling their limbs to make sure they were still attached. While this was all happening the overhead luggage compartment slowly opened and Trigger peaked out, giving the place the quick once over to make sure that the coast was clear.

Trigger and Richie scarpered across the mucky field, watched by Baxter who was standing in the doorway of the bus. The police sirens were getting uncomfortably close. Richie checked over his shoulder, giving the boss a questioning look.

"About a mile that way," Baxter called out through cupped hands before pointing towards a quaint church steeple in the near distance.

As Richie was giving Baxter the thumbs up Fran, Mick and Davey edged past him and climbed off.

"Everyone's alrigh'," Fran reassured the worried manager.

"Thank God for that," the gaffer replied, fearing the worst. He suddenly remembered the elderly brothers who had tagged along. "How are Larry and Mo?"

"Not a bother on them, once they got hold of their solicitor," Fran said with a wry smile.

The manager gave his player a quizzical look.

"I gave them a loan of me phone so they could register their latest claim," Fran added, "And they reckon they might've hit the jackpot with this one."

Baxter was alarmed. "Surely they're not going to land Power in it?"

"There's no fear of that. Them lads are professionals," Davey said, "They've already worked out their story. Something about being asleep and disorientated, oh and they're also playin' the elderly card."

Fran looked in the direction of the nearing sirens. "The law will be here shortly, wha' are we gonna tell them?"

"If they find out Paddy was driving..." Baxter said, shaking his head, "I can't believe he lost his license over a stupid bet."

"Trying to squeeze a double-decker bus at eighty miles an hour through a narrow tunnel will do it for you every time," Mick said, more like his usual sympathetic self.

At that precise moment they heard loud banging coming from the luggage hold under the coach. The men looked at one another. The day had been full of enough surprises as it was. Fran cautiously opened the door to the luggage hold revealing the dazed driver who was gingerly rubbing the top of his head.

The circus was packed with the big bank knobs and their spoilt families, staring in anticipation at a circular paper wall which was lit up with a bright spotlight. The circus band did a drum roll followed by a 'Dah, Dah,' but nothing happened. The drummer looked over at the furious ringmaster who had both his hands planted on hips. He motioned for the band to do the drum roll again. 'Dah, Dah,' they repeated with the same unsatisfactory result. There was a long pause then the female assistant who had only moments earlier checked in with Birdy peered from around the paper wall. She turned her palms skywards in defeat.

Meanwhile, Birdy, still dressed as a clown, wig and all, was already tearing along the road, riding his powerful scrambler motorbike hard in an attempt to make the football game or at least the second half.

A large, powerful tractor with concrete filled barrels attached to the rear acting as counterweights, pulled the coach out of the field and back onto the road. The bus appeared to have surprisingly only sustained superficial damage to its paintwork despite the accident and only a slightly dented bumper from the earlier shunt with the squad car.

Larry gave Baxter a discreet wink as he was stretchered past and loaded into the back of a waiting ambulance where his brother was already being tended to. Things could have turned out a lot worse and the manager was well aware of the fact as he chomped rapidly on his gum. This was something he did when his anxiety levels were sky high and having a Garda sergeant standing next to him definitely wasn't helping.

He wedged the chewing gum between the inside of his cheek and his teeth before speaking. "Fair play for getting us sorted," he said to the copper.

The sergeant didn't acknowledge Baxter's words of thanks. "One of our cars will give you an escort and Garda Conway will take command of your vehicle," said the sergeant.

The manager glanced over to where the dazed coach driver was being breathalysed. "Is that really necessary?" he asked.

"It's procedure."

"Could he not have at least been brought to the ozzy first?"

"He volunteered," the lawman bluntly replied, "We'll be in touch regarding this, alleged hijacking incident."

Baxter wasn't going to drop anyone in it if he could help it, so he kept his trap shut and said no more. He could only imagine how much his actions were annoying the sergeant who was now glaring at him, hoping to spot some sign of weakness. The manager retrieved his chewing gum from inside his cheek with the tip of his tongue and began to blow a bubble. The longer the sergeant continued to stare the bigger the bubble became. The lawman eventually relented and twisted his head away in defeat. Baxter burst his bubble.

Without warning the sergeant started to walk back towards his parked car. "Tell your players that we'll need to speak to them again before the week is out, to go through their statements in more detail," he said, not bothering to turn his head around. "The non-white fella in particular."

Baxter was going to say something smart but decided now was not the time. "Will do," he simply replied instead. The Gardaí who were manning the earlier checkpoint had said that the coach driver had a black face and of course Power was the only player on the team who fit that description. However, everybody on board the bus was sticking to the same story, the high-jacker was wearing a black balaclava.

The police sergeant reached his car, pulled open the door and climbed in. He started the engine and while continuing to stare straight ahead, lowered the window. "We've rang Real Roscrea to let them know about the delay," he said.

"Ta. You've been very understanding," the manager sarcastically replied.

The lawman angled his head and looked Baxter square in the eye. "If there's one thing I hate more than Jackeens, its Scouse Jackeens. Hope they kick the living daylights out of ye," he said. The car was then put into gear and departed the scene.

Baxter spat out his gum. "So much for impartiality."

4th Round: Real Roscrea v Sporting Les Behans'

Podge sort of half fell, half dived for a low shot but couldn't get to the ball in time to prevent it from crossing the goal line. The Real Roscrea players hugged one another in jubilant celebration as Fran kicked the patchy turf in frustration. While all of this was happening Birdy was going full throttle on his overworked scrambler down a narrow, uneven road not too far away. The game continued to ebb and flow with Sporting having the lion's share of possession but still looking vulnerable at the back. Charlie pulled out of a tackle at the last second but the Roscrea opposition player did a blatant dive, rolling around in agony and clutching his knee. The referee immediately blew his whistle having bought the free.

"A dive," Charlie shouted, protesting wildly about his opponent's theatrics.

The referee raced over to him, reached into his pocket and produced a yellow card.

"Ye can't be serious. Should be bookin' him for simulation," Charlie complained. He recreated the cheat's diving action for the benefit of the official.

The referee waved him away dismissively. "I know what I saw, lad. No more of yer lip or it'll be a red next time."

"The Les Behans' are gettin' it from all angles now," Gonzales commentated through his megaphone.

The opposition player who had supposedly been fouled, slowly got to his feet as Sporting Les Behans' formed a wall for the imminent free kick. Jigsaw stood next to Charlie as the opposition player slowly jogged past the pair of them, smirking at Charlie.

"Ask your sister about simulation. She was all the business in that lap dancing club the other night," the opponent said.

Charlie clenched his fist. "Yer gonna get it for real next time, bud, and with interest."

"Yeah, right. You and whose army?" the opposition player said, further taunting his opponent.

"Wait and see," Charlie promised, "Just wait and see."

Jigsaw turned to his teammate, a big smiley head on him. "He knows yer sister, Simone, isn't that gas? Small world all the same."

"Don't be so stupid," said Charlie, "He's never met me sister, the pox is only tryin' to wind me up."

"Oh, righ'. So is Simone not still a stripper then?" Jigsaw asked.

Charlie screwed up his face. "For the last bleedin' time, she's not a stripper. She's never been a stripper."

"I thought she took her clothes off for money?" Jigsaw said, scratching his head.

"She's an exotic dancer, righ'. And there's a difference," snapped Charlie.

Jigsaw said no more. He couldn't understand why his teammate was getting so upset. He'd seen Simone in action and she was very good at what she did, some great moves. And that was before she'd even taken her skimpy clothing off.

Real Roscrea took the free kick and the ball sailed over the Sporting defence. Podge ran out of his goal towards the bouncing ball but stumbled and somehow somersaulted forward, landing flat on his arse.

"Send in the clowns, where are the clowns..." Mick drolly sang.

At that precise moment Birdy appeared behind the Sporting goal, standing upright while riding his motorbike, both his hands clasped to the side of his head. He watched in horror as the ball bobbled into the empty net. The Real Roscrea players spun away, celebrating. Mick spotted Birdy's arrival and continued his song, "...they're already here."

The agitated circus performer raced up the sideline where Baxter was standing with his hands on his hips and threw the motorbike forcefully to the ground next to him.

"I thought you were doing a show?" Baxter said.

"Yes," answered Birdy. He made a swift, slitting of the throat action with his index finger and added, "No more for me."

"I've heard of lads running away with the circus but never running away from one," the manager admitted.

Les Behans' tipped off to resume the match after conceding the soft goal.

"I want to play football," Birdy angrily explained.

"Good for you," said the boss.

"What score, please?"

"Podge has let in four..."

"Fuck. Shit."

"Could be worse though, we've scored seven," Baxter revealed. He looked out onto the pitch towards the Assassin and shouted, "Watch your house."

The Assassin made a powerful header sending the ball almost thirty yards clear.

"Well done, lad," the manager called out, giving his player some encouragement. He then turned to Birdy and said, "He'd head a concrete block if it fell out of an aeroplane."

Birdy was confused. He stared skywards. Baxter glanced at the runaway clown before also checking out the sky. He then looked back at Birdy who was still staring into the air and shook his head. "Don't just stand there, get changed," he ordered sharply.

Mick, Fran, Baxter and Davey stood at the bar chatting with Frank the Publican, filling him in on their away game in Tipperary that day.

Mick said, "When the police breathalysed the coach driver I thought the poor sap was going to be incarcerated."

"He was poxed alrigh'," Fran agreed, "Said his liver's bandjaxed these last few months so he's been off the sauce."

"So that's why he volunteered to take the breathalyser," Baxter said, smiling.

The publican held up his hand for the lads to stop as he was having difficulty trying to follow their earlier escapades. "But I thought the driver was locked in the baggage hold and that Power was the one drivin'?"

"After gettin' the bangs on his loaf of bread the driver had no idea how he ended up in there," explained Davey.

"It was just as well," Baxter added, "When Davey told the driver we'd been hijacked and that he'd been bashed over the head by the attacker, he bought it hook, line and sinker. Ended up being a very convincing witness for the old bill."

They all laughed.

"And do ye think it'll wash with the law about the driver appearin' to be black only because he was wearin' a balaclava?" the publican asked.

"These are very sensitive times," Fran said, "And it'll be very hard to confirm a positive I.D. Any brief worth his salt would get the case thrown out if it ever got to court."

Davey felt a vibration in his jeans pocket and retrieved his mobile. It was Lily. He left the lads to the match postmortem, slipping outside to where it was a bit quieter and answered his phone. "Howya, darlin'. We won again," he proudly announced.

Yoyo and Charlie came out of the pub and lit up their cigarettes. Yoyo offered Davey one but he politely declined with a wave of the hand.

"Sorry, wha' was that?" Davey said into his phone, hoping that he'd misheard Lily. "Me Ma? How bad?"

Chapter 15

Davey's Ma was propped up in her hospital bed with several, crisp, white pillows. She was rigged up to a drip and some other complicated looking machine who's function Davey hadn't a bull's notion about, but it looked serious enough. He sat on the edge of the bed with his head bowed.

"Look, son, the fact of the matter is that I'm on me way out," his Ma told him, not trying to sugarcoat the truth.

"Cause they're all the same, tell ye there's nothin' they can do until ye produce the reddies," said Davey, trance-like. His Ma squeezed his hand and smiled. He looked into her kind but tired eyes. "Wha' about more chemo?" he urged.

"Just gonna prolong things, love. I want me last few days on this earth to have some quality," she bravely replied.

Tears were welling up in Davey's eyes. "What'll I do, when yer gone?" he asked, a droplet of water escaping from the corner of his eye.

"Yer gonna become a man, son. And yer to promise me that ye'll give up the robbin'..."

"I haven't stroked in..."

"Who d'ye think yer talkin' to? Now go and get me bag out of that press," she ordered.

Davey shuffled off the bed and retrieved his Ma's favourite handbag from the bedside locker and handed it over. He remembered buying it for her birthday one year, legitimately, cost him a nice few quid as well, only to bump into an old acquaintance the very next day who was offloading the exact same bags at a quarter of the price.

"How long, do ye know?" he asked.

"Until ye get yer inheritance?" Mrs. Byrne said, trying to lighten the situation, if only a smidgeon.

Davey jumped to his feet. "I don't want..."

"Sit down ye flippin' eejit, I was only jokin'," his mother gave out.

Davey did as he was told, feeling stupid. "I haven't got long," she answered truthfully. She took a Credit Union book and an envelope from her bag. "The instructions are all in here and yer to use this money to bury me." She waved the Credit Union book then handed it to him. In their part of the world it was of huge comfort for an older person to know that when it was their time to depart this earth, they wouldn't be burdening their loved ones with the funeral expenses.

"Stop..." pleaded Davey.

"Don't interrupt yer mother. I want ye to make sure the neighbours are well looked after, send them all home locked."

Davey flicked through the savings book, confused.

"Every shillin' ye've ever given me is in there," his Ma explained.

"I don't understand. It was to make things easier for ye," Davey said, choking back the tears, "So ye wouldn't have to be runnin' around lookin' after all those old people."

"Ah I know that, son. Yer heart was always in the righ' place," she said, consoling him, "But I loved mindin' the poor little elderly men and women. I learned so much from them and it was never a hardship. Now, I want ye to buy somethin' out of the money for the hospital, they've been very good to me. Don't give them cash though. In my experience the hierarchy have a way of divertin' the funds away from where it's most needed."

"How am I supposed to know wha' to buy?" he asked, behaving like a petulant schoolboy.

"That nice nurse will be able to tell ye..."

"Who?"

"...what's needed. I also want ye to try yer best to help people out who are less fortunate than yerself, who for wha'ever reason have nowhere else to turn. It'll help with the grievin' process and will give ye somethin' to focus on goin' forward. One last thing," She handed him a business card.

He cautiously accepted it and looked it over, pulling a face. "A shrink?"

"I've made an appointment for ye and yer to keep it, d'ye hear me?" she sternly instructed.

"Ma!" he said, protesting.

"I'll haunt ye if ye don't," she threatened.

Mick wandered sheepishly along the lingerie aisle of the large, upmarket department store, pausing every now and then to scan his surroundings. After the ridicule he'd received from the paralyzed Yank and his beefcake boyfriend Mick knew that he needed more modern clothes if his 'Camming' enterprise was going to be successful. The trouble was the clothes here looked expensive and he wasn't exactly flush with cash at the moment. He could only imagine the slagging from the lads if he got caught stealing women's knickers, he'd never be able to live it down. He tentatively touched some of the delicate undergarments not really sure if they were suitable. The elegant shop manager who was in her late forties noticed the customer's antics.

She sidled up behind Mick. "Can I help you, sir?"

The customer spun around knocking a lace corset to the ground. He immediately bent down, fumbling to pick it up, his face reddening by the second. "No, thanks. Just something for the wife," Mick lied, saying the first thing that entered his head.

The store manager didn't believe him of course. There was no sign of a wedding ring or any kind of a mark suggesting that he normally wore one. Besides, it was her job to notice these things. "Well, if I can be of assistance, just give me a call. My name is Wendy." She began to move away but paused. Turning around, she said, "Look, I'm locking up this evening, so I'll be the last one out of here if you'd like to give a call back for some personal assistance, say about six-fifteen."

Mick stood on the pavement opposite the store watching as the lights went out, section by section. The staff dispersed in small groups, chatting animatedly as they left. Mick checked the time on his phone, it was almost quarter past six. He crossed the road and tapped gently on the glass door with his car keys before he had time to change his mind. There was no sign of life at first and he was seriously considering walking away when Wendy appeared out of the darkness and opened up. She touched his arm and welcomed him inside with a warm, reassuring smile. Mick felt a surge of electricity pulse down his spine, something he hadn't experienced in quite a while.

The store manager had laid out a selection of women's lingerie on the spotlessly clean counter.

"They're all in your size..." Wendy said.

"You've got this wrong," Mick protested, half-heartedly.

Undeterred, she pointed to a row of cubicles, "The changing rooms are over there."

He hesitated.

She folded her arms, tilted her head to one side and said, "It's up to you."

It hadn't taken much for Wendy to persuade Mick to try on the new outfits despite his initial denial. He examined his reflection in the changing room mirror.

"Ready?" Wendy called from the other side of the cubicle curtain.

Here goes," Mick said to himself, feeling absolutely ridiculous. He coughed and said, "Ready."

Wendy pulled back the curtain and grinned. "Perfect fit," she complimented as she further checked him out.

Mick stood with his arms folded, dressed in a white basque and knickers.

"Give us a twirl," Wendy said, gushing like a teenager.

Mick reluctantly turned around. This was definitely new territory for him and he'd seen and done an awful lot of fucked up shit in his day. The tiniest piece of string divided the tanned, muscular cheeks of his ass. Wendy slipped out of her conservative dress, letting it slide to the floor and revealing sexy underwear of her own. She then licked her lips seductively.

Tracey was sitting alone on Fran's couch, sipping coffee when he came into the room carrying a baby monitor.

"Job done," he said, placing the listening device down on the dresser.

"Is she asleep already?" asked Tracey, pleasantly surprised.

Fran remembered the framed photo of his late partner, Vicky, sitting on the dresser. He checked over his shoulder then slipped it into a drawer.

"Out for the count. Thank God for Dozol," he replied.

Tracey was more than a little alarmed. "Are you supposed to give that to a child so young?"

"I'm only jokin'."

"Swine. She's a lovely girl and you're very lucky to have her."

Fran gave a wry smile. "That's just it. Don't know for how long more."

Tracey gave him a quizzical look.

"Got a letter today, a date's been set for court for the custody case," he revealed.

Tracey got up off the couch and gave him a reassuring hug. "You're a lovely chap and a brilliant father to that child. A blind man could see that."

"Thanks."

"And you've got some great friends for support, not that I can fathom how you're still mates after all these years. None of you seem to have much in common," Tracey noted.

"That's the power of football I suppose," Fran said.

Tracey eased her arms from around Fran and leaned back on the edge of the dresser. "No, there has to be more to it than that. Take Mick for example, if he was a bar of chocolate he'd have eaten himself by now."

"He's not that bad," laughed Fran.

"Right," Tracey replied, failing to see any redeeming qualities in the man. She remembered him from her primary school days and he hadn't been a particularly nice person back then. He wasn't a bully or anything like that. It was just that he was so self-centred and inconsiderate.

Fran knew only too well that his friend wasn't perfect but still felt that he had to stand up for him. "It was his parents who messed him up, packin' him off to private school when we hit second level so he could reach his full potential and all that shite. They even tried to bar him from hangin' around with us when we were teenagers, can ye believe that?"

"With the likes of Davey and Yoyo, I can fully understand why. How did Mick's father make his money?" she asked out of curiosity.

"Somethin' to do with computers, a software programme, I think. I'm not that well up on technology to be honest. Mick was tellin' me that his aul fella couldn't even spend all of his money if he tried to, there's that much of the stuff."

"Mick would want to make sure he keeps in with the old man, so," Tracey joked.

"It's a strange setup. He hasn't really spoken to either of his parents in years but they still give him a hefty allowance," Fran explained.

"I knew I picked the wrong bloke," said Tracey, giving Fran a cheeky wink.

Fran smiled and said, "Nice to know where I stand."

"I think you know very well where you stand." She leaned in closer and kissed him fully on the lips, "And by the way, you don't have to hide Vicky's photo in the drawer every time I call around."

Fran was impressed by his date's powers of observation. "Did ye ever consider a career as a detective?"

Following on from the impromptu fashion show back at the department store and the subsequent 'after party', Wendy had invited Mick back to her place for drinks. Mick wasn't in a hurry to return home to his pauper's pad and was more than happy to take up the generous offer. He waited patiently in the middle of Wendy's kitchen. It was modern and tastefully furnished with all the latest and most expensive appliances. Definitely the work of an interior designer not curtailed by even the hint of a budget.

"Help yourself to a drink. There's beer in the fridge and spirits in the press next to that," Wendy instructed from an adjoining room, "Pour me a vodka, darling, and make it a double."

After Mick had sorted himself out with a beer he went searching for a glass for Wendy's drink. An immaculately groomed, Bichon Frise trotted into the room, gave him the once over and started to yelp.

"What's your problem, fur ball?" Mick asked, retrieving a glass from the press and fixing the hostess a drink.

Wendy appeared, wearing a figure hugging, almost see through, silk nightdress that emphasised her womanly curves.

"Shush, Fluffy," she scolded her almost toy-like dog before turning her attentions back to Mick. "Take no notice of her. The bitch gets a little jealous when I have company over." She took her drink from Mick, "Cheers," and took a sip. "Head into the lounge and make yourself at home."

Mick did as he was told and made his way, beer in hand, into the adjoining room through the open double doors. He cautiously sat down on the spotless white leather suite, terrified that he'd mark it in some way.

"Mind the rug, cost me a fortune," warned Wendy from the kitchen where she was rummaging through some drawers.

Right on cue Mick's drink slipped from his grasp but he somehow managed to catch the now upturned glass before it crashed to the floor. "Shit," he whispered.

The beer snaked across the polished walnut floor like liquid mercury, setting a course for the expensive rug sitting in the centre of the room. He desperately looked around for something, anything, to mop up the amber lager with when he noticed Fluffy out of the corner of his eye. She reminded him of a giant cotton wool bud on legs.

Wendy sauntered into the lounge moments later carrying a leather bag. All traces of the beer had miraculously vanished along with Fluffy who was sulking behind the couch.

"Fantastic place you've got here. What does your ex do again?" asked Mick.

"A wanker. No, sorry. A banker but I could never quite tell the difference," Wendy said.

"What happened?"

"Threw him out," she answered, indifferently.

"And why was that?"

Wendy set the open leather bag on Mick's lap. It contained a selection of adult toys.

"Neglect," she replied.

"Neglect?"

"That and a lack of imagination."

While Mick and his latest conquest were getting to grips with one another in the jacuzzi of the expensive penthouse apartment a darkened figure was hurrying up the paved garden pathway of a terraced house not too far away. The doorbell was repeatedly pressed by the distraught caller who was also hammering on the door with their hand for good measure. Inside the terraced house, the upstairs toilet flushed and Davey emerged, carrying a folded newspaper under his arm. The banging and ringing continued in earnest.

"Can a man not have a gick in peace," he said, trudging down the stairs.

He hadn't yet reached the bottom step when the hammering became more fervent. "For fuck's sake," he complained, his pace quickening. He paused to look out through the spy-hole then quickly reefed open the door. Lily was stood there with tears streaming down her pale cheeks.

Chapter 16

Rain pelted down as the undertakers removed the small white coffin from the back of the hearse. A delicate floral arrangement, mostly made up of white chrysanthemums and gypsophila, rested against the inside glass of the funeral car spelling out the name 'MILLIE'. Davey, Lily and a scattering of other mourners sheltered as best they could under windswept umbrellas, watching in numbed silence.

"Sorry I can't be there, later on. Official stuff at work needs sorting," explained Lily, trying to keep it together, "I tried my best..."

"I know ye did, babe," Davey whispered. He would have loved to have Lily by his side later that day but he fully understood her predicament and wasn't going to add to her burden by making a scene.

An old man with an even older face, sang a lonesome ballad in the corner of Frank the Publican's bar respectfully watched by the gathered mourners including the Sporting Les Behans' team. When he finished his song, everyone clapped and a fresh pint of stout was set down in front of him. Most of the football team were sat around a group of tables, tucking into the stew and sandwiches that had been laid on for the funeral.

"Everythin' okay there, lads?" Frank the Publican said, referring to the grub.

"Magic," thanked Trigger.

"At least it'll put some linin' on yer stomach," Frank said before walking away to check on his other customers.

Podge greedily slurped down the tasty stew as if it was going out of fashion.

"It's not bad," said Gitsy, licking his lips, "But ye can't beat an aul Dublin coddle."

"What's that?" Baxter asked. Although he'd been living in the capital for over a decade he wasn't familiar with the dish.

"A poor man's stew," said Trigger.

"It's basically boiled sausages, rashers, potatoes, onions and carrots," Gitsy explained.

"Me granny never made it with carrots and she always used pearl barley," Split said.

"It's far from pearl barely you were reared," slagged Trigger.

"Now lads, you can't go wrong with a bit of Scouse inside of you," said Baxter.

"Is that an offer?" joked Charlie.

"Scouse the dish, you divvy," the manager said. "A favourite with sailors from the Northern European ports, made with beef or lamb."

Birdy wiped his teak strong hands in a napkin and said, "No, best food is Goulash. Favourite with shepherds."

"So, yer Hungarian then," Trigger said. Nobody in the team had bothered asking Birdy where he was from, presuming he was Polish or maybe Lithuanian.

"I'm Irish," the goalkeeper proudly said.

"Ah when did ye get yer citizenship?" Split asked.

Birdy shook his head. "I was born here, in Rotunda."

"You?" Gitsy said, finding it hard to believe, "G'wan outta that."

"Yes, it's fact. My mother was Irish, my father from Budapest," Birdy explained.

"Jaysus, ye learn somethin' new every day," said Trigger. He'd never been west of Holyhead, mostly due to bail conditions but he'd love to travel farther someday if he got the chance. Maybe he'd look into getting a bent passport.

"So how come ye don't speak like us? Split asked.

"Lucky I think," Birdy said with a cheesy smile.

Some of the lads laughed.

"No, seriously," said Split.

Birdy looked at each man sitting around him and paused for a moment. He then cleared his throat. "I was two, my mother died. My father, Gabor, take me back to Hungary."

"Sorry to hear that," said Trigger.

"How d'ye end up in the circus?" Podge asked, in between shovelling the stew down his neck, barely taking a breath.

"My mother and father were trapeze artists. My mother's brother, he owns circus," Birdy revealed.

"I get ye now," said Gitsy.

"How'd d'yer Ma die then?" Podge asked. Tact had never been his strong point.

The Assassin walloped him across the head nearly knocking him into his stew.

Trigger glared at Podge. "Yer some fuckin' eejit."

"It's okay," Birdy answered. "She died in accident."

Jigsaw let out an audible gasp, imagining a mid-air mishap where hands bathed in chalk dust slipped from each other's desperate grasp.

"Car crash," Birdy revealed, "We left Ireland, Gabor never married again."

"That's very sad," Leonard said, almost in tears.

The circus performer nodded his head solemnly. "My father died last year, I am here now."

Davey, Fran and Mick, dressed in black suits, white shirts and loosened black ties, sat around a low table away from the rest of their teammates. Every available space was practically taken up with both empty and full pint glasses of stout. Fran stacked some of the glasses to make room so that Baxter could set down the three whiskeys he had just ordered for the boys.

"It was a beautiful ceremony, ar kid," the manager said, giving Davey's shoulder a consoling squeeze, "You did your Mam proud."

Davey nodded and the gaffer returned to the counter to chat with the bar owner. "Like a bus," Davey mumbled before downing his whiskey in one go.

Fran and Mick exchanged puzzled glances.

"Ye wait all year for a funeral to come along then two come together," added Davey. After earlier attending Millie's burial, his partner, Lily, had insisted on bringing him home so that he could change out of his wet clothes for his mother's funeral that afternoon. Lily had then reluctantly headed back to work but promised to meet up with him as soon as she could get away.

"It's sad when a child dies alrigh'. Not that yer Ma dyin' wasn't, isn't..." Fran said, flustered.

"It's okay, bud, I know wha' ye mean," Davey said, "I just can't get me head around it, why she hadn't told me she was that sick, pretendin' to go on holidays with her pal, Vera."

"Sometimes people just need time to figure things out for themselves first," Mick said.

"Bollox," said Davey.

"Or maybe she felt that you know, you were too immature and perhaps incapable of dealing with the truth," Mick continued. Although genuinely trying to be sympathetic he was making a complete balls of it.

Davey's addled mind was trying to process what Mick had just said but no matter what way he threw it around it didn't sit well. He suddenly pointed a finger at his teammate, turning on him. "And wha' the fuck would you know, Mr. Perfect? With yer posh accent and yer rich Daddy."

Mick gulped down his whiskey. "It's just, you know..."

"No, I don't know. Like wha'?"

Mick was caught totally off guard by his friend's confrontational manner and couldn't make his mouth manufacture words quickly enough to respond with.

"Come on, seems how yer such an expert on every fuckin' thing," Davey said, pushing for an answer.

Mick gave a polite cough then said, "Well, I haven't told anyone this yet but, but I dress up in women's clothes..."

"D'ye think this is a poxy comedy show?" Davey roared, waving his hand around the pub, not letting Mick finish his sentence.

The ballad singer stopped abruptly. Sporting Les Behans', Frank the Publican, Vera and the rest of the mourners looked over at the three lads.

"No," replied Mick in a low, apologetic voice, "I didn't mean it like that..."

Davey eyeballed his teammate. "Yer fuckin' serious?" he shouted. "Aren't ye?"

"This isn't the time or the place for this conversation, lads," Fran advised. He had plenty of drink taken but he was still relatively sober, and enough to realise that this was turning nasty.

"I was only trying to help," Mick meekly answered.

Davey rose unsteadily to his feet. Swaying from side to side he pushed his face into Mick's. Fran immediately stuck his hand between the two men, holding Davey back.

Davey turned to Fran. "Don't," he warned. He then looked back at Mick, his face ready for war. "And how dare ye bring up filth like that and me Ma barely cold in the grave?"

"You don't understand, I meant..." said Mick.

Davey was having none of it. "Oh no, I get it. It all makes perfect sense now."

Mick knew that he was fighting a losing battle. He'd wait until his friend was sober so that he could explain himself properly. He stood up and headed for the door having had his fill.

"Go on, run home and try on another dress, ye fuckin' freak," jeered Davey.

"That's enough," Fran said, shoving his friend forcefully back into his seat.

Everyone in the pub was stunned. They were all gawking at Mick as he fled from the bar, absolutely mortified. Davey was incensed. He tried to get to his feet but stumbled backwards, being too pissed to pose any real threat.

Fran cocked his head as if to say, 'Are we good?'

A notice which was stuck to the glass door read: 'Alcohol a problem? Christians Together can help.' A slightly camp Christian lad, wearing a grey suit and clerical type collar accompanied a deathly thin man out of the building. They paused outside.

"Are we ready for this?" the Christian chap asked, enthusiastically.

"Going to have to go back into a pub at some stage," his companion nervously replied.

Mick staggered along the footpath more out of disbelief than intoxication. He barged his way through the Christian man and his slight companion as they were making their way towards Frank the Publican's place.

"Happy hour must be well and truly over," the Christian lad quietly joked to his friend.

They entered the unusually silent bar and headed for the counter where the publican was standing with a rag in his hand not really knowing what to be doing after Davey's outburst moments earlier.

"Soup and sandwiches for two, please," ordered the Christian lad, shaking Frank from his thoughts. He surveyed the other customers who were mostly dressed in black and wearing gloomy expressions then turned back to his friend. "What do you think, Kevin, it's like a funeral around here?" he quipped.

His companion was all jittery and barely said, "It is," in agreement.

The Christian man then spotted Davey out of the corner of his eye. "Holy Moly, I don't believe this," he said, marching straight over to where Davey was slouched with a pint held up to his mouth. "Roger, Roger, Roger," the Christian geezer said, his hands planted firmly on his hips and shaking his head in utter disappointment.

Davey lowered his glass but didn't bother making eye contact with whatever fool was nagging him now. "Fuck off," was his only reply.

"Now's not a good time for a sermon, padre," Fran said, advising the overzealous Christian lad to leave it out.

The clergyman ignored the warning. He narrowed his eyes, focusing in on Davey. "You need to be strong, Roger."

An ambulance and several squad cars were parked outside Frank the Publican's bar. Paramedics wheeled the injured Christian man out of the premises and loaded him into the waiting ambulance. Kevin, his companion, was inside the boozer downing a large brandy, the day's events having taking their toll. Moments later, Davey, handcuffed, was dragged kicking and screaming from the pub by four burly Guards as Fran and the rest of the Sporting Les Behans' players looked on.

"Go easy, lads, he's only after buryin' his Ma," Fran said, pleading for leniency.

"Back off," ordered one of the policemen.

"I'm just tryin' to help..."

"We don't need it. And if you don't go away you'll be spending the night in a cell with your associate."

"Bleeding Gestapo!" shouted Baxter.

The Assassin, his considerable muscle mass tensed to the last, took a step forward but Vera gripped his arm. He looked at her questioningly.

"It's not worth it, son," Vera said softly. "Besides, he needs to grow up."

One of the policemen raised his baton threateningly towards the Assassin but his show of bravado wasn't fooling anyone. Al glanced at the weapon then stared the guy dead in the eyes. "Ye'll do nothin'," he warned.

The guard wisely took a step back knowing that he'd need a hell of a lot more back-up than what was presently available to him. His colleagues had successfully bundled Davey into the back of one of the waiting squad cars and fearing that it was all about to kick off they promptly left the scene.

The detergent used to clean the Garda interview room did nothing to disguise the underlying smell of sweat and alcohol from previous detainees. Detectives Lyons and Cartland sat across the table from Davey who was slouched forward with his chin resting on his folded arms, taking in everything but saying nothing in return. Although he'd consumed a gallon of porter earlier in the day, being lagged had a queer way of rapidly sobering up a man. Lyons broke off a square of chocolate from a purple tinfoil wrapped bar and popped it into her mouth, savouring the taste.

"Better than sex, that," she commented as she secretly rubbed Cartland's crotch under the cheap Formica covered table.

The young detective shifted uncomfortably but didn't give the game away.

"Well, I suppose that depends on who you're doing it with," Lyons said, sneering at Davey, "In your case it'll probably be between the baldy bloke with the 'I love me Mammy' tattoos and the muscular lad with the 'Who's your Daddy' tats."

Davey remained silent, doing his best not to rise to the bait.

The female detective gave a fake laugh. "GBH. Who would have thought?" she said in a further attempt to provoke the suspect.

There was a knock on the door quickly followed by the appearance of the officer on duty. He handed Lyons a note and looked away already knowing its contents and having a fair idea of how his boss would react. Lyons read the piece of paper in silence, her facial expression changing from one of gloating to one similarly found in deranged people.

"I don't fucking believe this!" she shouted, scrunching the paper into a ball and firing it at the wall.

Davey strolled out of the cop shop, hands deep in his pockets. Lyons had done a song and dance about his impending release and had exhausted every possible channel trying to have him retained but without any luck. The Sporting Les Behans' player checked up and down the empty street, a cool, refreshing breeze washing over him. The two detectives followed him out to the doorway.

"Billy no mates," Lyons sarcastically said, unable to accept defeat. She'd been the same at boarding school, once breaking her own teammate's nose in a game of hockey after the girl had missed a penalty to win some Mickey Mouse cup.

Davey lit a cigarette, remaining chilled. Having just escaped the hangman's noose he wasn't going to push his luck any farther, not tonight. Minutes later a taxi pulled up on the far side of the street and sounded its horn. Davey squinted in its direction as the rear window was lowered.

Fran stuck his head out. "Get in, ye muppet."

Davey didn't need to be told twice. He dropped his smoke onto the concrete and stubbed it out with his shoe. Cartland was about to pull him on it but before he could say anything Davey picked up the extinguished butt and pocketed it.

"Don't want them feckin' crows causin' any more hassle," he said, ever so innocently.

Lyons was going to respond but held her tongue.

"Nigh' so," said Davey. He sprinted across the road and climbed into the back of the waiting cab to join his friend.

"It would have to be a bible fucking basher that he assaults," Lyons said through clenched teeth, watching Davey slip through her fingers yet again.

Inside the taxi Fran turned to his pal. "Well, Roger?"

"Don't start," said Davey, cringing at what he'd done, "Thanks for collectin' me in anyway."

Fran nodded. "Tracey was stayin' over so she's mindin' the young wan for me."

"That's handy."

"There's nothin' handy about it. It's nearly one a.m. Ye better apologise to Mick," Fran insisted, "Ye were bang out of order."

"I know. I was an absolute prick," his friend said, completely accepting his inexcusable behaviour earlier on at his Ma's send off.

Davey sat across from Fran in the busy American-style diner, stirring his black coffee with disinterest. An assortment of empty plates and bowls were stacked in front of Fran who was devouring the last piece of a very tasty chicken fillet burger. He had to admit that the secret ingredient in the sauce which the diner proudly boasted about in their radio ads was to die for. He glanced up from his feast as a fit looking waitress cruised by.

"Everything okay?" she enquired, batting her long eyelashes.

"Stuffed, thanks," answered Fran, politely covering his mouth with his hand.

The waitress gave him a playful smile. "Well, if you need anything, you know where to find me." She slowly walked away, seductively smoothing the ass of her tight-fitting uniform as Fran looked on admiringly.

"Glad to see yer gettin' yer appetite back," said Davey. He remembered how a part of his pal seemed to die when Vicky had tragically overdosed and he was glad to see some sort of a spark being reignited.

Fran quietly burped, giving his chest a light tap. "So let me get this straight," he said, "usin' the alias, Roger, ye joined an Alcoholics Anonymous type group so ye could find out, while people were at their most vulnerable I might add, details about their backgrounds for personal gain."

"Pretty much," Davey admitted.

"Yer Ma would've bleedin' killed ye for that kind of carry on."

A security guard stood just inside the entrance of the fast food restaurant. He was wearing a cheap suit with his chest puffed out like a silverback gorilla and seemed to be more interested in fixing his hair in the wall mounted mirror than doing his job. He caught Davey watching him. The pair stared one another out of it, their alpha male animal instincts not allowing either man to turn away. The security guard straightened his tie, rotating his neck in an elaborate stretching motion.

"Check out the ponce. Thinks he knows it all," Davey remarked, still eyeballing the security guard.

"I'm over here," Fran reminded his companion. "And don't go changin' the subject." He wanted to know more about his pal's his alter ego, Roger, and the latest fiddle.

Davey faced his friend, leaning forward. "Look, I went to several meetin's. There were a lot of genuine people with some very sad stories there and ye'd have to feel sorry for them but there were also a few absolute gobshites."

"And of course ye were able to justify yer actions by only targetin' those same gobshites..."

"I never scammed the individual, only their place of work," Davey explained, trying to diminish his actions.

"Righ'. So this Christian geezer still thinks yer an Alco?"

Davey gave a slight bow of the head.

"And that's why he won't press charges?" Fran asked.

"That and I promised him I'd continue to attend meetin's," Davey said.

"Yer goin' to hell, buddy. Just as well yer man's into the turnin' the other cheek lark, otherwise ye could have been facin' a long stretch inside."

"I know. Reckon the Ma was watchin' over me."

The two friends got to their feet and put their jackets on.

Davey picked up the bill from the cluttered table. "I'll get this."

"G'away outta that," said Fran, holding out his hand, "Sure ye ate fuck all."

"My way of sayin' thanks," Davey said, not letting go of the bill, "I know it was a massive inconvenience..."

Fran shrugged his shoulders and told his friend to forget about it. The pair headed for the till.

"Hang on a sec," said Davey, suddenly remembering something. He went over to where a couple in their late twenties was sitting, chatting over coffee but not having ordered anything to eat. The security guard monitored Davey like a hawk.

Davey put his hand on the man's shoulder and said loud enough for the security guard to hear, "There ye are, Johnny, how's it goin'?"

The man wore a blank expression.

"It's me, Johnny," Davey tried again, smiling broadly.

"Think you have the wrong person, mate," the stranger answered in a strong northern English accent, "I'm not from around these parts."

"Sorry about that, bud," Davey said, apologising profusely, "Jaysus, yer a ringer for Johnny O'Leary."

He left the couple to have their coffee in peace and went back to the till where Fran was waiting. Davey swung around again, not fully satisfied with the Englishman's answer. "Not even a cousin?"

The lad smiled warmly, giving his head a gentle shake.

"A double for Johnny all the same," Davey said to no one in particular.

He grinned at the security guard as he handed the bill to the cashier and paid up. Fran left a generous tip for the helpful waitress who was busy cleaning a table at the far end of the diner to notice that he was leaving.

The lads left the restaurant and strolled down the narrow, cobbled street doing their best to avoid the numerous tourists aimlessly wandering about even at this late hour.

"Look at them," Davey loudly said, waving his hand about at the visitors, "The hungry fuckers won't spend a shillin', happy to walk around all nigh' gettin' in people's way."

"I heard there's a job goin' with the tourist board, think ye should apply," Fran suggested.

"Wha'ever," said Davey.

Fran suddenly stopped. "Yer man in the diner looked nothin' like Johnny O'Leary."

"I know that, but I had to teach that dipshit of a security guard a lesson," replied Davey, continuing to walk but noticeably picking up the pace.

Fran caught up with his friend just as he turned the corner only for Davey to take off at speed.

"Ye switched the bleedin' bill, didn't ye?" shouted Fran, running after his pal, knowing that it was wrong but still getting a buzz out of it. He could only imagine the head on the security bloke when it was time for the English couple to settle their end of things.

Davey finally arrived home, exhausted from the day's proceedings.

"It's only me, Ma," he shouted up the stairs before realising that she wasn't there. It had finally dawned on him that his best friend in the whole wide world was gone, and forever. He sat down on the bottom stair and despite his best efforts began to sob uncontrollably.

Chapter 17

A bonfire blazed away in the middle of the communal back garden which Mick shared with about half a dozen other tenants. Although he had gotten a few dirty looks from some of the residents when he had first started the fire none of them dared say a word due to his demeanour. They had instead hurriedly shut their windows to keep out the toxic smoke. Flames had torn indiscriminately through the heaped pile of various women's garments reducing the remnants to an unrecognisable pile of flaky ash. Inside the house in a dingy upstairs room which Mick now called home, he was hammering the living daylights out of a punch-bag he had lashed to an exposed beam in the ceiling. Sweat was pouring out of him as he sent the bag swinging in all directions. A telephone which was sitting on the scuffed linoleum floor rang several times before switching over to the messaging service.

"Sorry I can't take your call right now but if you leave your name, you know the drill," instructed Mick's pre-recorded voice.

Mick, breathing heavily, held the punch-bag between his gloved hands as his listened to the phone message.

"Hi, it's Wendy, you know, from the department store? Thought you might like to go shopping, pick up a few more nice bits and pieces and perhaps do some modelling for me. Give me a ring."

The call ended. Mick resumed battering his punch-bag but with a renewed vigour. To the outsider everything appeared normal in Mick's world. In truth, the only bit of luck he'd had recently in a sea of misfortune was that there was a working landline in his bedsit. The previous tenant, who was now deceased, had paid for the telephone rental in full for the remainder of the year. This meant that Mick had only to pay a nominal fee to switch the existing telephone number over to his old one. It also meant that he could still use his answering machine to vet calls, a facility that had served him extremely well over the years especially when it came to the stalker ex-girlfriends who had difficulty accepting closure and moving on.

Wendy held her mobile to her ear while caressing Fluffy, her spoilt pooch, with her free hand. She was disappointed not to have heard back from Mick these last few days as she'd felt that they'd made a real connection despite promising herself never to get involved with another man again. Of course it was primarily a physical arrangement and they were having plenty of fun but she was secretly hoping that there was more to it than just raw sex.

Demanding attention of her own, Fluffy used her snout to snuggle in closer to her owner. The action brought Wendy back to the here and now. She sniffed the air, immediately screwed up her face then leaned in closer to her beloved pet.

"Good God, you still smell like a fucking brewery."

Davey finally awoke from his drink induced slumber sometime about one in the afternoon. He sat up slowly, somewhat disorientated, not quite sure where he was, let alone what day of the week it was. Coarse, dark stubble covered most of his haggard face. As he stumbled out of bed he stood on an array of squashed beer cans that seemed to litter most of the available floor space like some sort of knacker-drinking minefield.

"Bastard" he cried out after one of the aluminium tins had pierced through the skin on the sole of his bare right foot. He attempted to kick the can but stubbed his toe instead and fell to the ground in even more agony. Despite the immense pain a thought popped into his fuzzy head. When did he last have a tetanus jab?

After eventually making it down the stairs, hopping on one foot and almost breaking his neck, Davey went to the fridge in search of sustenance. He retrieved a milk carton and with a less than steady hand gulped down a large quantity. The sour liquid was immediately spat back out with Davey retching several times before eventually gathering himself together. He squinted hard tying to focus on the best before date only to discover it had long since passed. The carton was closed and shoved back into the fridge with the door following suit with force. It was only then that he noticed the psychologist's business card stuck to the fridge door with a colourful magnate from the Balearic Islands. 'Santa Ponsa, Ballymun in the Sun,' popped into his head. The psychologist's card was promptly removed and tossed away.

"Quack," he just about managed to croak, his throat dryer than an Arab's flip flop. He reopened the fridge, took out a can of beer and swallowed down some of the golden nectar, hoping to cleanse his palate of the scaldy tasting milk. Satisfied, he made his way over to the kitchen table where he spotted a box of cornflakes sitting on the counter. An idea came to him. He got a breakfast bowl from one of the laminated presses, filling it with the cereal and dumping the rest of the can of beer on top. After cautiously tasting a spoonful he made a contented face, sat down and began to devour the rest.

It was late in the evening and Davey was snuggled up on the couch, snoring loudly, a quilted duvet covering him. A DVD cover of the musical version of the film 'Oliver', one of his Ma's favourites and his too if he was being honest with himself, sat on the coffee table that was also littered with empty lager cans and half eaten Chinese take-away cartons. Loud banging on the front door echoed throughout the still house. Lily was outside hammering away with her fist, trying to get in but without success. She shielded her eyes with her hand in order to get a better view through the living-room window. Squinting, she could just about make Davey out, slumped on the couch. At first she feared that he was dead and her heart went into freefall. That was until Davey pulled the duvet up over his head and turned his back on her. This infuriated Lily to no end. She smacked the window with the flat of her palm.

"Fuck off," Davey swore aloud, not realising who was making the racket and presuming it was some eejit trying to sell him cheap electricity, a vacuum cleaner or Jesus.

Lily had had enough. She searched the garden and found a large, moss covered rock and promptly smashed the window.

"Wha' the fuck!" shouted Davey, reefing the duvet away from his face.

Lily peered through the broken glass. "May Christ be me witness but if ye don't get yer scrawny wee arse off that couch, I'm gonna bash yer feckin' head in. D'ye hear me, Davey Byrne?" she screamed.

Davey, wrapped in his blanket, reluctantly opened the front door allowing his girlfriend to storm inside.

"Aye. The state of ye. Yer an absolute disgrace to the memory of yer poor Mammy," she yelled.

Davey rubbed the side of his temple, wincing with the pain as he shuffled zombie-like back into the living-room after Lily. His girlfriend stood in the middle of the room holding up the 'Oliver' DVD cover.

"Ah, ye poor wee orphan," she mocked. She then flung the film cover unceremoniously out through the broken windowpane. "Get yer act together or ye can forget about us," she threatened, "And ye better get this place cleaned up, it's like a flippin' pigsty."

With that Lily abruptly turned on her heels and left, slamming the door in her wake. The Tasmanian Devil cartoon character from the telly was the first thing that came to Davey's mind. He plopped down on the couch, the stench of stale beer and Chinese food escaping from his body in an exaggerated loud sigh. He was in an absolute jocker. He looked down at his bare foot with a puzzled expression, lifted it up and peeled off the psychologist's card that had somehow managed to end up there. Maybe it was a sign? If you believed it that sort of shite. Then again, was it worth tempting faith? He turned the card over several times in his fingers, contemplating his next move.

Tracey accompanied Fran as he wheeled his mother, Mrs. Reilly, down the ramp outside the stained granite courthouse following the custody hearing for Laura.

"The judge didn't make a decision one way or the other," Tracey said, offering some encouragement, "That has to be a good sign, doesn't it?"

"I've still no job and in this climate," Fran complained, shaking his head in defeat, "Ye heard the fat wig goin' on about stability in a child's life." Having no proper job was wrecking his head. It was a far cry from when he'd completed his apprenticeship during the boom. Firms couldn't fill positions quick enough back then. But now, they only wanted subcontractors and getting paid for a decent day's work was always complicated.

Mrs. Reilly spotted Laura's other Granny, Mrs. Flynn and her daughter, Tina, as they exited the same building but over on the far side.

"All them Flynn's are the same. Heartless bitches. I've a good mind to go over there," said Mrs. Reilly, her anger rising dangerously close to tipping point.

"She'd love that, be straight back into the Judge," Fran warned, knowing that if things were to escalate outside the courthouse, he wouldn't have a hope in hell of ever having his young daughter living with him.

Mrs. Flynn glared back at Mrs. Reilly. "Look at her," she said to Tina, "Brazen wagon. One son a jailbird and the other a layabout."

Tina absentmindedly flicked her long hair away from her face and arched back her shoulders which in turn hoisted her cleavage like some breed of exotic bird performing an ancient mating ritual. "He's fit though," she couldn't stop herself from saying.

Mrs. Flynn glared at her daughter not bothering to disguise her disappointment in bringing this eejit into the world. "There's no way I'll ever allow that shower of degenerates rear any grandchild of mine," she vowed.

Davey had rung Lily the day after her tumultuous visit to his home with a grovelling apology, promising to clean up his act. His girlfriend had been equally sorry for smashing the window and completely blowing her top. She even offered to pay for the damage but Davey was having none of it. The eventual outcome was amazing make up sex and a promise from him that he'd seek professional help. So here he was, sitting in an expensive, reclining leather chair in the psychologist's office. The surrounding walls were adorned with an assortment of fancy framed awards and certificates for this that and the other from various colleges most of which he'd never heard of. 'It's all ballsology,' he thought, if not a bit envious of such a lucrative gig where a sham could earn over one hundred euros an hour. The psychologist held the end of his ballpoint pen in his mouth, a thoughtful look on his face. A Newton's Cradle with its four gold plated balls rested on the desk in front of him.

"Ye haven't a clue," Davey said, challenging the shrink.

"So tell me then," the psychologist suggested.

"D'ye really want to know?" Davey asked, trying to keep a lid on his growing frustrations.

The psychologist nodded before casually flicking the balls on the pendulum, setting them in motion. He then turned towards the window looking out into the distance, running his hand through his highlighted hair. The clinking balls momentarily derailed Davey from his train of thought. He re-gathered himself and said, "I wanted to know who I was, where I came from."

"Like that programme? What is it called again?" interrupted the psychologist who was still gazing out into the distance, "Who Do You Think You Are? That's it."

Davey bit his lower lip.

"An intriguing exercise," continued the shrink totally oblivious to Davey's worsening change in mood, "Although, one's never quite sure what skeletons might pop out of one's closet," he chuckled. When there was no response forthcoming the shrink turned his head towards his patient. Davey was glaring at him.

"Go on. You were saying," the shrink quickly backtracked, sitting upright in his chair, trying to act more professional.

Davey hesitated before deciding to go on but only because he'd promised Lily and his late Ma. He wasn't happy with how things were proceeding but maybe this was all part of the process, to get you angry so that you might let things spill out that you'd normally keep bottled up.

"I'd asked the Ma a few times about me background, but she always changed the subject. I should've just left it there, but I couldn't," he said with more than a little regret. He chewed off a piece of his fingernail and spat it out then began to inspect the rest of his jagged, stunted nails. The psychologist was appalled but said nothing. "D'ye know wha' I found out?" Davey asked, suddenly sitting forward.

The psychologist motioned with his hands for his patient to continue.

"Me Ma, that easy-goin', lovely little woman who never harmed a fly in her whole life and who'd do anythin' for anyone… She was raped."

There was complete silence as the horrendous crime hung in the air like a bad smell. The psychologist was in no rush to talk, he was on the clock after all and was getting well paid.

Davey finally spoke. "She could have gotten rid of me or given me up for adoption and gotten on with her life as best she could, and who would have blamed her. But no, she accepted that wha' happened, happened. I never told her I'd found out but deep down I think she knew." He cupped his face in his hands exhaling noisily through the narrow gaps in his nicotine stained fingers. Moments passed before he lowered his hands. "And d'ye know wha'? In all the years that she reared me, she never once, not once, looked at me or treated me with even a hint of regret."

"Interesting," pondered the psychologist, trying to sound oh-so intelligent. "So Mr. Byrne, Davey if I may. Do you think that this feeling of regret might be in fact some kind of suppressed sexual tension?"

A nervous patient who was sitting in the psychologist's waiting room jumped up from his seat on hearing the commotion in the adjoining room. He made for the exit but couldn't force himself to leave and returned to his seat instead, rapidly pumping his hands open and closed trying to combat his rising anxiety. Davey came storming out and slammed the door behind him so hard that it bounced back open. He stared at the shaking patient who was seriously contemplating legging it for real this time.

"The only letters that bleedin' sham should have after his name are D.O.P.E.!" shouted Davey. He picked up a chair, flung it against an ornately framed certificate hanging on the wall, smashing it to pieces and left.

The terrified patient ran his hands busily over one another, wondering what he should do next. He looked towards the door where the madman had stormed out through. There was complete silence. Convinced that the man wasn't going to return, he got to his feet and cautiously peeked inside the office. He spotted the psychologist's legs sticking out from where he was buried beneath a mountain of broken furniture.

The ringmaster stepped in front of Birdy's slow travelling motorbike and caught hold of the handlebars not allowing his nephew to go any further.

Birdy deftly stepped off the bike leaving the ringmaster holding onto it and strode away towards the circus tent without so much as a by your leave.

"Why do you want to waste your time with this stupid football team?" his furious uncle demanded. He was still smarting from Birdy's no show during the special performance for the bankers. And to make matters worse the financiers had insisted on a full refund. The ringmaster had held tough and fobbed them off with a few free passes instead but not before he had to listen to a foul-mouthed tirade from the company's CEO.

Birdy looked over his shoulder at his uncle and shouted, "I left because the team is fun, like circus was!" He disappeared inside the large tent without another word.

Two circus workers walked by, carrying a heavy piece of timber. They glanced at their boss who was still holding onto the motorbike.

"What?" he yelled at the men. He then threw the machine to the ground and gave it a boot for good measure.

Davey was completely disillusioned with the world after his recent visit to the psychologist, psychiatrist or whatever the fuck he was supposed to be. The quack had no intention of reporting the assault for fear that his credentials would be checked out and someone would discover that they were courtesy of the internet and a laminating machine. Instead, he counted his lucky stars not to have sustained more serious injuries other than a broken nose and two black eyes and reminded himself that he'd need to act more professionally in the future for his scam to continue.

On the ride back from the shrink, Davey inexplicably turned into the car park of the granite built, ornate church, a place he hadn't previously noticed even though he must have passed it by a hundred times or more before. Perhaps another sign. He parked his bike and looked up, drawn to the looming spire.

After biting the bullet and deciding to enter the eerily quiet building Davey made a beeline for the sole confessional box with a red bulb alight. He went inside, sat down on the cushioned seat and waited. Father O'Brien, an elderly priest with a kind, creased face, slid the hatch across and blessed himself, piously gazing towards the heavens.

"Father, son, holy spirit, Amen," the priest began.

Davey remained silent, twisting his sovereign ring on his finger. The priest finally looked across at God's latest customer.

"Go on, my son?" he gently prompted.

"Howya, buddy," greeted Davey.

"Grand, thanks. Would you like to confess?" Father O'Brien asked.

"Someone said somethin'?" answered Davey, all defensive.

"Sorry?" asked the elderly clergyman.

"No need to be. Sure ye can't help it if some fuc... fella tells ye things."

The priest massaged the bridge of his nose and said, "I think we have our wires crossed. Let's start again, shall we. Are you here to make a confession for your sins?"

"Ah Jaysus no, father, sure we'd be here all nigh'. Wanted more of a yap like," Davey said.

"Okay?"

"Religion's not really my thing but the late Ma was mad into it and to be honest, I don't really know where else to turn."

A little over an hour later, Davey and Father O'Brien emerged from the church the best of friends. They shook hands and Davey started to walk away but paused and returned to where the priest was standing. He took the psychologist's gold, four ball pendulum from his jacket pocket and gave it to the clergyman. Father O'Brien at first refused the gift but reluctantly accepted it after some 'gentle' persuasion normally reserved for a Marrakesh marketplace.

Derek and the rest of the kids that hung around the Stadium of Light watched with keen interest as Davey retrieved a large sports bag from the boot of a car. The player gave the side of the jammer two quick taps and it drove away, beeping its horn. He then turned to the young lads.

"There's some spare sports gear in the bag, the aul fella with the cap said to hang on to it if ye wanted," he casually said.

The gang looked on suspiciously. Davey dropped the bag on the ground and as he headed for the truck container dressing room, he looked over his shoulder and said, "He's not always that grumpy ye know."

The lads glanced at one another before charging towards the bulky sports bag, flailing each other. It reminded Davey of the grushies he'd been involved in as a young fella outside the churches when someone got married. There'd be absolute pandemonium as the local kids would scramble for the coins thrown into the air by the wedding guests. It was a miracle that no one was ever killed. Happy days but sadly another tradition long gone by the wayside.

With the exception of Mick, the Sporting Les Behans' players were inside the dressing room getting changed.

Davey turned to his pal, Fran. "I met a priest today, a lovely little man."

Fran grabbed Podge, who just happened to be walking by and sat him on his knee like a ventriloquist's dummy.

"D'ye want to show me on the doll where he touched ye?" Fran said.

Podge acted limp, pretending to be the doll and doing an excellent job into the bargain.

"I'm serious," said Davey, ignoring the shenanigans.

Paddy Power overheard the conversation and decided to throw his oar in for good measure. "Davey's been touched by God," he announced to the rest of the team.

"Ye can bang in a claim for that," Charlie said.

The team laughed.

"Would yis ever fuck off and mind yer own business," said Davey. He turned back to Fran. "He was sound, the priest. Was tellin' him about Sporting Les Behans'. He got a bit confused though, asked if I was a man or a woman, then said it didn't matter, that we were all God's children in the eyes of our Lord. Told me he'd give us a mention at mass."

"That's eh, lovely," Fran said, not knowing whether to take his mate seriously or not. Davey had never shown an interest in the church, not even as a kid. "Any word from Mick?" he asked, trying to get onto more pressing matters.

Davey looked glum and said, "Nah. Called around but got no answer.

Not sure what's goin' on but there was a 'For Sale' sign up on his gaff. I left several messages on his phone as well."

He was extremely sorry for the way he'd carried on at his Ma's funeral and the appalling things he'd said to his friend and was desperate to make amends.

Fran was baffled. "A 'For Sale' sign? He never mentioned anythin' about it to me," he said.

Davey shrugged his shoulders. "How'd ye get on in court?"

"Don't ask," said Fran.

Father O'Brien stood next to the altar in front of his sparse congregation. If the age profile was anything to go by the vast majority of his audience were destined to meet their maker in the very near future.

"And before I forget, I'd like to just quickly mention that I hope the Lesbians have a great day out and that please God they'll score," he said with a beaming smile.

Two elderly female parishioners sitting in the front row turned to one another.

"Disgustin'," they condemned in unison.

"I might even drop up to the park later on and watch them in action," Father O'Brien innocently added.

Chapter 18

5th Round: United Dunboyne v Sporting Les Behans'

The Sporting team arrived at the away ground in a convoy of cars approximately one hour prior to kick-off. This allowed plenty of time for the players to get changed and to do a half decent warm up without getting bored. Davey retrieved two large wheelie cases from the back of the Assassin's cab and set them down on the pavement.

"Travelling light, I see?" Baxter said, with regards to the extra baggage.

"And that's just his make-up," Fran said, grinning.

"I like to keep me options open, Boss," Davey half explained.

The not too helpful home official grunted some kind of directions when Baxter had asked where the away dressing room was located. The team followed their manager into the pavilion, which appeared to be a relatively new building, and found their changing room at the end of a corridor that was tastefully decorated with numerous prints of modern art. Baxter was first into the dressing room and was happy enough with what he saw. It was clean and there was plenty of room as well as being brightly lit. The players filed inside and nodded their approval having togged off in some awful shitholes over the years. Davey headed straight for an electric socket and plugged in one of his wheelie cases.

Baxter was puzzled. "Do you have to recharge it or something?" he asked, thinking it was like a battery-operated golf trolley.

"Nah," replied Davey, "It's a boom-box. Am mindin' it for some scanger who owes me a few quid." He switched it on and a quick-mouthed rapper was doing his thing.

"Ok, boys, no dilly dallying," said the manager, "I'll take a wander around and suss out the pitch but if this place is anything to go by, you'll be playing on a billiard table."

"Righ' Boss," answered a few of lads, already retrieving their boots, shin guards and the likes from their gear bags.

"And Davey," said Baxter.

"Yeah, Pa?"

Baxter twisted an imaginary dial and said, "Give it some volume like a good man," then left.

Davey did as he was told and turned up the rapper who was singing about 'Doin' some hoe, high on blow, puttin' lead into the fuckin' Five O'. He opened up his second case. Hidden amongst his football kit were a few hand tools and a lot of empty space. The tools included a handy sized crowbar, a hammer, a selection of spanners and a battery powered drill. He turned to Al. "Give us a bunt, will ye?"

The Assassin duly obliged, lifting Davey onto his wide shoulders with ease. The player didn't hesitate and began in earnest to unscrew every second energy saving bulb from the ceiling.

"Will ye tell them ballbags to turn that excuse for music down!" the irate opposition coach roared at Baxter after he spotted him coming in from his pitch inspection. "I've been bangin' on the door these last ten minutes, but the fuckers won't answer."

"What?" yelled Baxter.

"We can't hear ourselves think with the racket yis are makin'!" shouted the coach, his face growing redder by the second.

Baxter raised a cupped hand to his ear. "You'll have to speak up, lad, I can't hear a single word you're saying with the music."

"Isn't that wha' I'm tryin' to tell ye, ye dozy auld git!" Baxter's opposite number screamed. "Lower it down or turn the shaggin' thing off."

"Switch off the music?" said Baxter, shaking his head. "Sure I couldn't do that, it's part of their warm up."

The opposition coach glared at Baxter, but he was failing miserably if he thought he could intimidate the Scouser. He finally stormed off knowing that he might as well have being talking to the wall. Baxter went back into the dressing room where his players were dancing around, psyching themselves up.

"Everythin' alrigh', gaffer?" Fran shouted.

Baxter smiled as he rubbed his hands together. "Just getting inside their heads, ar kid."

"Ye never miss a trick," complemented Fran.

The manager looked around and said, "Is it my imagination or is the lighting not great in here?"

"Probably old age. Should get yer eyes tested," Davey cheekily suggested.

Baxter was about to reply when the music abruptly stopped. Davey immediately went to the socket and checked the plug on his wheelie boombox but everything seemed to be in working order. He decided to open the dressing room door and have a look, expecting to see the whole place out. Instead he saw the opposition coach standing in the hallway wearing a dopey smirk while holding a fuse aloft in his right hand.

Davey turned his head back inside the dressing room and called out to his teammates, "Their tosser of a manager has only gone and turned our leccy off."

"Who?" the Assassin asked, barging his way through his own players.

"Where are you going?" asked Baxter, "We don't need any trouble, Al, not before the match."

The Assassin had already escaped into the hallway where the opposition coach went the colour of boiled shite on seeing the size of him and his less than friendly facial expression.

The coach made a rapid retreat back inside the safety of the home dressing room, locking the door after him for good measure.

Al was not impressed. "I'll get this sorted."

Davey stepped in front of his outraged teammate. "It's alrigh', bud, I have this," he said, hoping to calm the madman down.

The Assassin stared at Davey, weighing up in his mind whether or not to go to war with the crowd next door. Davey gave Al a goofy smile doin' his best to diffuse the situation. "I have an idea and sure if it doesn't work can't ye slaughter them when the match is over?" he said.

The Assassin slowly nodded after weighing up the pros and cons. "Ok. But it better be a good plan or I migh' have to batter you as well."

Davey hoped his teammate was joking.

As soon as Davey had ushered the Assassin back into the confines of the dressing room, he headed outside the clubhouse still togged out in his football kit. Jigsaw spotted him leaving and followed.

"Where are ye goin'?" he asked.

"The shops," Davey said, checking out the people who were hanging around the pavilion.

"Will ye get us a quarter pound of bonbons?" the waif-like striker asked, "I've a hankerin' for them all of a sudden."

"Yer not pregnant, are ye?"

"No," replied Jigsaw, "I never have unprotected sex."

"No love without the glove, glad to hear yer bein' responsible," said Davey, "It's kilo's now, by the way."

His teammate pulled a face. "Are ye sure?"

"Positive," said Davey, still doing a recce on the assembled crowd, "Somethin' to do with Europe."

"Well in that case get us a quarter pound of kilo's then," said Jigsaw.

Davey didn't bother trying to explain. "Will do."

"Thanks," said the happy-go-lucky striker before disappearing back inside.

Davey spotted what he was looking for, a young fella with a bike. "Heore, you, give us a loan of yer BMX for a few minutes?"

"Not a chance," the lad replied.

"I'll bring it straigh' back, I promise," Davey said, making the sign of the cross over his heart.

The youngster shook his head 'no'.

"Look, I'll give ye a few euros when I get back, I'm only goin' to the nearest shop," said Davey, "I'll even bring ye back a few sweets."

"Are you on the sex offender's register?"

"Yeah, next to yer aul fella's name."

The young lad grinned. "How much?" he asked.

"A fiver," said Davey.

"Do I look like an innocent kid to you? A score," said the youngster.

"Yer a tough little negotiator," Davey said, liking the lad's entrepreneurial trait.

The boy spat on the ground, delighted with the compliment but too cool to show it.

"Fair enough, a score it is," agreed Davey.

"Upfront," the boy said, holding out his hand.

"But me cash is in me sports bag."

"And how were ye gonna buy stuff in the shop?"

"None of yer fuckin' business," said Davey.

The young fella shrugged his shoulders like it was water off a duck's back.

Davey thought for a moment before deciding to remove his massive sovereign ring from his finger. "Okay, hold onto this. Don't do a leggin' job or I'll bleedin' bate the head off of ye when I find ye. And I'll give yer aul fella the slaps too. Have ye got a dog?"

The boy gave a reluctant nod.

"And I'll kill yer dog as well."

The youngster handed his bike over and watched the player peddle away, wondering would he ever see it again.

Davey stopped off at the first shop he saw, letting the bicycle drop to the ground in the middle of the doorway. It didn't dawn on him that someone could possibly trip over it, he was a man on a mission and that was his entire focus.

"Sorry, love, ye migh' be able to help me out," he said to the nice looking blonde behind the counter in the tight fitting red and white Polska top, "I'm looking for the local GAA pitch, have a match and I missed the bus."

"I'm not sure. I'll ask manager. Wait, please," said the helpful shop assistant.

"Good girl yerself. Warsaw's loss is Ireland's gain," Davey said, not knowing any other places in Poland. He admired people who had the strength to leave their families and friends behind to try and make a better life for themselves in some strange country. A bit like the Irish in days gone by he supposed, hardworkers who got nothing easy, not like that other shower with their hands constantly held out.

The helpful shop worker found her manager towards the rear of the shop but when she looked back to where she'd left the customer waiting, he was nowhere to be seen.

On arriving back at the dressing room Davey pulled out a jumbo pack of batteries from inside his jersey.

"I've got the power," he badly sang Snap's nineties hit.

Some of the lads groaned.

"I was just about to sing that," Split, the king of puns, moaned.

"Hurry up," said the Assassin, "I'm losin' me buzz."

Davey did as he was told. He unclipped the back of the boom-box, tore open the pack of new batteries and stuck them into the ghetto blaster. The machine burst back into life.

"Did ye forget about me kilos?" asked Jigsaw when he didn't see any sign of the bonbons.

"Ah shit, bud. We'll stop at a shop on the way home and I'll get ye a moxy load, I promise." Jigsaw was more than satisfied with that. Davey took a twenty euro note from his kit bag, went back outside and handed it to the young fella, retrieving his ring in return. The kid snatched the money from his hand just in case it was a trick and fled the scene. Davey knew that the young fella would be thinking that it was the easiest twenty he ever made. However, in all the youngster's haste he hadn't noticed that the note was a dud and not a great one at that. Maybe he'd be able to offload it somewhere, if the shopkeeper was blind. It suddenly dawned on Davey that unlike when he was a child you never saw a blind shopkeeper nowadays. Maybe ordinary people were far more trustworthy back then.

The pub was hopping after the Les Behans' latest victory. Frank had his hands full trying to keep everyone happy, especially his new customers. He'd noticed that there were a lot more younger women now frequenting his establishment, especially on match days. Groupies, he supposed. He'd even had the offer of the ride from one of them himself, a fit, top-heavy lass half his age. Although seriously tempted he had resisted but he wasn't sure how much longer he could hold out. Regardless of what these forward women were called they were certainly good for business, with fancy gins being the tipple of choice and as a result the coffers were filling very nicely indeed. Whoever said gin was a depressing drink was obviously not selling it.

"D'ye know wha' would look great in here," Davey said to Frank who was busily adding bits and bobs to various glasses of spirits.

"What's that, then?" Frank asked, feeling more like an interior designer than a publican.

Davey opened his wheelie case and retrieved a pair of prints which he'd lifted from the United Dunboyne clubhouse earlier in the day.

"Not bad," said Frank. He placed two freshly made gins in front of a cute girl with great cheekbones who was standing next to Davey. She paid for her drinks and went to find her friend but not before checking out several of the Sporting players first.

Frank looked at the framed prints and asked, "How much?"

"Fifty each or a hundred and twenty for the pair," Davey replied.

The publican furrowed his brow.

Davey winked. "Ninety for the two, was just seein' were ye awake."

Frank pursed his lips. "I don't know," he replied, already serving another eager customer.

"Look, I'll throw in half a dozen energy savin' bulbs for good measure. Ye can never have enough of those babies and they're not cheap."

"It's a deal," said Frank.

"Good man," Davey said. He handed over the newly purchased prints and light bulbs, zipped up his case and wheeled it back to the table, parking it next to Fran.

"Yer an awful man," said Fran, having noticed the transaction. "Didn't they have CCTV in the hallway?"

Davey opened the case again and took out two wall mounted security cameras. "Ye mean these yokes?"

Fran raised his eyebrows even though he wasn't surprised.

"Basic enough set-up. Didn't have the footage backed up or anythin'," his friend added.

The lads were enjoying the craic and the beer was flowing freely. Baxter knew that he couldn't put a total embargo on the drink situation otherwise the players would revolt. This was amateur football not the premiership after all. He hoped that by allowing these blowouts after a win the lads would remain keen and keep putting in the effort at training.

"The little bastards," Gitsy said, looking at his phone.

"Everythin' all righ'?" Charlie asked.

"It's me sister's young fella," Gitsy said, grinding his teeth, "He's after gettin' an awful hidin' from scumbags in his school. Look at the state of his poor face." He showed Charlie the picture his sister had just sent him.

Charlie took the phone and examined the image. "Toe-rags."

"Gis a look," Davey said.

The phone was passed over. Davey was disgusted by what he saw. The poor lad's face was badly bruised and swollen as well as having a nasty looking cut on the bridge of his nose. "Fuckin' animals."

The entire team took it in turns to examine the photo.

"An animal wouldn't do somethin' like that," Fran said.

"Liam's only twelve and he's a nice kid, very quiet," said Gitsy, clenching his fist. "It's been goin' on for ages and the sister's gone into the school a few times to complain but they've done fuck all about it. If anythin' it only makes it worse. He won't go back to school now and she's terrified he'll do himself harm."

"Where's this poxy school in anyway?" asked the Assassin, already visualizing the carnage he was going to cause.

Fran leaned forward. "We know ye mean well, Al, but ye'll get lagged if ye hit the fuckers. Ye'll be up before a judge and they'll all be wearin' their school uniforms actin' as if butter wouldn't melt in their mouths."

The players watched the Assassin with understandable apprehension.

Al digested what Fran had said. "I suppose yer righ'," he agreed.

Fran nodded in relief.

"I'll mangle the principal instead," said Al.

"Will he not fight back, Gitsy, what's yer nephew's name again?" Trigger asked.

"Liam," Gitsy replied. "Nah, he's not like us, he's very placid."

"I blame the imbalance in the ratio of male and female teachers in schools these days for causin' all the aggro," Charlie said out of nowhere.

His teammates looked at him wanting a further explanation.

"The kids are gettin' softer, they're not taught how to stand up for themselves anymore," he said.

Not all of the lads were convinced.

"Take a look at sports for example. Schools are findin' it almost impossible to get teachers to lend a hand," Charlie added.

"If they're not gettin' paid then I don't blame them," said Split.

"That's a cop out," Trigger interrupted. "Even when the games are played durin' school time a lot of the teachers won't help. No wonder half the country's over fuckin' weight."

A few of the lads mumbled in agreement.

"Diabetes is one of the biggest growth markets in the pharmaceutical industry," Yoyo expertly informed the lads having already done some research into the sector.

"Boys need sport to toughen them up and to give them an outlet for all that testosterone," Trigger said.

Leonard gave a polite cough. "I'm not sayin' that Charlie or Trigger are right or wrong," he tentatively began, "But in a recent article that I came across..."

"The last article I came across was in Playboy," offered Split, unable to resist the pun.

"Shut up ye dirtbird, the man was speakin'," Fran said, motioning for Leonard to continue.

"The article was about gender inequality and stated that Ireland was way above the European average for having more female teachers and not just at primary level. It said that nine out of every ten national schoolteachers were women."

"And have absolutely no interest in physical education. I rest my case," Charlie said, folding his arms.

"That's an awful generalisation, I know a lot of fit teachers who are birds," joked Power.

Davey nodded his head. "I heard a fella callin' the kids nowadays the Snowflake Generation."

"D'ye remember when we were at school and there was a disagreement," Power said, "The masters would let fellas sort it out for themselves in the yard, so long as it didn't get out of hand. Ye migh' not always have won the scrap but ye gave as good as ye got."

"I always won," said the Assassin.

Nobody could disagree with that. Even as a child Al was the size of a man. He never took a backwards step in a fight, just like his idol, world heavyweight champion, Rocky Marciano, who was also undefeated.

"I firmly believe that it's to do with the chicken nowadays," Yoyo said after letting the others have their say.

"Wha'?" asked Huey.

"I was listenin' to them pair of aul wans on the radio," Yoyo said, "I think one of them stalked his wife before she was his wife. In anyways, they were goin' on about women's hormones bein' injected into chickens and that's why boys are becomin' more feminine and growin' diddys and all."

"Fuck off, they never said that," Huey interrupted.

"More or less," Yoyo insisted.

"Does yer nephew eat a lot of chicken?" Podge asked Gitsy, feeling empathy for the youngster.

"Bucket loads of fried chicken by the looks of it," Split said.

Gitsy pointed at Split. "Shut it, asshole."

"I was just havin' a laugh," the chop-chop merchant said, quickly apologising.

Baxter, fearful that Gitsy might bash Split, decided to intervene. "We'll have none of that body shaming talk here."

"That's a bit rich comin' from you," Podge said, "I'm always bein' called fat."

The manager raised a finger and pointed it at his disgruntled player. "We're talking about a child here. You're a grown man and should know better."

Podge wasn't happy but didn't challenge the double standards.

"I seen a documentary on the chicken hormones thing about a year ago," said Davey, "Apparently the American military were considerin' usin' it as a weapon to make their enemies more emotional."

Baxter laughed. "If those crazy Yanks think that turning the enemy into women will make them weaker, they've an awful lot to learn about the opposite sex."

"So wha' are we gonna do about the little shits?" Trigger asked, referring to Liam's bullies.

Davey grinned thinking about Derek and the gang of young fellas who hung out around the Stadium of Light. "Don't worry about it. I know a few boyos who'd be perfect for the job," he said but didn't reveal their identities.

Quarter Final: Sporting Les Behans' v Cork Rovers

After disposing of United Dunboyne by three goals to one and then Galway City F.C., four-two in the sixth round, the lads were now into the quarter finals. Another home draw was on the cards, this time against one of the best sides to have come out of Cork in recent years. Baxter was only too aware of just how vulnerable his team was at the back without Mick's anticipation and clever reading of the game but what could he do. He'd been onto Davey several times with regards to getting the absent player back into the fold and to be fair to the chap he seemed to be doing his utmost to make contact with Mick but with little success to date. Although the away tie to United Dunboyne had been a potential banana skin, the lads had done well, containing their opponents to a couple of long-range shots. On top of that, Dunboyne couldn't handle the pace of Sporting's wingers down both flanks.

The match against Galway City F.C. had been a much more difficult affair with their powerful centre-halves causing all sorts of problems every time they got a corner or a free. Fortunately for the Les Behans' the away side seemed to run out of steam in the last fifteen minutes and this was when Richie ran riot, scoring one himself and setting Trigger up for a simple tap in at the far post. Home advantage had definitely been a bonus for Baxter's side who didn't have to stray from their match day routine. People often underestimated just how much it took out of players having to travel for hours by coach. It didn't help the visiting team either that persons unknown had placed several misleading signposts close to the Stadium of Light adding another very frustrating hour and a quarter onto their trip.

Derek led the large gang of kids, armed with black plastic bags and litter pickers, up and down the pitch, scouring the bobbly surface to within an inch of its life. Even the tiniest scraps of rubbish were promptly gathered and bagged. Another group of young lads were busy touching up the paint job which they'd done the previous day on the truck container dressing room to cover over the scorch marks from the torchings as well as the mindless graffiti. This was all part of the intensive clean-up operation. The kids felt kind of good to be helping out and doing something constructive for a change but were reluctant to say it aloud for fear of being ridiculed by their peers.

An additional truck container had been sourced, albeit a smaller one measuring twenty feet long, which served as the away dressing room. The council were under strict instructions from Baxter to leave a band of uncut vegetation approximately two yards wide directly in front of its double doors. They were only too happy to oblige as their job had become noticeably easier since the arrival of the Sporting Les Behans' team. Nobody now tried to steal the lawnmowers and the dirty nappy bombardment had ceased. The lack of grass cutting directly outside the entrance to the smaller truck container had resulted in a fine patch of nettles establishing itself. This without fail led to at least every second opposition player ending up getting stung to bits and in turn disrupting their warmup. The game was about inches and fine margins after all.

The Sporting Les Behans' team was assembled inside their converted truck container, changing into their freshly washed and ironed kit. Trigger watched as Jigsaw slowly put on the number twelve jersey. He patted his good pal on the back.

"Don't worry, ye'll be back in the startin' eleven before ye know it," he said.

Jigsaw didn't believe his friend but appreciated the kind words none the less.

Baxter, wearing a perplexed expression, made his way over to Davey. "Did you see them kids outside?" he asked, not sure what the hell was going on.

"I did," said Davey, "Hearts and minds, Boss."

"Hearts and minds, my arse," Baxter replied, "Keep an eye on them, they're up to no good, I can tell," He turned to the rest of his players, "Right, you lot. Get stuck into them from the off. And remember, if you can't get the ball..."

"Get the fuckin' man," the team loudly finished, having heard the gaffer's mantra a thousand times before.

"Yeah, yeah," Baxter said, "Let's see how smart you are out there."

The lads bounded out of the dressing room, pumped up for action accompanied by Gonna Fly Now or as everyone else knew it, the theme song from Rocky belting out through the powerful speakers which had recently been bolted onto the top of the dressing room.

The Assassin discreetly caught Fran by the arm and held him back allowing the room to clear. "I heard ye could do with a bit of work for the aul custody battle, migh' help sway things with the judge?"

"Good news travels fast," said Fran, feeling more than a little sorry for himself.

"Shit happens, deal with it," Al said, chastising his friend, "Ye can use me taxi for as long as ye want, do a bit of cosyin' in it."

"Pardon?"

"Ye heard."

"Thanks, Al, but I don't have a PSV license or anythin' like that," explained Fran, taken aback by the unexpected but very generous offer from his teammate.

"Don't be worrin' about that end of things. I have an agent that'll sort it out, owes me a few favours for stuff I can't talk about." The Assassin gave a swift look around as if he was listening for something then turned back to his teammate, "And I don't want any rent for the plate or the car, just put wha'ever juice ye use back into it."

Fran felt like hugging the giant towering over him but knew that it wouldn't go down too well. Al was definitely old school when it came to that sort of touchy feely thing. "I don't know wha' to say," he said instead.

"Thanks will do," Al said.

"Thanks."

"Sure I know ye'd do the same for me or any of the other lads under the same circumstances."

The makeshift scoreboard read: Sporting Les Behans' 2, Cork Rovers 1. Baxter chomped rapidly on his exhausted chewing gum almost grinding his teeth to the last with the nerves. Jigsaw wasn't much better as he gnawed his way through what remained of his fingernails.

The manager turned to Split. "What's left?" he demanded.

"One minute less than the last time ye asked," Split smartly replied.

"Do you want me to kick the living shite outta you?" barked the manager, his eyes bulging out of his head.

"Sorry Boss, times up," Split immediately apologised. He'd never seen the gaffer this jittery before.

Baxter left his excuse of a technical area and trespassed onto the edge of the pitch. "Come on, ref! Blow it up!" he roared.

When the Assassin headed the ball out for a throw-in Yoyo spotted an elderly priest over at the far sideline. Putting two and two together he deducted that this must be the same priest that Davey had been talking about earlier on.

"Davey, yer Sugar Daddy's come to watch ye play!" he shouted.

Davey checked the sideline and saw Father O'Brien. The priest waved over and he sheepishly saluted back. Moments later the full-time whistle was blown and the Les Behans' hugged one another in scenes of delirious celebration. Baxter raced onto the pitch and picked Fran up, almost throwing him into the air.

"That wasn't good for the heart," he said with nervous laughter.

Charlie ruffled Davey's hair. "Ye comin' back to Frank's for a few celebratory scoops?"

"Maybe later. There's somethin' I have to do first," he answered, already jogging towards Father O'Brien. Once he reached the holy man he nearly reefed the arm out of his socket with his energetic handshake.

Fran caught up with Trigger, patting him on the back. "Ye'd some game, bud."

"Ah, all the lads were great," said the in-form striker, "I feel a bit sorry for Jigsaw though."

"Yeah, his confidence has really taken a hammerin' these last few weeks," Fran agreed, "Don't suppose ye could take him for a bit of shootin' practice?"

Trigger licked his lips trying to moisten them and although surprised at Fran's suggestion he was more than willing to help out. "If ye think it'll do him some good I don't have a problem."

"Top man," said Fran.

Davey stood in the darkness of his shed, his mobile stuck to his ear. The phone was eventually answered at the far end. "Jacko? It's Davey."

The line remained silent which he took as his cue to continue. "D'ye still do the security thing with yer mate at the Internationals? Wha' d'ye mean do I know wha' time it is? Buddy, business never sleeps. Ye'd better change that mindset of yers if ye ever wanna get out of that hovel yer livin' in... Tell yer mate to put me down as a steward for next week's match... Don't give me that bullshit... Of course I know we're playin' Brazil... Look, I'd some bleedin' job off loadin' that furniture, ye let me down big time, pal."

He hung up on Jacko, determined not to let the man ruin his buzz. He'd promised his Ma prior to her passing that he would help out people who were less fortunate than himself and he was determined to deliver on that promise. When he'd first approached Derek, the young lad from the flats, and broached the subject of tackling a group of bullies he wasn't quite sure how he would react. He needn't have worried however. Derek was mad for action and the fact that Davey had also offered him a few quid made it all the sweeter.

Gitsy's nephew, Liam, had returned to school without the fear of being picked on after Derek and a few of his pals had ambushed the bullies outside the school and gave them a right good kicking. Derek had informed the little shits as they cowered on the ground that Liam was his cousin and warned them that if he even got so much as a whisper that they were looking crooked at Liam he would give them a worse hammering. Problem solved.

Davey was pleased that he'd been able to help but the idea had also popped into his head that there was money to be made here. He was in no doubt that there were other children out there being picked on and whose parents would gladly pay for something to be done. This was a real community project in the making he convinced himself. He'd be providing jobs, albeit on a casual, non-taxable basis for Derek and the other young lads from the flats as well as putting an end to bullying. His Ma had told him to help the less fortunate, which he was now doing and if he could turn a profit from it then maybe he could ease back on the robbing too.

The exclusive department store was busy with customers who had a lot more money than sense, paying a fortune for the latest must have brands. Bloggers had a lot to answer for, not that the shop owners were complaining. Davey wore a baseball cap pulled down low on his head as he casually wheeled a clothes rack through the shop. Dozens of identical, colourful dresses in various sizes hung from the rail. An alert young shop assistant noticed Davey heading for the exit. She walked briskly up to her colleague, tapped her on the shoulder and pointed towards the man with the baseball cap.

"What's he up to?" she asked, her tone a mixture of concern and curiosity.

"Something about a recall on a defective line. Said management had cleared it," replied her less than enthusiastic colleague who was more interested in her phone than store security.

Fran and Tracey strolled through the town centre carrying a couple of handy sized shopping bags. They were so comfortable in one another's company that they could easily have been mistaken for a couple who had been together for years.

Fran squinted as he looked into the near distance. "That looks like Davey Byrne."

"Where?" asked Tracey, trying to spot him through the crowd.

Davey, his head down, hurried towards the couple, pushing the packed clothes rack.

"Wanna watch ye don't get a speedin' ticket there, mate," said Fran.

"Ask me bollo..." began Davey before looking up and seeing his friend.

"Ye were sayin'?" Fran said.

Davey smiled then gave a quick check over his shoulder.

"How are you keeping?" Tracey said kindly, "I was very sorry to hear about your Mum."

"Ye know yerself, takes time to readjust," answered Davey. He really appreciated people remembering his Ma, but things were still a little too raw for him to be able to open up and to talk about her death.

Fran nodded towards the dresses.

"Special delivery, better head," Davey half explained before hurrying off down the street.

Fran and Tracey watched him make his exit.

"I thought he was a motorbike courier?" Tracey said.

Fran cocked his head to one side. "Cutbacks, I suppose."

Tracey gave him a puzzled look but her new partner didn't elaborate. They walked on a little further pausing next to a bicycle rack where Tracey fixed the strap on her shoe with the sensible heel. Functional yet stylish was how she thought of this particular set of footwear.

Trigger, dressed in a navy tracksuit, came tearing around the corner almost flattening the couple. He was carrying a bulky satchel and perspiring heavily.

"There ye are, Fran," he gasped.

He looked questioningly from Fran to Tracey as he whipped off the tracksuit bottoms revealing Lycra shorts underneath. He then retrieved a cycling helmet and sunglasses from the satchel and shoved them on.

"Sorry. Tracey, Trigger. Trigger, Tracey," Fran said, introducing the pair. "Trigger was the boy with the mop of curls in the school photo I showed ye? The one you said was a ringer for Shirley Temple."

"I never said that," Tracey replied, absolutely mortified. She thumped Fran hard in the shoulder.

"Yer alrigh', love," Trigger said, gulping in some air, "I wouldn't believe a word out of his mouth. He's a born liar." He pulled a piece of black tape off the side of his satchel revealing the logo 'No Messin' Couriers'. "Nice to meet ye all the same."

"You too," said Tracey.

Trigger then reefed off his navy tracksuit top and turned it inside out. It was now bright yellow.

"I'm sure I'll bump into ye again," he said, panting heavily as he unlocked one of the bicycles in the rack, hopped on it and raced away.

The young couple watched him narrowly dodge furious shoppers as he sped away.

"I'm absolutely exhausted just looking at him," Tracey said, frowning. "He'd want to be careful not to overdo it or he'll end up having a fecking banger."

"Yeah. Think it's the triathlon he's trainin' for. He'll probably jump into the Liffey and swim home," said Fran.

Garda sirens wailed in the distance as two Gardaí ran past.

"No sign of him here," reported one of the policemen into his radio.

Tracey shot Fran a puzzled look, but he just gazed skywards and whistled.

"Come on, better get back or your Mum will think we've eloped," Tracey finally said, having resigned herself to the fact that Fran wasn't prepared to reveal any of his mate's secrets.

Frank the Publican was behind the counter busily cleaning beer trays when Davey called in laden down with the stolen dresses, having discarded the wheelie clothes rail in a nearby skip.

He dumped the clothes onto the bar. "Mind these for me like a good man, I'll explain later. And here..." He tossed a wad of notes onto the counter, "...put that behind the bar for the lads for later on."

He then disappeared just as quickly as he had arrived. Frank put the sizeable wedge in the till, not bothering to count it. He picked up one of the short dresses and held it aloft for closer inspection. Larry and Mo watched closely from where they were seated at a far table.

Mo nudged his brother and said, "Another one."

Larry shook his head unable to hide his disappointment. The world was a lot different from the one he and his brother were familiar with growing up.

Irish football supporters marched along the patchwork of narrow streets that led the way to the stadium. The football ground was lit up with powerful floodlights and the boisterous chanting that was echoing from the modern arena was almost deafening. Fans eager to see their team take on the South American champions squeezed their way through the numerous turnstiles.

Davey, dressed in an official luminous yellow jacket with security pass attached, was positioned at the mouth of one of the stadium's many tunnels. Despite Jacko's protests that he hadn't a hope in hell of getting a pass for Davey he had somehow managed to come up trumps. Davey's name was added to the list of stewards on duty giving him unrestricted access to all areas.

The match had been a very entertaining affair with the crowds treated to some classy football punctuated with outrageous skills. Ireland did their best to kick lumps out of the Brazilians but struggled for the most part to get anywhere near the silky-smooth South Americans. A voice came through Davey's earpiece notifying that all stewards should take up their end of match positions. Following orders, he made his way inside the ground and sat on the edge of the pitch next to Jacko. They were facing the crowd along with the numerous other stewards. When the additional time was almost up Davey turned to Jacko.

"Mind these for me," he said, pulling off his tracksuit bottoms and unzipping his luminous jacket. He was wearing the brand-new Ireland kit underneath.

Jacko was more than a little alarmed. "Wha' d'ye think yer bleedin' doin'?"

"Makin' me international debut, buddy," Davey replied with a beaming smile.

Seconds later the referee blew his whistle three times and signalled the end of the match.

Being a private investigator was a pain in the hole as Tina was finding out to her dismay. She was slumped behind the wheel of her parked car with her mother sat in the passenger seat next to her. Since the custody battle for Laura when the judge had failed to commit one way or the other, Mrs. Flynn had become even more determined in her quest. She'd decided to get proactive to ensure that Laura would be made a ward of court even if it meant stalking Fran twenty-four-seven. And once she was appointed guardian for the child the Reilly clan could take a flying leap for all she cared. She had no doubt that Fran would slip up and when that happened she'd be there to take full advantage.

A smart looking taxi pulled up outside Fran's place, honking its horn loudly. After a few short moments the young father emerged holding Laura, wrapped snugly in a warm blanket, while also balancing a travel bag in his other hand. The alert taxi driver hopped out and opened the rear door allowing Fran and his child easier access into the cab. After his passengers were safely on board the driver got back in and began to pull away.

Tina turned to her mother. "Do we have to?"

Mrs. Flynn glared at her daughter who wisely decided to shut her trap. She turned the key in the ignition and gave pursuit.

Davey squirted water over his head and jersey as he casually jogged onto the pitch past the Irish captain, Bobbie Kane. The record-breaking international striker stared at Davey as he went by.

"Story, head," Davey cheerfully greeted. Although there were thousands of people watching from the stands and countless others glued to the box he wasn't the least bit nervous. Knowing that you were doing the right thing for the right reason was empowering. It was all about being positive. Kane rubbed his prominent chin, unsure of what to do next. The kit that this bloke was wearing looked remarkably similar to the gear which had recently been stolen from the warehouse. He knew it had caused untold headaches for the football association to reorder a new set and to get them delivered in the nick of time. Oblivious to the repercussions of his theft, Davey headed straight for Padjo, the latest superstar to have come off the Brazilian production line.

"Good game, me amigo," the Les Behans' player said to Padjo.

The diminutive South American didn't recognise this Irish player and he glanced around for reassurance from his fellow teammates, but they were too busy interacting with their Irish counterparts. Davey wasted no time in removing his own jersey, revealing a t-shirt underneath with a photo of Millie and the dates of her short life printed on it. He handed the jersey to Padjo who cautiously accepted it.

"Obrigado," said the Brazilian, his answer barely audible over the boisterous crowd.

Davey glanced around and saw the Irish captain speaking to another one of his players, tugging on the chest of his football shirt. Kane then pointed over at the imposter.

"Areeba, areeba, underlay!" Davey encouraged in his best pigeon Spanish much to the bewilderment of the Portuguese speaking footballer, "I'm doin' an interview with *Sky Sports* in an uno momento, comprende?" he added, holding up an imaginary microphone to help with the language barrier.

As Padjo was slowly removing his shirt Bobby Kane and his teammate were marching towards Davey. The Brazilian star reluctantly handed his top to Davey who snatched it and jogged away in the opposite direction of the approaching, irate Irish players.

Padjo held up Davey's shirt and looked at the name on the back. "By...r... ne?" he did his best to pronounce.

Davey checked over his shoulder and called out, "It's Byrne, as in wha' yer doin' to the rainforests for fuckin' burgers."

Padjo stood in the middle of the pitch watching the crazy Irishman flee and being chased by his fellow countrymen. He presumed that the man was some kind of environmental activist and he admired his ingenuity in getting access onto the football pitch to make his protest. However, if the eco-warrior had properly done his research, he would have discovered that the Brazilian star had recently bought ten thousand acres of precious rainforest solely for conservation purposes.

Jigsaw and Podge were at the counter in Frank the Publican's bar, nursing pints. They were trying to pace themselves in anticipation of the monster session that was going to happen later on. Frank was busying himself removing trays of steaming glasses from the cleaning machine when Podge glanced up at the television.

"Fuck. Did ye see that?" he said, excitedly jabbing his sausage-like finger at the screen.

"No, wha'?" asked Jigsaw, almost as excited.

Podge hopped off his high stool, nodding vigorously at the television. "Davey Byrne. He's just swapped jerseys with yer man, Padjo," he spluttered.

"Our Davey Byrne?" Jigsaw giddily asked.

"The one and only," Podge confirmed, chuffed with his powers of observation.

"Go on outta that," said Jigsaw. Although the lads were always winding him up he still wanted to believe his teammate.

Podge was adamant. "May Christ be me witness."

Jigsaw scratched his head. "Surely he'd have told us if he got called up to the Irish squad, wouldn't he?" he asked, looking to Frank the Publican for reassurance.

Frank stared at the telly but could only see the usual suspects.

"I must be a worse feckin' fool," he said to himself, shaking his head. He leaned across the counter, "I'm not tryin' to tell ye yer business or anythin', Podge, but I really think ye should flush wha'ever tablets that hospital has ye on down the bog."

"But I'm serious, I know wha' I saw," Podge protested.

Frank glanced over at Jigsaw, but the beanpole striker was too busy trying to spot Davey on the box.

"With all the weight yer after losin', Podge, maybe yer hallucinatin'," Frank said, careful not to offend his customer.

"Bollox, I know wha' I saw," cursed Podge, his agitation growing.

"Okay, okay," the publican said, holding up his two hands in an attempt to appease his customer. "Look, why don't we ask Davey when he comes in later on."

Podge scratched the stubble on his chin and decided to sit back down on his stool.

"Unless he's havin' a few sneaky scoops with his new Irish teammates," Jigsaw innocently said.

Frank looked at Jigsaw and was going to tell him how ludicrous his suggestion was but refrained. "Time's pushin' on, lads," he reminded them instead, "Ye better get ready, the rest of the gang are due in about ten." He looked over at Larry and Mo, "You'll have to drink up, lads, there's a private party on here tonight."

"Can we not stay?" asked Larry, feeling miffed.

"I don't know. There's a strict dress code," the publican replied.

"I can see the headlines now," Mo said, turning his back on Frank and looking at his brother, "Old age pensioners thrown out of their local by money grabbin' publican."

Frank was appalled. "It's not like that," he said, defending his actions. He didn't want any unwarranted bad press. Mo immediately sniffed a weakness and pounced on the opportunity which had fortuitously presented itself.

"All the good money we've spent in this kip and this is how we're treated," he complained.

Larry shook his head and said, "Deplorable. Wha' do they call it again?"

"Ageism," said Mo.

"That's it, ageism," Larry repeated.

"Alrigh', alrigh'," the publican said, stroking his wrinkled forehead, almost losing the will to live. The elderly brothers were a formidable tag team, "If it's okay with Davey then its fine by me."

Larry coughed and gave his chest a gentle tap. "I think a few compensatory pints migh' be in order."

"Compensation, for wha'?" asked Frank.

"Ah lads, we're all friends here now, aren't we?" Mo said, suddenly switching from shit stirrer to that of peacemaker, "Let's have three or maybe four free pints each and we can call it a goodwill gesture. Then there'd be no need of even of thinkin' about gettin' journalists or barristers involved."

The bar owner gave a sigh but otherwise remained silent. He knew when to accept defeat and on this occasion, he was well and truly beaten.

Fran Reilly got out of the taxi, awkwardly trying to balance both Laura and her accompanying baby care paraphernalia in his strong arms.

"Give us a minute," he told the driver before hurrying inside the safe house.

Mrs. Flynn and Tina hadn't had much trouble following Fran's ride to its new destination, apart from breaking the odd red light or two under the strict orders of the older woman. They'd kept watch all the way and were now parked a relatively safe distance up the street.

"This is takin' ages," Tina complained, "And I'm gonna miss the party."

"Ye can be one selfish cow," Mrs. Flynn said, scolding her daughter.

Tina folded her arms across her chest and slumped back into her seat without another word.

"That's yer niece in there and my grandchild," her mother added.

As tough as Tina was she was wary of her mother. Mrs. Flynn was a formidable adversary and when she lost it, she lost it big time.

As much as Fran wanted to go to the party in Frank's pub he was still quite apprehensive about leaving his young daughter in the care of her uncle. Richie on the other hand had no such worries. He stood in the centre of the living-room holding Laura, watched closely by Fran.

"She'll be grand with her uncle," Richie promised, trying to alleviate his brother's concerns. He then smiled at the precious infant, "Won't ye, honey bunny?" He thrust her playfully into the air, caught her as she deftly returned to earth then threw her up again. Laura laughed heartily.

"Wouldn't do too much of that, bro, if I was you," Fran warned, "She's not long after her tea."

"Righ'," said Richie, immediately turning the young child around so that she now faced away from him. He also held her at arm's length, just in case, "Go on, will ye and have a good time."

"I shouldn't be too late," said Fran, glancing over at the web cam, "Are ye sure ye know how to use this?"

"Prison has its perks. Did all that stuff on a course while banged up."

"Glad to see the taxpayer's money was put to good use."

"And when ye get a proper job ye'll be able to contribute to that pot too," Richie said, sticking out his tongue.

Fran missed having the buzz with his brother. "Give me a ring if ye need anythin'," he said.

"Just get Mick to the pub and get things sorted," Richie ordered.

The brothers walked out to the hall door where Richie watched Fran climb into the waiting cab. The taxi pulled away leaving Laura and her doting uncle to wave it off.

"Yer aul fella's an awful worrier, d'ye know that?" joked Richie.

Less than forty yards up the street Tina shot forward in the parked car, peering out through the windscreen. "Is that Richie Reilly?" she asked in disbelief.

Mrs. Flynn was grinning like a Cheshire cat. She retrieved her mobile and dialled. The call was answered within seconds.

"Garda, please," she said.

The police station was starting to get busy as the duty officer made his way past two of his colleagues who were dealing with a well-oiled, elderly man intent on finishing his party piece. The duty officer tapped on the glass door of his superior's office and was immediately beckoned inside by his boss.

"Sorry for disturbing you, sir, but this woman just rang in about an escaped prisoner," the officer said, handing over a note, "She refused to give her name."

The senior lawman carefully read the piece of paper. "Check out this Reilly character. Unless he's a mass murderer he'll have to wait 'til we clear the backlog from tonight's football match."

There was no shortage of parking spaces outside Frank the Publican's bar as the Assassin arrived in his taxi. Within seconds Trigger freewheeled into the car park riding a top of the range racing bike that you could probably lift with one finger. The striker dismounted in one smooth motion and left the bicycle leaning against the exposed brick wall of the pub. Baxter, Charlie, Yoyo and Paddy Power climbed out of the Assassin's cab.

Trigger gave them a salute. "There ye are, lads."

"Bud," Charlie said, acknowledging his pal.

The Assassin stuck his head out the driver's window. "Trig," he greeted.

Paddy Power attempted to give Al money for the fare but his hand was instantly knocked away.

"Would ye ever fuck off. I'll stick this yoke around the back. Get the gargle in, I've an awful goo on me," he ordered.

Trigger opened the pub door and was about to go in when Yoyo caught his sleeve. "Are ye not gonna lock yer bike, looks mad expensive?" he said.

"It's not mine," replied Trigger, already disappearing inside for the party which Davey had decided to throw at short notice.

"Now there's a surprise," said Charlie, knowing his friend's history when it came to owning bicycles.

Although Trigger had risen through the ranks of the criminal fraternity and was now a very accomplished and highly respected armed robber, he still had a thing for stroking pushbikes. When he was a nipper, he would go rambling most weekends around the city robbing bicycles. There wasn't a lock he couldn't pick with his pocket-sized, fold-up scissors. He'd hand the bikes into various Garda stations saying that he'd found them dumped but was clever enough not to go to the closest station where the owner would most likely have reported the theft. Instead, Trigger travelled several miles in all directions making use of the many stations dotted around the city which in turn kept him fit. He'd lift two to three bicycles a day, between racers, mountain bikes, BMX's, ladies bikes, etc., whatever was in demand. Back then there was no interconnecting computer data base and even if there was, inputting information regarding stolen bicycles wouldn't have been a priority. A year and a day later Trigger would rock up to the various Garda stations and find that nine times out of ten the bikes would be thrown out the back, having remained unclaimed. He would then collect his prize and become the new lawful owner. And anyone who wanted a bike for a half decent price had only to leave word with his Ma and they'd be sorted. It was a thriving business for a ten-year-old.

It was a sad reflection on society when hospitals needed security personnel to guard them twenty-four hours a day, Davey thought as he slid past the stocky man in the high viz jacket. Normal visiting hours were long over but this wasn't a regular visit. Davey moved stealthily along the deserted corridor that led to St. Michael's ward. He stopped outside the locked door, stuck his face to the glass and knocked. One of the nurses on duty who was tucking in the edges of a sheet in a cot leapt with the fright. Davey shot his hands into the air by way of an apology, thankful that the woman hadn't screamed aloud. It took a few seconds for the startled nurse to recognise him as her colleague's fella. She walked to the far end of the ward, her hand placed on her heart and lightly nudged Lily who was busy reading a thermometer. Lily turned around and was pleasantly surprised to see her on/off boyfriend at the door.

Lily joined Davey out in the corridor for some privacy. He handed her a plastic bag.

"I want ye to auction this," he said.

Lily checked inside and saw the Brazilian player's soccer jersey. "The girls were sayin' that a footballer resemblin' a certain somebody was on the television with a picture of Millie on his t-shirt," she said, lightly poking Davey in the chest.

"I make the odd guest appearance on the box but it's usually on Crime Line," Davey said, trying to make light of the situation.

It was corny but it still brought a smile to Lily's face, something that was thin on the ground these last few days.

"Get onto a few radio shows, try the one where yer man used to be a keeper, with Leeds I think, about auctioning the jersey but don't let them know that it's you personally who has it," Davey explained, "Then let the bids build up."

"Will ye get arrested for this?" his concerned girlfriend asked.

"Probably but it's for a good cause. Have to leggit now, need to try and save a friendship."

Lily planted a sloppy kiss on her boyfriend's lips. "Yer Ma would've been so proud," she said, tears welling up in her kind eyes.

Richie sat on the couch while Laura played on the floor with some sort of a musical twirly yoke that you had to hit every few minutes to keep it playing. The evening had gone a lot smoother than he'd imagined and he wouldn't hesitate helping out again in the future if asked. He sniffed the air and glanced over at his niece. "Is that Peggy Dell comin' from you?" he asked, pulling a funny face while pretending to be deeply offended by the smell.

Laura looked up at her silly uncle and giggled.

Fran and Mick sat in the back of the stationery cab outside Frank's pub.

"I thought I could do this, but I can't," Mick said, having second thoughts.

"Come on. If ye saw the hassle I've had tryin' to organise a babysitter," said Fran, doing his best to encourage his pal.

Mick shook his head. "I'm sorry."

Although Fran could see the conflicting emotions in his friend's eyes, he wasn't going to let him give up so easily. "Ye can't stay hidden in yer gaff forever. Anyway, everyone knows yer secret by now."

The nosey taxi driver who was hanging onto his passengers every word, spun his head around. "I don't," he said, the curiosity finally getting the better of him.

Mick and Fran looked at one another before bursting into laughter. The driver had unwittingly sealed the deal.

The two friends headed through the pub doors with Fran hanging back slightly just in case Mick had a change of heart and tried to scarper. The room was in total darkness.

"That Frank fella mustn't have paid his leccy bill," said Fran.

The double doors had no sooner swung closed behind the two lads when Frank the Publican switched on the lights, illuminating the entire room. The Sporting Les Behans' players were standing in line, side by side with their hands behind their backs as if waiting for their equipment to be checked before a match by a referee. They were all wearing the identical dresses that Davey had nicked earlier in the day. Larry and Mo were sat in the corner also dolled up in the stolen gowns, not really sure what was going on except that there was free gargle on offer and that was all the reason they needed. Mick tried to retreat but Fran blocked his way.

Davey stepped forward from the assembled gang. "I just want ye to know that I was bang out of order the last day and said some shitty things," he apologised, "And this is me way of sayin' sorry."

He held out one of the stolen dresses for Mick. There was complete silence for a few tense moments with no one really sure how he was going to react. They needn't have worried, however.

Mick smiled and said, "I saw you on the television earlier, at the Ireland game. I have to say it took some neck, but it was a wonderful gesture, remembering the little girl like that."

Podge immediately spun around and pointed an accusatory finger at Frank the Publican and Jigsaw. "I fuckin' told yis I saw Davey, didn't I?"

The publican gave an apologetic nod, but Podge wasn't finished having his rant. "Blamin' the medication I was on as if I was some sort of crackhead..." He caught Yoyo's eye, "Nothin' personal, bud."

"Yer grand," said his teammate.

"Heore, mouthpiece, enough," ordered Al.

Podge did what he was told and immediately shut his gob.

"Would you two ever kiss and make up," Charlie said, referring to Mick and Davey.

No sooner had Mick accepted the dress from his friend when Frank stabbed the play button on the pub stereo. Music belted out from the sound system and with that the entire Sporting team produced pompons from behind their backs and began to dance and sing to Toni Basil's eighties classic 'Mickey' much to Mick's delight. If he was the soppy type he might have even shed a tear but he wasn't.

Richie closed the seals on Laura's new nappy. "Piece of piss, that," he boasted. He looked his niece in the eyes, "Pardon the pun." He then proudly stood her up straight after managing such an enormous feat, "There. And the way that the birds do be always goin' on about how hard they have things."

The nappy promptly fell to the floor causing Laura to shriek with delight. Richie scratched his head. Maybe there was a bit more to this childminding business than met the eye. He'd have to come up with plan B.

The atmosphere back in the pub was electric and had all the makings of the sort of night that would be talked about for years to come.

The Assassin collared Frank the Publican. "C'mere. I'm nearly after disappearing down a hole bigger than the one the Chilean miners were stuck in."

"Round the side?" said the bar owner.

Al nodded.

"It's got nothin' to do with me, Al," said Frank, "That bit of ground belongs to the council and I've lost count at this stage of how many times I've been on the blower to them and sent emails."

"They're leavin' themselves wide open for a claim," the Assassin said.

"I agree with ye," said Frank, "I'm amazed Larry or Mo haven't thrown themselves down it yet."

"They know better than to shit on their own doorstep."

"Suppose yer right. I better get this thing started," said Frank, lowering the big screen using the remote control, "If that's ok with ye?"

"Work away," said Al, "It's yer shop."

"A bit of hush," Frank ordered, "We're going over live to an undisclosed location, somewhere in Dublin."

Sporting Les Behans' looked up at the big screen where Richie now appeared. He was also wearing one of the stolen dresses that Davey had dropped around to him earlier that day.

"All righ', girls," Richie said, buzzing.

The team cheered.

Although Richie enjoyed a drink, he could take it or leave it and anyhow he knew it was far more important that things with Mick got sorted tonight so he didn't mind babysitting.

"Go on, ye ride!" Davey shouted.

Richie blew his pal a kiss which Davey pretended to catch and pull to his heart.

"I want ye to know, Mick, that like the rest of the lads I couldn't give a shite wha' floats yer boat so long as yer happy," Richie said, genuinely not giving a toss.

The team cheered again, only louder this time.

"And just to let ye know, that if ye ever get banged up, there's plenty of yer type inside," he added with a cheeky grin, "I can make some introductions for ye if ye like."

All the lads laughed and some clapped.

"Bitch," Mick retorted but in a jovial manner.

"Enjoy the session, ladies," Richie said then signed off.

The party was living up to its billing. Everyone was having a great time, not that they'd remember much about it in the morning. Mick and Jigsaw, their dresses hitched up around their waists, stood next to one another relieving themselves against the sheet of stainless steel which served as the urinal.

"So are ye bent or wha'?" Jigsaw asked.

"Would it make a difference?" Mick said, subconsciously chasing a cigarette butt with his urine down the channel which ran along the base.

"Not to me. Sure me Da's a gay," Jigsaw revealed with complete frankness.

Mick finished his slash, washed his hands and pressed the hand dryer but remembered it was broken. He dried himself with the end of his dress instead.

"How can your father be gay?" he asked but immediately regretted it, "Forget it, it's none of my business."

"No, yer alrigh'. I'm not ashamed to discuss these things. It's a modern world we're livin' in nowadays," Jigsaw insisted, gently swaying from side to side, "Ask away, buddy."

Mick felt that he'd no option now but to indulge his teammate. "How can your father be gay?" he asked.

Jigsaw did his best to remain still. "He ran off with me Ma's hairdresser and he's a man."

"I see. And was she very upset about it, your Mam?" Mick asked, sensing that Jigsaw needed to get it off his chest.

"Upset! She went bleedin' ballistic. Said the baldy bastard had no idea how hard it was to find a decent hairdresser in this town."

"Priorities, I suppose," Mick said. He smartly left the bathroom to rejoin the party having done his bit for charity.

Just as Jigsaw finished his whiz and was tidying away his tackle Podge stumbled in.

"That fizzy lemonade is some powerful tac," Jigsaw said, trying to be funny.

Podge managed a barely audible grunt by way of a response as he stumbled his way into one of the cubicles. He gathered up the ends of his dress with some difficulty, dragged his jocks down with one hand and plonked himself onto the bowl not bothering to close the door.

"Yer a gas man. Really gettin' into this women's thing, big time," Jigsaw said.

"Wha'?" Podge asked, his voice more than a little slurred.

"Sittin' down while havin' a slash," Jigsaw pointed out.

"Habit I suppose," replied Podge, trying to unravel some toilet roll. He eventually managed to tear off a piece of paper, wiped himself dry and climbed to his feet with the aid of the wall a bit like Spiderman after twenty pints.

"Wha' d'ye mean habit?" asked Jigsaw, not quite following things.

Podge pulled up his jocks. "Sharon doesn't allow me to have a jimmy riddle while standin'."

Jigsaw wasn't sure if his teammate was being serious.

Podge looked at him, trying hard to focus. "Don't open your gob, the lads will be on me case," he said as a distant warning bell rang from deep inside his alcohol-soaked brain.

"Me? Lips tighter than a nun's fanny," Jigsaw said, his mouth pressed closed to reinforce the point but already knowing that he was going to blab to the boys the first chance he got.

Podge grunted once more as he made his way unsteadily towards the door, unaware that the back of his dress was tucked into his underpants.

Jigsaw was going to tell him but figured that his friend would find out soon enough. As he was checking himself out in the large wall mounted mirror Davey ambled in. The nervous striker tried to act all normal hoping that he hadn't been caught.

Davey hoisted his dress and started to drain the spuds. "It's alrigh', yer arse doesn't look big."

Jigsaw smiled. He scanned himself in the mirror once again. "Would I be a zero?"

Davey looked Jigsaw up and down then said, "Definitely a zero, buddy, no doubt about it."

At that precise moment the Assassin bounded in and caught Jigsaw examining his reflection. "Howya gorgeous. Any chance of a lash?" he joked.

Jigsaw scarpered.

Al turned to Davey. "And there's me thinkin' there were no more virgins left on the Northside."

Back at the safe house Richie was sat on the couch playing a soccer game on the computer console while Laura was stretched out on an armchair across from him, covered with a blanket, sound asleep.

Richie scored a goal. "Get in there, my son!" he roared.

Laura woke with a start and began to cry. Her uncle bolted off the couch and hurried over to her, accidentally standing on her plastic feeding bottle and crushing it into the bargain.

"Bollox," he swore.

He picked Laura up. She was wearing one of the stolen Irish jerseys with a plastic bag sellotaped over a towel as a makeshift nappy.

"Shush, it's okay," he said in an attempt to console his niece. "Come on. Ye have to admit, it was a crackin' goal."

After a few minutes of cajoling, Laura finally stopped crying and he placed her gently back down on the armchair, sticking a cushion under the seat to prevent her from rolling off. The little girl was beautiful, and he had to admit that his brother was doing a fantastic job in rearing her. He was glad of what had happened the night that the drug-pushing scumbag Murphy had met his end. And if push came to shove, he'd wish for the exact same result all over again. Picking Laura's broken bottle up, he checked the damage. It was fooked as they might say in China. He caressed his chin hoping for inspiration.

The craic was deadly back in Frank the Publican's place. Everyone had made up and the stories were flying.

"So wait an ye hear this one, lads," the Assassin said. "Go on, Fran, tell them wha' happened to ye the other nigh'."

Fran leaned forward and checked that he had everyone's attention. "As most of yis know, I'm now doin' a bit of taxi-in' thanks to our good friend, the one and only, Mr. Al Caffrey, to help me keep me young wan."

"Fair play," Baxter acknowledged.

The rest of the lads nodded solemnly in their approval while others clapped. The Assassin was a nutter, but he was their nutter and that's all that mattered.

"So, I gets this call on the radio to collect a woman," Fran continued. "She'd just finished the late shift."

"This is priceless," Al interrupted, loving the banter.

"So I pulled up outside her job," said Fran, "and out she comes, all smiles. Not a bad lookin' mot in her day I'd say but with a fair bit of mileage up on the clock by now. Anyway, she slides into the passenger seat beside me and I thought this was a bit odd. Normally women on their own jump into the back but I said to meself she just seems to be a friendly sort."

"Did ye ride her?" asked Split, getting all excited.

The Assassin gave him a dig in the shoulder. "Will ye let the man tell his bleedin' story," he ordered.

"Sorry," Split apologised, rubbing his upper arm tenderly knowing too well that he'd have a massive bruise in the morning.

"We're drivin' along," said Fran, "and she was wearin' a long dress, the ones with the buttons runnin' up the front. Next of all she starts to undo them from the bottom up. I didn't know where to look."

"Ye bleedin' liar," Davey said, laughing.

"Well, ye know wha' I mean," said Fran. "Of course I had an aul gander. By the time we arrived outside her gaff nearly all of her buttons were undone. She then lifts one leg up onto the dash and exposes the whole shebang."

"Was the wagon not even wearin' knickers?" Charlie blurted out. This was one of his many unfilled fantasies.

"Not a stitch," said Fran. "Then she turned to me and said all seductive like 'Can I pay ye with this?' And I says, have ye got nothin' smaller, love?"

The lads were in hysterics. Tears were rolling down the Assassin's cheeks even though he'd heard the story a hundred times already.

"Did ye give her one in the end?" asked Charlie, already on a boner.

"Which end?" joked Davey.

The lads erupted into fresh laughter.

"Ah, lads. She must have been at least sixty," said Fran.

"Older people need a lot of loving too," Baxter reminded them.

"D'ye hear the geriatric," Davey slagged.

"You know what they say," said the manager, "An old one closing is like a young one opening."

Stevo was behind the wheel of the stationary stolen car with Scully sat next to him. They were keeping tabs on Frank's bar hoping that their target would come out of the woodwork at some stage or that they'd at least catch some sort of a lead. It had been a long night, hanging around but this was all part and parcel of the business they were in. Shortly after midnight, Fran, now changed back into his own clothes, emerged from the boozer and got into a waiting taxi.

Stevo turned the key in the engine. "That's Richie Reilly's brother."

"About fuckin' time," said Scully. He took a small, cylindrical shaped container from his jeans pocket and popped two pills. He then turned to Stevo who was watching him closely and offered him some.

His partner in crime looked at him with disdain.

"Suit yerself," Scully said, clearly getting the message.

Richie was back on the sofa, relaxing while playing the game console, conscious this time not to get overexcited. Laura was sitting happily next to him, drinking from an improvised feeding bottle that Richie had fashioned out of an empty beer bottle he'd rinsed clean.

Outside, Mrs. Flynn and Tina were still holed up in their car keeping watch on the safe house. Tina received a text message on her phone.

"Wer r u? Prty n Sineads???" read the text.

"This is a load of nonsense," Tina snapped, unable to hide her annoyance any longer. "The law are never gonna show." She reefed open the car door and got out.

"Where are ye goin'?" her mother demanded.

"For a smoke," Tina replied, slamming the door closed after her. She lit a cigarette and took a deep drag, moodily dwelling on what she was missing out on and who she could be shagging at the party. Enough was enough. She sneakily dialled a number on her phone. While it was ringing, she checked over her shoulder to make sure that her Ma was staying put. "Officer," she said, pretending to be in shock, "I'm just after seein' men with guns runnin' into a house." 'That should put a fire up their holes,' she thought.

Minutes after Tina's call to the police, the taxi carrying Fran arrived back at the safe house. He paid the driver, giving him a generous tip and the cab took off in search of a fresh fare. Stevo and Scully had followed Fran from the pub and had quietly pulled in down the street, still hoping to catch a break. They watched as Fran knocked on the front door.

"Some gaff. Must have a posh tart on the go," said Scully, putting two and two together and coming up with five.

Richie, still wearing his stolen dress, opened the hall door.

"Sweet Jesus, d'ye see the state of yer wan?" Scully said, almost choking, "Don't care how much money she's got, that's one ugly yoke."

Fran disappeared inside the house.

"That's the brother, Richie Reilly, ye dope," said Stevo.

Scully glared at his companion and was about to say something he might regret but managed to stop himself in time. Stevo casually opened the glove compartment, retrieved a pair of snug fitting leather gloves and pulled them on. He then took out a revolver and silencer and expertly screwed both parts of the deadly weapon together. Sensing that Scully was still eyeballing him Stevo turned his head sideways and said in a voice that meant business, "Problem?"

Scully quickly backed down. "No, no. Didn't know he was a fag, that's all," he muttered.

Back at the Garda station, the officer on duty hurried along a corridor almost colliding with several of his colleagues who were in no hurry to get out of the way. They gave him a curious look, but on this occasion he didn't hang about to offer an explanation. Instead he kept on going until he reached the door to his superior's office. He tapped at the glass but didn't wait to be asked inside this time.

"Another caller just rang in, a young woman, about armed men at the same address as that Reilly fugitive," he explained with growing urgency.

The rear garden of the safe house was dimly lit with spot lighting strategically placed within the shrub beds to highlight the more architectural plants. Stevo and Scully jumped off the top of the boundary wall into the garden. The older man landed upright in a standing position with his knees slightly bent to absorb the impact while Scully did a theatrical series of rolls before eventually getting back to his feet.

Stevo looked at his pathetic associate and shook his head. "Gotta be easier ways of makin' a fuckin' livin'," he said to himself.

Fran stood in the middle of the living-room looking from Laura, dressed in the Irish jersey and makeshift nappy and drinking from the modified beer bottle, to Richie, wearing the lady's dress and a cheeky smile.

"Couldn't get the hang of the nappies and all her little clothes got ruined," Richie explained, "I left them in the sink for ye."

"Thanks."

"Who would have known that so much stuff could come out of someone that small," Richie said, baffled.

"Tell me about it. And wha' about the beer?" asked Fran, nodding towards his daughter's choice of beverage.

Richie picked up the broken feeding bottle and held it aloft. "Improvisation, bro," he said, delighted with his ingenuity, "I gave it a good rinse before givin' it to her. I'm not that stupid."

Stevo and Scully crept along the rear of the building, hugging the walls where the garden lights failed to illuminate. They paused next to a large window where Scully popped another couple of pills from his container. Stevo peered through the glass pane and could see Fran and Richie sitting on the couch, sipping beers and laughing, with Laura propped up between the two brothers.

"Fuck, there's a kid inside," Stevo quietly cursed.

"So? We do the brat as well," said Scully, giving it the 'big I am.'

"Are you off yer fuckin' chomp?" said Stevo.

Scully shrugged his shoulders, started rotating his neck in a manly fashion, the drugs giving him a false sense of bravado. "A casualty of war, shit happens," he smugly replied.

"Get back to the bleedin' car ye dozy bastard," Stevo said, doing his best not to slap Scully in the mush.

"But they've made us look like poxy amateurs," Scully protested, "This needs sortin', once and for all."

Stevo grabbed the skinny thug by the throat and stuck the gun to his forehead. "And yer the hero to do it, are ye? I won't tell ye again, get back to that fuckin' car while ye still have a breath left in ye."

Scully sat in the passenger seat of the stolen jammer with his arms folded across his chest and a demented look plastered across his face. Stevo dismantled the gun, carefully placed it back in the glove compartment and began to peel off his leather gloves. Scully stared at the unguarded revolver. He suddenly lurched forward, snatched the gun and bailed out of the car at speed.

"Ye little bollox," swore Stevo, swinging an arm in a failed attempt to grab his fleeing accomplice.

Scully sprinted towards the high wall and leapt over it with surprising agility as Stevo clambered out of the motor in pursuit. He was forced to pull up when he noticed several vehicles in his peripheral vision, including two squad cars with their lights off, cruising silently up to the front gates of the safe house. Reluctantly, he turned around and made his way back to the stolen vehicle, hopping in. Furious with himself, he thumped the steering wheel several times before slipping away from the scene.

As Fran was rinsing Laura's baby-grows in the kitchen sink he was almost certain that he'd seen something move outside. He paused what he was doing and squinted hard, trying to focus on possible activity in the garden but with little joy. Although it was probably a stray cat he couldn't help himself from leaning his head closer to the window pane and staring even harder.

Scully slid up to the living-room window holding the loaded gun with both hands. Richie was still on the couch next to Laura keeping her entertained with funny faces and silly talk.

"Yer Da's definitely comin' along since he met that nice lady," Richie said to his young niece while crossing his eyes at the same time.

Laura gave him a big smile in return as if she understood exactly what he was saying even though he looked stupid. Outside in the garden Scully had Richie in his sights and took aim. His hands were shaking but he knew he needed to see this thing through. He had no doubt that he would go up in his uncle's estimations and maybe get promoted too. Word would filter onto the streets too that he wasn't a man to be fucked with. Then he could get rid of that fucking know-it-all, Stevo, once and for all. He cocked the gun. There was no way he was going to miss, not from this distance.

"Isn't that righ', bro?" Richie called out to Fran in the kitchen but there was no reply. Sensing that there was something amiss, he slowly got to his feet.

Scully placed his finger carefully on the trigger, preparing to squeeze. He was just about to fire when Fran came out of nowhere and brought a large saucepan down on the scumbag's head. Scully's legs wobbled before he collapsed to the ground like the way one of those giant smokestacks imploded after being dynamited. The gun was sent skittering across the patio slabs and thankfully didn't go off. At that exact same moment, armed police came crashing through the front door using a battering ram sending timber fragments flying in all directions. Fran glanced towards the racket but when he turned back a split second later to where Scully had fallen, the would-be assassin was already gone, scarpering over the boundary wall. Fran noticed the loaded revolver lying on the ground and instinctively bent down and picked it up.

"Drop it!" shouted one of the armed officers who had stormed the property. Members of the Garda rapid response unit had their weapons trained on Richie's torso. Their target held his hands high above his head in the universal sign of surrender.

"Stall the ball, lads," Richie calmly appealed, not wanting any jittery fingers squeezing triggers. "There's a small child present."

Detective Lyons strolled into the room and glanced over at Richie and Laura. "Playing happy families, I see," she commented.

An armed officer escorted Fran into the living-room accompanied by his law enforcement colleague who was holding a transparent evidence bag containing the recovered weapon. Seconds later Detective Cartland entered the room carrying the pile of stolen Ireland jerseys.

Lyons looked at the football gear before turning her attentions back to the Reilly brothers. "Can't wait to hear the excuses, lads," she said with a smirk.

Stevo watched the stolen car from the botched hit blaze violently away on the deserted waste ground, its berserk flames almost mirroring his own feelings. Fire usually gave him some comfort but not tonight. Things were really fucked up and he'd been around long enough to know where this was all heading. He didn't want to end up as just another punctured piece of meat on a slab in some stinking morgue. No, he knew what needed to be done and the sooner he took care of business the better. He almost missed his mobile phone ringing above the loud groaning noises that the van was making as it twisted and turned in protest under the intense heat of the bonfire. He checked the caller I.D. and Scully's name appeared on screen. He pressed cancel and said, "Gee bag."

Chapter 19

Noises from a speeding 4x4 off-road vehicle broke the early morning silence as it bounced its way through the coniferous woods. Trigger steered the jeep along the bumpy track which was only occasionally frequented by forestry workers when the spruce trees needed thinning. Jigsaw hung tightly onto the leather strap just above the passenger door as the vehicle jerked violently from side to side.

"Corners well," Jigsaw offered, having heard the saying on the telly but having absolutely no idea what the phrase meant.

Trigger held the wheel firmly. "Yeah, it's a decent enough bit of kit."

"When d'ye buy it?" Jigsaw asked.

"Are ye for real?" laughed Trigger, "Robbed it yesterday."

Jigsaw feigned laughter. His teammate leaned over and opened the glove compartment, pulling out a blindfold. He tossed it to his companion and said, "Put that on."

"Wha'?" asked Jigsaw, more than a little alarmed.

"Don't be worryin', will ye. I'm not into the kinky business," Trigger said, "Let's just say it's for yer own safety." This did absolutely nothing to allay his passenger's concerns.

The paperboy fed the cumbersome bundle of newspapers and magazines through the letterbox of the luxury apartment, cursing the extra unpaid work involved. 'It'd be alright if it was like the States where you could just cycle by the gaffs and fuck the papers at the doors,' he thought. Department store manager, Wendy, still dressed in her white silk pyjamas with the black pinstripe and red velvet, high-heeled slippers, retrieved the publications from the floor. One of the papers fell to the ground and happened to open up on a photo of Sporting Les Behans' wearing the stolen dresses under the heading 'LES BEHANS' ENJOY GIRLS' NIGHT OUT'. Wendy dropped the rest of the papers before bending down and snapping up the one with the team photo. She studied the picture closely and frowned. "What an absolute bastard," she said when she realised that Mick was one of the grinning men in the picture.

Detectives Lyons and Cartland sat po-faced across from Davey in the police interview room, a sense of déjà vu hanging in the air. Davey had his spindly legs stretched out fully in front of him with his hands resting behind his head.

"You look like a man who hasn't a care in the world?" Lyons prodded.

Davey gave a wry smile but remained tight lipped.

"We have you red-handed for the stolen Irish kit," Cartland said.

"Boyhood dream, was it?" said Lyons, teasing her suspect, "Playing for your country instead of that shitty excuse of a team." She turned to her colleague, "What are they called again?"

Davey casually chewed off a piece of his fingernail and spat it out onto the floor.

"Sporting Lesbians," answered Cartland with a dirty schoolboy smirk.

"Sporting Les Behans'," Davey said, correcting Cartland but not getting the least bit annoyed at the detective's mispronunciation. Afterall this was Davey's reason for jokingly choosing it in the first place.

Lyons shook her head. "You can imagine my surprise when I switched on the T.V. and there you were, in glorious Technicolor, wearing one of the stolen jerseys."

"I found it," Davey casually offered. He knew well that it was a brutal excuse but he couldn't care less.

"Yeah, right," interrupted Cartland.

"Anyway, I gave it to that nice Brazilian lad and he gifted me his shirt in return. And because I'm charitable by nature I then gave his jersey away to someone more deservin'. I'm led to believe it's now bein' auctioned for a good cause," Davey said, dismissing the male detective's remark, "So there's no harm done and everyone's a winner. Can I go home now?"

"Not just yet," said Lyons, smiling at the audacity of her suspect. She nodded to her colleague who in turn produced a clear evidence bag containing a cigarette butt.

"Do you know what this is?" she asked.

Davey carefully studied the exhibit. "A Johnny Blue, I'm guessing?" he eventually said, "Not that there's much left to go on."

"For the benefit of the tape we have just shown the accused an evidence bag containing a partially smoked cigarette butt," Lyons said aloud.

Cartland's inexperience in playing the game was beginning to show. He dragged his chair forward and rested both elbows on the table which in turn made his powerful arms look even bulkier. "We found it at the warehouse where the jerseys were taken from," he said in a raised voice, trying to push the suspect.

"And this is somethin' that should be of interest to me?" Davey asked.

"We had it tested and guess what – it has your DNA written all over it. Any ideas?" quizzed Lyons.

Davey stroked his chin slowly, a pensive look on his face. "Crows?" he finally suggested, "They're always pickin' things up and droppin' them again."

"What?" asked Lyons, more than a little baffled.

The suspect cocked his head to one side. "Ye know, crows. Black birds that fly but not the other type of blackbirds that also fly and they're definitely not the black birds who look fly, if ye catch me drift," Davey helpfully explained.

"You want to be very careful with your racial slurs or we could have you up for hate speech," Cartland threatened.

Davey pointed his finger at Cartland. "I think it's you, detective, who'd want to be mindin' wha' they say," he said, "Inferrin' that bein' black is somehow a negative in itself doesn't sound righ' to me."

"What?" said Cartland, not sure where the detainee was going with this.

"I've some great mates that are black and are very proud of the fact. And me teammate, Paddy, sure he's a double for the Black Pearl of Inchicore."

Neither Lyons nor Cartland were following Davey. "Ooh aah, Paul McGrath, I said ooh aah, Paul McGrath," he sang to his distinctly unimpressed audience. He smiled then said, "I've also got super friends that happen to be white. People come in different colours so get over yerself and stop pretendin' to be offended for everyone else on the planet."

"Stop wasting our time. We know you were there. We have proof!" Cartland shouted.

Davey was the epitome of calm. "There's a chance I was there of course or at least in the vicinity at some point in time," he said, "I'm a courier after all, I've been all over this town and back again."

"And the cigarette butt that we found on the roof?" demanded Cartland.

Davey caught a subtle change in Lyons' facial expression. He knew that she was going to roast her colleague later on for his amateur slip up in revealing precisely where the spent cigarette had been found.

"He's not the brightest star in the constellation, is he?" Davey teased, "I mean, that Hubble telescope would have a job pickin' him out." Lyons pretended to be less than amused but Davey knew he had hit a nerve and besides, he loved messing with their heads.

"I smoke," he said. "And maybe I flicked the butt away and who knows, and this is just an educated guess," he leaned forward. "For the benefit of the tape, like. A crow could have picked it up and flown onto the roof with it." He elaborately checked left then right, "I'm not into grassin' or anythin' like that but they're always hangin' around in bunches, actin' suspicious." He then sat back, smiled broadly, satisfied with his contribution in trying to help the guards solve a crime. Was this not what civic duty was all about then?

Lyons balled her two hands threateningly into fists. "I'll wipe that smug grin off your face."

"Murder!" Davey loudly exclaimed.

Both detectives gave a little jump much to Davey's delight.

"What are you on about?" Cartland asked, utterly exasperated.

"I'd like to set the record straight. I said bunches of crows, but I should have said a murder of crows. See I've been doin' a bit of readin' since the fishin' lesson," Davey said, giving Lyons a mischievous wink, reminding her of the recent visit to his house when she had corrected him about the natural habitat of pike.

Lyons had had enough of the little upstart. She suddenly rose to her feet knocking her chair backwards in the process onto the grubby, tiled floor with a crash. "Interview suspended," she barked.

"Ye can take it off now," said Trigger.

Jigsaw removed the blindfold and blinked his eyes a few times, trying to adjust to the dim light. He could just about make out that he was standing in a dry passageway where the walls on both sides were built up with sandbags and the ceiling was made out of what appeared to be lengths of timber logs. Trigger took the blindfold back from his teammate, stuffing it into his trouser pocket.

"It was in case ye were ever captured and interrogated," he explained.

"By who?" Jigsaw nervously asked, his eyes darting about.

Trigger looked serious. "On a need to know basis, buddy, but sure there's no need to worry about any of that now. And even if they tortured ye and killed ye, sure ye know fuck all and that's the best way to have it."

This did absolutely nothing to reassure his friend. "Wha' is this place?" asked Jigsaw, sniffing the earthy smell.

His teammate excitedly rubbed his hands together. "Come on an I'll show ye. It's bleedin' deadly even if I say so meself."

Trigger clipped a paper target onto a battery-operated line and pulley system before pressing a button and sending it off into the distance. He then went over to a large metal trunk and unlocked it revealing an assortment of weapons including a heavy, Soviet made machine gun. Jigsaw's eyes nearly fell out of his head. He immediately picked up the powerful automatic firearm with no small effort and threw a few shapes.

"How in the name of Jaysus did ye get yer hands on this bad boy?" the gangly striker asked.

"The PK?" said Trigger. Jigsaw had no idea what the gun was called but still nodded vigorously, resembling one of those toy dogs with the bobbly heads you saw in the back windows of cars.

"Another example of Mr. Kalashnikov's exemplary work," Trigger said, "And it was a lot easier to get hold of than ye'd imagine, my friend. Sure,

I'm only after bein' offered a helicopter gunship by me Russian contact but I had to turn it down, for practicalities sake."

Jigsaw nodded. "Know wha' ye mean. Sure, ye'd have to hire a pilot and find somewhere to stash it."

"Ah I wouldn't have been too worried about that end of things," Trigger said, "It'd be more like the local kids callin' around all hours of the nigh', lookin' for a spin around the block. Yer head'd be melted."

"Can I have a go?" Jigsaw asked, switching the attention back to the heavy machine gun, the thoughts of the helicopter having already departed the limited hangar space inside his skull. Images of a pumped-up Rambo, armed to the teeth, emerging from a blazing jungle came rushing through his mind instead.

"That's the whole point," said Trigger, taking the weapon back from Jigsaw and returning it to the strongbox, "but we need to take things a little slower first." He then took a slingshot from his jacket pocket and handed it carefully, with both hands, to his friend.

"A gat?" moaned Jigsaw. The last time he'd used a catapult he was in short pants and a bag of Taytos cost less than twenty pence.

"Baby steps, buddy, baby steps. This yoke could take yer eye out," Trigger warned.

Jigsaw was deflated but gave an obedient bow of the head.

"The bleedin' puss on ye," laughed Trigger. He then presented his pal with a gleaming six-shooter from his waistband instead, "Ye can start off with this."

Jigsaw's eyes lit up as if all of his birthdays and Crimbos had come at once.

With protective glasses pushed back on his head, Trigger pressed the button to retrieve the paper target. Jigsaw, also wearing protective glasses, stood next to his pal while still gripping the revolver tightly in his hand in anticipation. As the target neared, Jigsaw could clearly see that he had shot six bullets through the head of the paper man.

"Yer a natural, me aul flower," Trigger said, absolutely gobsmacked at how well his teammate had done.

Jigsaw looked puzzled. His mentor pointed to his ears to let him know that he still had his ear plugs in. Jigsaw, getting the message, gave a crooked smile before removing them.

"That was A one," Trigger said, affectionately slapping his teammate across the back.

Jigsaw reluctantly handed back the gun and said, "Thanks very much, that was some buzz."

"Yer more than welcome. Fran thought it migh' help if I did a bit of shootin' practice with ye. Seemed to think it'd give yer confidence a boost."

"Righ'," said Jigsaw even though he thought it sounded a bit strange, "So wha' about havin' a go of the machine gun?"

"Another day, I promise. I'll need to get me hands on some more ammo first."

The cell door was unceremoniously slammed shut in Davey's face. He banged on it several times with his tightly bunched fists just for the sake of making a racket as opposed to any real expectation of being released.

"I'm an innocent mon!" he shouted in a mock Northern Irish accent. He paused his histrionics, feeling that he was being watched and slowly turned around. Fran, Mick, Yoyo and Frank the Publican were all sitting on a bench, staring back at him.

"Love that film, In the Name of the Father," Davey said, giving the lads an embarrassed smile. "Why are youse all in here?"

Yoyo coughed. "I refused to share a chocolate fountain with other people," he admitted.

"Wha'?" asked Davey.

"I've been cuttin' back on the drugs the last coupla months, like the boss warned us to. And I was at me cousin Sandra's weddin' and they had this chocolate thing with marshmallows and strawberries and ye know yerself, the munchies just grabbed hold of me and I couldn't wait."

"There's nothin' illegal about that?" Davey said, puzzled.

Yoyo sucked in his lips. "There is when ye won't give it back and ye threaten to stab the groom in the heart with a skewer for interferin'."

"I give up," said Davey. He looked questioningly at Frank the Publican. "The whiskey?" he asked, fearing that the law had somehow found out about Baxter's nest egg and it had been seized.

Frank shook his head. "No, that's safely stashed away. An inspector from Sky called around to the pub and spotted the fake pint symbol. Apparently it's supposed to disappear during the ads," he revealed.

"That's fraud. Could be lookin' at five to ten, minimum," said Yoyo, sticking his oar in.

"No, he couldn't," Davey replied. He looked the bar owner in the eye, "Don't mind that gobshite. I'll sort it out." He glanced at Yoyo, "I liked ye better when ye were on the gear." He then turned back to Fran and raised an eyebrow.

"The law raided the safe house..." Fran began.

"Wha' the fuck? How'd they find out?" his pal asked.

Fran shrugged his shoulders having no idea that it was his in-laws who had landed him in it.

"That's gonna mess up yer custody battle, big time," Davey said.

"Yep. But what's worse is that there was some toe-rag in the back garden gettin' ready to take a pop at Richie and Laura sittin' righ' there beside him," said Fran.

"Ye mean with a shooter?" Davey asked, incredulously.

"Yep," answered Fran, barely believing it himself.

"The dirty rotten poxbottle. Any idea who it was?" his friend asked, unable to mask his fury.

"Reckon it was somethin' to do with the row Richie had in the nick but he wouldn't tell me."

"Where's he now?"

"Back in the 'Joy'."

Dave looked questioningly at Mick. "I'm half afraid to ask."

"Wendy..." Mick started to say but was interrupted by Yoyo.

"Who's she?" he asked.

"That's his new mot," Davey said, "Now will ye let the man finish."

"I'm not stoppin'..." said Yoyo.

"Will ye just shut the fuck up," swore Davey. He looked at the rest of his captive audience. "Has anyone got a Snickers for him."

Yoyo placed a hand across his mouth to show that he'd gotten the message.

Davey arched an eyebrow at Mick. "Wendy spotted a photo of us in the paper wearing the dresses from the team bonding night in Frank's pub," Mick explained.

"How'd our picture end up there?" asked Davey.

"Jigsaw. He had it on his Facebook page and some journalist copied it."

"And what's it got to do with yer bird in anyway? Don't tell me she's jealous?"

"Funny. You stole the dresses from her shop," Mick revealed.

"Shit. Sorry about that, bud." Davey meant well but everything he touched at the moment seemed to be going tits up. "Look, I'll get things sorted, I promise."

You'd have needed a chainsaw to cut the atmosphere in Mrs. Reilly's kitchen it was that thick. Fran's Ma was parked next to her low sized table, puffing hard on a cigarette while Fran stood with his back to the sink, apprehensively watching her every move.

"Wha' were ye thinkin' about, hidin' that waster of a brother of yers?" Mrs. Reilly finally said, exploding with anger towards her favourite son.

"Don't, Ma, please," Fran said, trying to keep a lid on things.

His mother forcefully stubbed her cigarette out in the packed ashtray, spilling other butts onto the table in the process. "All he's ever done is cause aggro. Every single bar of his father."

"He means well..."

"Means well, me arse. Look where it's got ye?" she shouted. "Yer gonna end up losin' that child." She gripped her thinning grey hair with both her hands and began to sob uncontrollably.

Fran dropped to his knees next to her and gently prised open her hands, taking them away from her head before she could do any real harm. His Ma looked so forlorn, so vulnerable, slumped in her wheelchair.

"I owe him," Fran said, trying his best to explain.

"Owe him? Have ye gone fuckin' simple!" she screamed, pushing her son back into a sitting position on the linoleum floor.

Fran slowly got to his feet, taking his time to gather his thoughts. He looked his mother directly in the eyes and was heartbroken at what he saw. He knew he had to tell her the truth no matter how much more pain it caused. It was the only chance he had of ever making things right. He took a deep breath before finally speaking. "I was the one who killed that drug pusher, Johnny Murphy," he finally admitted.

"Wha'?" said his mother, totally taken aback by the revelation.

"The one who was fightin' with him the nigh' he died, not Richie."

"Stop."

"The one who caused him to smack his head off the concrete footpath for wha' he done to my Vicky."

"Stop this, son," she pleaded. "It was Richie, he's the violent one. Sure, didn't he do the same thing to that poor man in England."

"D'ye really want to know wha' happened to our Richie over there?"

Mrs. Reilly took a cigarette from the packet, her hand shaking uncontrollably, "It was easy enough to work out..."

"He was only a kid and he tried to tell ye, but ye wouldn't listen."

His mother tried to light her cigarette but couldn't get the lighter to work. Instead she flung it across the room in frustration, smashing it against a wall.

"Ma?"

Mrs. Reilly waved her arm dismissively. "Get out," she ordered, not having the stomach to hear any more, "Get out!"

Fran hesitated for a moment then stormed out of the flat, nearly taking the hall door off its hinges.

It hadn't been easy for Mick to convince Wendy to let him into her apartment once he'd been released from the Garda station. But here he was, sitting on the edge of her couch, watching her pacing back and forth as she spoke into her mobile phone trying to explain to the police about the stolen dresses.

"Yes, I'm fully aware that I have wasted your time... As I've already explained, it was a simple misunderstanding... Once again, I forgot that it was part of the publicity stunt that we were running... Of course, I'll drop by tomorrow to sort things out..." She looked at her phone. The person at the other end of the line had abruptly hung up. She tossed the mobile onto the sideboard.

"Thanks, that means a lot to me," Mick said, grovelling.

Wendy noticed a strap-on dildo on top of the gleaming glass unit. She licked her lips and turned to her visitor. "You owe me, big time," she said.

Chapter 20

Although the press conference had been called in a hurry, the organisers wasted no time in getting everything ready. England captain, Johnny Carter, sat behind a long table flanked by his glamorous but tired looking wife on one side and his concerned club manager on the other. His agent was hovering somewhere in the background no doubt wondering how this would impact on the potential earnings of his prized commodity and in turn his own fifteen percent cut.

"I ain't gonna sit here and make excuses for what I've done," began Johnny in a practiced accent that didn't completely disguise his Cockney roots, "I know I've let an awful lot of people down." He smiled apologetically at his wife and she gently squeezed his hand in return. "I'm well aware that I should have come forward a lot sooner and prevented other people from being hurt too and that really bothers me."

Davey and Mick snaked their way through the packed pub up to the counter. Everyone in the boozer seemed to be watching Johnny Carter's press conference which was being televised live on the big screen.

"Thanks again for gettin' Wendy to drop the charges," Davey said to his teammate.

"Are you joking?" Mick said, "When she heard what you did with the dresses as part of a peace offering following on from our misunderstanding at your Mam's funeral you were back in her good books. And then when she found out about the stunt you pulled with the football jersey to raise money for sick children like Millie, you could literally do no wrong."

"Well, I hope it didn't cause ye too much hassle all the same."

"Let's just say that sometimes you just have to take one for the team," Mick said. He didn't elaborate any further on the subject despite the curious look from Davey, "What's the bid for the Brazilian's jersey up to now?" Mick asked.

"Sixty k plus change," replied Davey.

"Awesome," said Mick.

The amount had well exceeded Davey's expectations. He'd been hoping for about five grand if he was lucky, but the interest in owning the shirt had been truly staggering. And when Padjo heard about the good cause he'd gone on television promising to get the entire Brazilian team to sign it. After that things went absolutely bananas.

The two friends turned around and spotted Larry with Mo, now both parked in wheelchairs at their usual table with Gonzales pulled up next to them. Tommo, the patio man, was seated nearby, and he was also confined to a wheelchair as well as sporting a neck brace. He was in the company of a man who looked remarkably similar to the Assassin from the back.

"Gettin' more and more like Lourdes in here," quipped Davey.

Mick smiled. "Maybe there's an increase in the disability allowance coming down the pipeline and words gotten around."

"Cynic," Davey said, only half listening. He was more interested in Tommo and his familiar looking drinking companion.

The man who looked like the Assassin then turned around and he was indeed the one and only Al Caffrey. He immediately spotted Davey.

"Head the ball!" Al shouted, beckoning Davey over, "I want a word, quick smart."

"Shit," Davey cursed under his breath. It was at times like this that he wouldn't be too put out if a meteorite crashed into the boozer, albeit a very small one.

"I'll hang on here," Mick wisely said.

Davey pulled a face. "Thanks for the support, bud, I won't forget it in a hurry."

Mick blew him a kiss.

At the press conference, Johnny Carter was pouring his heart out. "I should have told someone a lot sooner but frankly I was ashamed." He bent his head down, ran two hands over the bristles that had sprouted from his usually closely shaven scalp and took a moment to gather his thoughts. He then looked back up, "Coming from the tough neighbourhood like the one I grew up in didn't make things any easier. I was sixteen, had a promising career ahead of me, the fam were so proud. I had the chance to change my life, all of our lives, forever."

Flashback...

A young Richie Reilly was lined up on the manicured surface of the training pitch with his fellow apprentices. Sixteen-year-olds with the world at their feet. They were being put through their paces by the coaching staff, dribbling balls around cones before shooting for goal against the apprentice keeper, a ruddy faced giant from Scotland. One of the lads tapped Richie on the shoulder. "See who's with the gaffer?" he said, indicating with his eyes towards the sideline.

Richie glanced over and saw the youth team manager having a friendly chat with the first team's Numero Uno, a heavy-set Spaniard who was like a walking advertisement for one of those 'cash for gold' joints.

"Looks like you're going to get your big break," Richie's teammate said, having absolutely no doubt who the first team coach had come to see. He was also genuinely pleased for his young teammate.

Richie received the ball and began his dribbling exercises, trying hard not to get too far ahead of himself and to concentrate on the task in hand.

"He's gifted and extremely determined, Mr. Garcia," praised Colin, the youth team manager, who knew talent when he saw it. He was a former professional footballer himself, forced to retire prematurely after twice doing his cruciate on the same knee.

"Excellente," said the Spaniard, "You think he has the cojones, it's good for me, no? Tell him to get his eh... how you say..."

"Kit," said Colin.

"Si, kit," thanked Mr. Garcia, "And come to first team."

The men shook hands before Mr. Garcia climbed into a luxurious motor that was polished to within an inch of its life and was whisked away by the smartly dressed chauffeur.

The youth team manager put two fingers in his mouth and whistled to get his apprentices' attention. All the lads stopped what they were doing and looked over.

"Richie, get your stuff!" Colin shouted.

Richie couldn't believe his luck as he raced into the youth academy's changing rooms to gather his gear. This was the dream. After years of being glued to the T.V. set, watching his idols play the beautiful game he was now going to get the opportunity to be a part of it all. To take on the best defences in the Premiership and with any luck beat them a few times too. He could just imagine the slagging back home if he got his face on the footie stickers that were all the rage. Then there was the latest FIFA video game that the kids would sell their granny's for. Rapid. He slowed down as he reached the tiled floor area of the dressing room not wanting to slip in his studded boots and ruin his career before it had even kicked off. It was a cardinal sin for players not to remove their boots when entering the building, but Richie's head was all over the shop with the excitement. He collected his kit bag, slung it over his shoulder and was just about to dash back out when he heard a young lad's voice.

"Please don't," begged the teenager.

Richie peeked around the corner into the adjoining shower area. He saw young Johnny Carter, naked, cowering in a corner with one of the football coaches, an extremely muscular man, standing menacingly over him. The coach's tracksuit bottoms were pulled down around his knees. Richie quietly edged back and sat down on the varnished timber bench that ran the entire length of the wall, his gear bag resting on his lap.

"Please don't," mimicked the coach from the adjoining area, "Little Johnny doesn't want to play ball."

Richie fiddled with the straps on his bag as he painfully listened to the goings on next door. His brain was telling him to get the hell out of there and to mind his own business but every other part of his entire being was screaming for him to intervene.

"Please," young Johnny repeated.

"I don't give a fuck what you want," threatened the coach.

Richie got to his feet, taking several agonising steps towards the exit as if he was wading through wet concrete but was unable to go any further. He returned to the bench and sat back down again. He looked up at the ceiling and closed his eyes hoping for divine intervention. Nothing was forthcoming so he reluctantly decided to take control of his own destiny. He dumped his bag on the ground and marched into the shower area. Both the coach and young Johnny looked his way, completely taken by surprise. No one uttered a word for what felt like an eternity.

"Walk away if you ever want to make it in this game, sonny, and forget whatever you think you've seen," the coach warned after recovering from the initial shock of the unannounced guest.

Richie ignored the threat and turned to Johnny instead. "Get dressed," he said kindly.

Johnny didn't move at first, but Richie nodded reassuringly. The terrified lad scrambled to his feet and rushed past his saviour into the changing room and began to hurriedly dress without drying himself first. The coach casually pulled back up his tracksuit bottoms and tied the strings at the waist.

"So what, you're going to report me?" the coach asked.

Richie remained silent.

"If I hear so much as a murmur about this, I'll tell them that I caught the pair of you in here, thieving. The thick Paddy and the light-fingered Cockney, what a perfect double act." The coach moved towards Richie. "Who do you think they're going to believe? In the meantime, you'll both be asked to leave the club while it pretends to investigate. Word will get around, you can be sure of that, and there won't be another academy the length and breadth of this country that'll touch either of you with a ten-foot barge pole."

"I'm not goin' to report ye," Richie calmly answered.

"There's a good lad. I knew you'd see sense," the smug coach said, resting his sweaty hand on Richie's shoulder. "And who knows, maybe we can become the best of friends too."

Richie glared the molester in the eye. "Take yer fuckin' hand off me."

Although scared, he felt an inner strength like he'd never sensed before pulsing through his veins.

The coach removed his limp hand and retreated a few steps. He smirked at the young apprentice. "Think of yourself as a bit of a hard man, do you, sonny? I'll give you one last chance to turn around and walk away," he said.

Richie glanced over at young Johnny who was now fully dressed, shivering next to the shower area entrance. Richie gave him a wink, letting him know that everything was going to be all right.

It was early evening in the prison, and all was quiet. Mr. Quinn sauntered towards one of his henchmen and discreetly handed him a crudely made shiv. The makeshift weapon had been constructed in the woodwork room out of a brush handle and a piece of metal piping scavenged from a radiator. Quinn's associate hid the blade under his shirt careful not to slice himself in the process. Both men paused, looking down from their gangway vantage point on the second-floor landing. The other inmates were glued to the flat screen television that was firmly bolted to the wall and protected by unbreakable Perspex. The lone exception was Richie who was sitting at a table rigidly fixed to the floor. He shuffled a deck of cards, playing solitaire, content in his own company. Mr. Quinn grabbed his partner in crime's arm, holding it in a vice-like grip.

"Do this for me and I'll look after ye when ye get out, make sure there's a hefty wedge waitin'," he promised.

The inmate gave a determined nod.

Back in the pub, Davey trudged over to where the Assassin was seated next to the wheelchair-bound Tommo.

"Take a pew," the Assassin ordered, pulling out a stool for Davey.

The player did as he was told.

"I know there's no need for me to be doin' any sort of introductions," Al said.

"Tommo," said Davey, acknowledging the patio man's presence.

"Davey," Tommo hesitantly replied.

"Like a bleedin' funeral around here. I mean it's not as if anyone died, am I righ'?" joked the Assassin, giving Tommo a playful clatter across the back of the head, "Well, not yet in anyway." Tommo winced with the pain of the friendly slap. "Although things could have worked out a lot differently when certain people tried to wrong me aul Ma," the Assassin said, eyeballing Tommo.

"I can explain, Al. It wasn't Tommo's fault," Davey confessed, not wanting the poor sham in the wheelchair to get into more trouble.

"There's no need, buddy. These things happen," Al said. "And I know it was nothin' personal, but I appreciate yer honesty all the same. Ye can't buy that sort of respect nowadays." He raised his shovel sized hand, catching Frank the Publican's attention, "Same again and wha'ever Davey's havin'," he called out.

Frank nodded.

"Yer alrigh', Al, I'll get these," said Davey.

The Assassin stood up, took a crispy fifty euro note from his pocket and planted it down on the table. "Don't be silly, we're celebratin'. Goin' to the jacks, be back in a minute." He then headed for the toilets.

Davey looked at Tommo questioningly, receiving a nervous smile in return. "The bloke tried to kill ye and yet here ye are, garglin' with him. Wha' am I missin'?" asked Davey.

Tommo leaned awkwardly forward in his wheelchair, his movements severely restricted by the 'accident' and pointed an accusing finger at Davey. "None of this would have happened if ye hadn't tampered with me measurin' tape in the first place. Me bleedin' nerves are gone."

"Yer a big boy, Tommo. Ye knew wha' ye were gettin' into so stop the whingin'," Davey said. "And anyway, how the fuck was I supposed to know ye'd be measurin' up his Ma's patio?" He gave a swift check towards the loo to make sure that the Assassin wasn't coming. "So wha' happened?"

Tommo took a sip of his drink through his straw. "I got outta the nutjob's gaff as quick as I could, but I was still tied up with the feckin' measurin' tape. And when I looked over me shoulder, I could see him comin' after me, swingin' a hatchet. A fuckin' hatchet for Christ's sake! And in this day and age. Like he's Geronimo him bleedin' self, runnin' riot around the reservation." He took another badly needed suck from his pint. "That was when I fell out in front of the oncomin' van and got smacked," he revealed.

"Ouch," said Davey.

"Tell me about it. I'll be wearin' this collar for the next two months at least. I remember lyin' there, lookin' up at this madman with the hatchet and him starin' back at me with these murderous eyes. D'ye know wha' he said to me?"

Davey motioned with his hands for Tommo to carry on.

"He said, matter of fact like, 'that's gotta hurt.' The driver who'd knocked me down sat frozen inside his van, hands welded to the steerin' wheel. I panicked and told Al I was sorry, and that Davey Byrne had made me do it."

"Ye hangin' little pox," swore Davey, tempted to give the bloke a few slaps.

"I know, I know! I'm sorry. I was in shock," Tommo said by way of a defence.

Davey took a few deep breaths, exhaling slowly each time, the way he'd been shown at the alcoholic anonymous meetings, giving him the chance to take a step back from the abyss. "Okay, I'll give ye the benefit of the doubt, this time. So wha' happened then?"

"Al asked me was it his Davey Byrne, the one who played for Sporting Les Behans'? I said yeah and his face changed in a flash, he became kinda, I don't know, friendly. Talk about Jekyll and Hyde. And that's when it all kicked off. He ran over to the van driver, who coincidentally happened to be me business competitor, the one I was tellin' ye about, in the pub that day?"

Davey nodded and said, "The one who was undercuttin' ye, I get it."

"Precisely. I mean, wha' were the chances of that happenin'? So Al grabs yer man by the throat and was tryin' to pull him out through the van window. He was roarin' and shoutin' at him and even though I was in agony I can clearly remember exactly wha' he said." Tommo put on his best impression of the Assassin, "Wha' are ye playin' at, ye bleedin' psycho! Swervin' like a lunatic, ye could have killed that poor chap. When he sues ye, and he is goin' to sue ye, I'm goin' to be a witness. Nutcase like you should be banned from drivin' for life."

Davey could vividly imagine the scene as if he'd been there himself.

The patio man returned to his normal accent. "I don't know wha' happened after that. I blacked out but I heard they had to get a second ambulance for yer man after Al was finished with him."

The Assassin returned from the toilet, full of the joys of spring. He rubbed his monstrous, coarse hands briskly together. Davey imagined that the man could make fire if he did it a bit quicker but didn't have the courage to mention this.

"Did he tell ye that we're gonna sue yer man?" Al said.

"He did indeed," Davey replied.

"There's already an offer on the table. And don't ye worry, bud, yer gonna get yer fair share. Ten percent alrigh'?" Al said.

There was no need to answer. Ten percent was a whole lot better than the hiding Davey imagined he was in for five minutes earlier.

The prison warders and the inmates were transfixed by Johnny Carter's revelations on the T.V. While the drama continued to unfold, Richie kept himself busy playing his card game.

"Like a coward I never spoke up for the lad who saved me from being, you know, even though his future was at stake. He on the other hand never revealed why he hammered that..." continued Johnny.

Richie glanced up at the telly.

Davey, having returned from his interrogation with Al, stood at the pub counter next to Mick. They watched Johnny's press conference on the big screen in silence along with the rest of the mesmerised customers. You could hear a pin drop.

"...hammered that animal," explained Johnny live on screen, "I'd like to take this opportunity to thank the lad for sacrificing his own career for my sake. I'm ashamed to say that I didn't speak up in his defence and that I never made any attempt to contact him after he was thrown out of the club. I have no idea where he is now but if anyone can help, I'd love to get in touch to finally apologise and to try and make amends."

A reporter jumped to his feet. "Johnny! Johnny!" he called out above the rest of his boisterous colleagues, "What was the lad's name?"

The prison inmate, who was armed with the sharpened implement, edged closer to Richie who was oblivious to the impending threat on his life.

"He was a young Irish chap, from Dublin," answered Johnny on the prison T.V.

The tooled-up inmate hesitated. He looked up at Mr. Quinn who was nodding vigorously, urging his associate to stick the target.

"His name was... Richie, Richie Reilly," Johnny revealed.

The astonished warders and inmates alike all turned to where the unassuming hero was sitting, still playing solitaire. The armed inmate lunged towards him with the jagged blade.

"Watch out!" shouted one of the prisoners.

Mrs. Reilly was at home watching the England captain's press conference on her television, a present from Davey, and one of many electrical gifts he had given to her over the years. She was numb with shock. In another part of the city, Tracey and Fran were sat on his couch also looking at the broadcast. Not a single word was exchanged. Tears of relief trickled down Fran's face as the truth was finally coming out. Tracey gently wiped the tears away with her fingers then tenderly kissed his cheek.

Frank the Publican's bar was filled with noisy, animated chatter from punters gobsmacked at Johnny Carter's revelations. Frank shuffled along the counter to where Davey and Mick were standing. "Did you two know?" he asked.

The lads shook their heads, both genuinely stunned. They knew their pal Fran could keep a secret having sought his advice on a number of sensitive issues over the years, but this was an unbelievable burden for anyone to have had to carry for all this time.

Extra prison warders hurriedly arrived at the scene of the stabbing, helping their colleagues to hold back the angry mob. They'd trained hard for scenarios similar to this one, but it didn't necessarily make things any easier when the real thing happened. The attacker lay across Richie's chest with both men lying motionless on the ground. Oceans of bright red blood oozed out from between the two men, spreading across the floor. One of the warders glanced up at Mr. Quinn who was still watching the proceedings from the safety of the landing. The gang boss wore a wide grin much to the disgust of the screw. One of the senior officers pulled the attacker off of Richie almost slipping on the blood. The place had become eerily silent all of a sudden. Some of the inmates turned away, not having the stomach for such an appalling sight. Richie's eyes suddenly shot open. He sat bolt upright, frantically feeling his chest with both hands for wounds but found none.

"The blood's not mine," he eventually managed to say. He then turned and looked to where his attacker lay. The thug was lifeless with the crudely made shiv firmly lodged in his heart. The senior warder extended his hand to Richie, helping him to his feet.

"Karma, lad, Karma," the officer said.

Chapter 21

Mrs. Reilly rolled up to Mrs. Flynn's house in her wheelchair, parking at an angle which allowed her to bang on the white aluminium door with the side of her fist. Laura's cries could be heard coming from within, sounds which Mrs. Reilly found very upsetting. The door was eventually opened by Tina Flynn who just stood there with her arms folded, chewing gum, looking down on the disabled caller.

"Yeah?" she barely managed to grunt.

Mrs. Reilly tried to look past her, but Tina partially closed the door blocking her view.

"Yer mother in?" Mrs. Reilly asked, all business-like, doing her best to conceal her true emotions.

A pink bubble ballooned from Tina's mouth, growing to almost the size of her face before eventually bursting. She then shut the door without saying another word. A full two minutes had passed when Mrs. Flynn finally appeared.

"Is that our Laura cryin'?" Mrs. Reilly asked, "She's makin' strange."

"She wouldn't be if we'd gotten the chance to see her more often now, would she?" Mrs. Flynn retorted, "Anyway, she'll have plenty of time to get used to us now we've won the custody battle." She had no intention of being dictated to by this woman or any other woman for that matter, and most definitely not on her own doorstep.

"I'm not here to beg, missus, but wha' yer doin' is very wrong. Takin' a child away from her father isn't righ'," said Mrs. Reilly, fighting her own corner.

Mrs. Flynn pointed her finger at her adversary. "Don't preach to me about righ' and wrong. That young child in there wouldn't stand a chance if she was left with a loser son like yers."

Fran's mother tried her best not to rise to the bait. "Ye know in yer heart he loves that little girl and would do anythin' for her," she said, defending her son.

"Like he did for my Vicky?"

"That's not fair."

"Fair? If he'd only gone outside with her that nigh' like I'd asked him to she'd still be here today."

"Yer daughter didn't want him to, ye know that."

Mrs. Flynn was having none of it. "She was vulnerable and he knew that."

"My son did the next best thing though," Mrs. Reilly said, "Stopped Murphy from killin' someone else's child."

Mrs. Flynn looked confused.

"Yeah, it was Fran who killed that drug-pusher," Mrs. Reilly revealed.

"Are ye finished?" the other woman asked, trying her best to hide her shock.

"Not by a long shot. I'll get that child back if it's the last thing I do," Mrs. Reilly promised.

Mrs. Flynn had suddenly lost her appetite for the argument and eased the door shut without uttering another word.

Not long after Fran's mother had left, Mrs. Flynn went into her bedroom and began searching through the drawers of her dresser, discarding trivial bits and bobs onto the floor until she found the photo she was looking for. She sat down on the edge of the bed, sinking into its softness and examined the picture. Richie was kneeling on a blue and white chequered picnic blanket holding Laura above his head in his strong, outstretched arms with Vicky cuddling into him. A sand dune sprouting prickly Marram grass made up the background. Vicky was pulling a funny face. They looked so happy, so young. Mrs. Flynn couldn't remember where the photo had been taken, probably Dollymount, but it looked like a glorious day wherever it was. She kissed her finger and placed it gently onto her late daughter's face before breaking down, her shoulders jerking uncontrollably.

After Johnny Carter's recent revelations on television Mrs. Reilly had decided to take the plunge and visit Richie in prison, a place she'd never before set foot in and had always swore she never would. She was more than a little nervous as she recalled her appalling attitude towards her son over the last number of years. Richie however wasn't the kind of lad who held grudges so his mother had nothing to worry about. They sat across from one another in the visiting area not yet sure what to say or where to begin. Further along the rows of other inmates and their guests were Mr. Quinn and his delinquent nephew, Scully. The young thug was wearing a baseball cap and sunglasses attempting to hide the injuries which Fran had inflicted upon him with the saucepan.

"I saw that English chap's interview the other nigh'," said Mrs. Reilly, tears welling up in her bloodshot eyes.

"Don't, Ma. That was a long time ago," Richie replied.

"Fran told me ye took the blame for killin' that animal, Murphy. I'm so sorry I never gave ye a chance," she said, almost choking on her words.

As Richie reached across and took hold of his mother's hands, he happened to glance sideways and spotted Quinn staring back at him. The gang boss ran a finger slowly across his throat. Richie ignored the threat and turned back to his Ma.

"It's grand, sure ye weren't to know," he said, consoling her.

Mrs. Reilly retrieved a tissue from her handbag and dabbed the corners of her eyes.

"For ye to take the blame so Fran would have a chance of keepin' his child was a beautiful thing to do, son."

"He'd have done the same for me," Richie said, brushing away the compliment.

Mrs. Reilly leaned forward all of a sudden. "The radio said that someone had been stabbed to death in here and I was sure it was you..."

"Yer not to be worryin' about me. That was in another part of the nick, where they keep all the head cases," he lied. "It's like a bleedin' creche where I am."

Scully was all jittery as he gave his uncle the run down on how things were going on the outside.

"Stevo's not up to the job," he repeatedly told his uncle.

"Relax, the walls have ears," warned Mr. Quinn.

Scully looked around, his eyes darting everywhere.

"Ye'd want to cut back on wha'ever shit yer stickin' into yer veins or shovin' up yer snout," the older man advised.

"Strictly recreational, no need to worry about me," his nephew insisted but try as he might he wasn't fooling anyone, least of all his uncle.

"I promised yer Ma before she died..."

"I know, I know," Scully said, "But that fucker Stevo left me stranded, I could've got caught."

Quinn gave a barely discernable nod. "Forget about it, its bein' dealt with."

Scully's eyes widened. "I want to do it," he eagerly volunteered.

"No, yer way too valuable, can't risk that," the gang boss lied.

Quinn knew and had known for a long time that his nephew was a liability. He would have to deal with him sooner rather than later, and permanently. Although it pained him because he was family, business was business and the young fella had gotten more than his fair share of breaks.

"By the way, there's nothin' to link ye to that house, is there?" the older man asked. He couldn't care less if his nephew got lifted but he knew that the junkie wouldn't be able to do his porridge and would sing like a canary.

Scully scratched his head, replaying the events from his jumbled memory. He remembered getting walloped and dropping the gun and having to leggit but not a lot else. "No," he finally answered.

"Tell me ye wore gloves?" his uncle said.

"Yeah, of course," Scully replied, less than convincingly.

Mr. Quinn cracked his knuckles and recalled a saying that his aul fella used to repeatedly say to him in between dishing out beatings with his favourite leather belt. 'Never send a boy to do a man's job.'

Christ looked down from the cross at Jacko and Fr. O'Brien who were deep in conversation at the base of the steps leading up to the impressive marble altar.

"I can't believe they've arrested Davey. Have they no comprehension of the amount of good work he's doing for the community?" asked the priest, still in shock.

"Ye know yerself, Father, once ye get a bad name," Jacko said.

Father O'Brien nodded his agreement only too aware of what the young man next to him was alluding to. He'd been a man of the cloth for over five decades now and had seen the enormous changes in people's attitudes towards the Catholic Church. While he was saddened by this he also fully understood the anger which they felt. The truth was that he was sickened to the core himself by the vile acts that people who were supposedly Christian and responsible for spreading the good word of our Lord had committed. And then for the hierarchy to cover the whole thing up was irreprehensible. He had given considerable thought to leaving the priesthood but that was the easy way out. There were good people in this world and if he could help even one of them, he would. That was his calling.

"Davey reminds me in a way of Dismas," the priest thought aloud.

"Is he from Cabra?" Jacko asked, slightly confused.

Fr. O'Brien laughed kindly. "No, my son. Dismas was the penitent thief."

Jacko looked blankly at the priest.

"You know, the good thief on the cross next to our Lord when he was crucified," Fr. O'Brien helpfully explained. "He repented of course and was later made a saint."

Jacko looked at the doddery old priest as if he was soft in the head. "Eh, righ', wha'ever yer into yerself, Father. Ye have to make sure that Detective Lyons gets this." He handed over a DVD, "Should help to get Davey off." He paused momentarily before adding, "I don't mean that kinda get him off. It's not that sort of video." He then leaned in closer to Father O'Brien, "But I can get me hands on them as well, if the mood ever takes ye."

The priest stood there not quite sure what the young chap was on about but he was determined to help poor Davey none the less.

Father O'Brien stormed into the police station waving the DVD around like a bible wielding evangelist, demanding to see detective Lyons. The

Garda behind the reception desk remained pan-faced as he listened to the elderly man's rant before picking up the phone and calling the duty officer. Moments later, a harried looking detective Lyons came rushing along the corridor with the duty officer doing his best to keep up.

"Sorry, Ma'am," the uniformed officer apologised, "But the priest insisted on handing the DVD to you in person. He was going on about sinister forces at play and that he wasn't prepared to sit idly by and let another innocent man be crucified."

Lyons stopped dead in her tracks and stared at her subordinate.

"His exact words, Ma'am," explained the officer.

Lyons and Cartland were in the video viewing room watching footage from the disc which Fr. O'Brien had handed over. The priest had also given Lyons a stern talking to into the bargain about the latest miscarriage of justice. The quality of the picture from the DVD was surprisingly good and the detectives could clearly see themselves romping in the underground car park. Neither of them in all their lustful excitement had thought about the security CCTV. They exchanged worried looks but no words were needed.

Detective Lyons was all smiles as she sat next to her anxious colleague opposite Davey in the interview room. The suspect noted that neither detective was in a rush to start recording the session. He would see what they were up to before screaming blue murder if and when it became necessary.

"I wouldn't have had you down as the religious type but that Fr. O'Brien holds you in some regard," Lyons gently probed.

"A nice man," was all Davey offered by way of a reply. He didn't trust the wagon's change in tactics and reminded himself that he needed to be on his A game here.

Cartland coughed.

"Look, we'll cut to the chase," Lyons said, "I don't know how the priest got hold of the security footage in question…"

"Wha' are ye bleedin' on about now?" asked Davey, presuming that he was about to be stitched up for something he had absolutely nothing to do with, on this occasion anyhow.

Lyons shifted in her chair causing its metal legs to make a muted screech. "Let's not play games here. I need you to give me a guarantee that there are no other copies and I'll make sure that all of the charges are dropped," she promised.

Davey stretched his arms high into the air and rotated his head, buying time while trying to figure things out. He surmised that Jacko was involved somehow but couldn't quite work out the connection between him and the priest and why Lyons was so worried about a CCTV tape. After almost a minute of silent contemplation that felt more like an hour to the anxious detectives, Davey was ready to talk. "I'll need to make a call," he politely requested.

Davey held his mobile close to his ear while making sure that no one else in the vicinity was able hear. "Nice one, Jacko," he whispered, barely able to contain his delight. "Of course we're quits for the furniture mix up... Yeah, I'll let ye know how I get on." He hit the cancel button and closed his hands together, praying style. "Thanks, God," he mimed, "I owe ye one."

Lyons silently read through Davey's list of demands from the sheet of paper he had just handed to her. Cartland looked on nervously, fearing for the future of his career after working so damned hard to get this far.

"This is a serious list of requests," said Lyons, playing hardball.

"It's a serious situation," Davey countered.

"I'll see what I can do but I'm not making any promises," said Lyons, not wishing to appear to be rolling over too easily.

Davey arched his eyebrows.

"Okay, it's a deal," Lyons said, feeling like she'd just done business with the devil himself.

"There's one last situation which needs sortin'," said Davey, chancing his arm.

"And that is?" Lyons said, exasperated.

"Sky Sports' stickers," said Davey.

Chapter 22

Sporting Les Behans' passed the ball around smartly as they trained hard. The pressure of the upcoming semi-final in the forefront of their minds. They were being closely watched by the gang of kids who were piled on top of the truck container which now had a bevy of scantily clad women painted on its side. Derek and some of the older boys were sitting on an old couch that they had just about managed to haul up. Apart from having the odd bent spring lurking just beneath the covering where the stuffing had worn thin, the couch was relatively comfortable to sit on for the few fortunate enough to have bagged a place.

"We love ye Les Behans', we do. We love ye Les Behans', we do. We love ye Les Behans', we do. Oh, Les Behans', we love you," the kids sang in surprisingly harmonious voices.

The Assassin was gone on the missing list with none of his teammates having even an inkling as to his whereabouts. It wasn't like him to be a no-show, his dedication to the cause was unquestionable, almost leading him to commit manslaughter in a couple of games. Baxter had rang him several times but to no avail and it was troubling him. A buxom woman, plastered with enough layers of make-up to give her a better chance of withstanding a nuclear fallout than a cockroach, made a beeline for the manager. She was dragging two small boys behind her by their grubby little hands.

"Ah Mandy, how are you?" Baxter cautiously greeted, reminding himself that this woman was high on his bunny boiler list.

"Been better. Seen yer picture in the newspaper," Mandy said.

Baxter gave her his best lady killing smile but was failing miserably.

"Never had ye down as a cross-dresser," she said, going straight for the jugular.

Baxter's smile immediately vanished. "That was just for a laugh," he said, defending his manly reputation.

Mandy dismissed him with a wave of her hand. "Wha'ever ye do in the company of other men is none of my business."

Baxter exhaled loadly thorough his nostrils. "How did you know where to find me?" he asked.

"Facebook. One of yer players, Ludo or Snakes and fuckin' Ladders, set up a team page, has all yer info on it."

"His name's Jigsaw," Baxter said, absentmindedly.

"A sap's name anyway," Mandy replied.

The manager ignored her caustic remark. He bent down to the two boys. "Hello there, eh..." he stammered, his mind drawing a complete blank.

"Jack," Mandy intervened.

"Jack, of course," said Baxter, giving the young boy his warmest smile. He turned to the other lad, "And you must be..."

"Somebody fuckin' else's," Mandy said, bitch written all over her caked face.

The manager straightened back up. "Right. Well fair play for bringing them along to support the team."

"Snap out of it," the single mother said, clicking her fingers into Baxter's face, "I couldn't give a shite about yer dopey football team. I'm only here for the maintenance."

A ball rolled towards Jack and he instinctively kicked it back onto the field with surprising accuracy.

Mandy reefed him roughly by his scrawny arm. "Ye little poxbottle, ye'll wreck them fuckin' runners," she screamed.

Baxter looked around, not only embarrassed for himself but also for the two boys. "Calm down, love," he pleaded, "Sure all the young lads are mad to play ball, it's only natural."

Mandy pointed a finger at the manager, her face twisting in anger. "When ye start contributin' to his upkeep ye can have a say in how I do things, until then butt the fuck out."

"What about the Mickey mon...," Baxter began then quickly corrected himself, "...the children's allowance? That must cover the boy's costs?"

"Get a life, will ye. That's barely enough for me nigh' out with the girls, stop me from goin' stir crazy, cooped up in the gaff all the time with the snotty nosed little bastards."

Baxter gave a sad smile. The poor kids didn't stand a chance. He dug deep into his trouser pocket and retrieved a wad of crisp twenty euro notes which Mandy grabbed from his hand without so much as a thank you.

The minute Mandy had cleared off, dragging her two sons after her, the manager beckoned Jigsaw over. The tall striker was all smiles as he galloped giraffe-like over to the boss. The smiley head soon disappeared when Baxter kicked him in the shin.

"What's that for?" Jigsaw complained, rubbing his leg.

"Get me off that Bookface on the computers or I'll be proper skint."

The team was working on a few set pieces including corner kicks. Mick jumped up to head the ball from a cross that was whipped in by Fran but lost the flight, missing it completely and falling to the ground in a heap.

"Ye big girl's blouse," joked Charlie.

Mick picked himself up and glared at his teammate.

"I didn't mean anythin' by it," Charlie quickly apologised.

Mick smirked.

"Ye little bollox, ye had me," laughed his relieved teammate.

Davey ran by, prancing about like some deranged ballerina. "He's had me too," he said, gaily.

At the end of the pitch where the lads parked their cars Jigsaw was chatting to a reporter who'd been sniffing around at some of their most recent training sessions. The team had already received interest from the local publications but as word spread about their unprecedented cup run and peculiar team name, some of the bigger newspapers began to take a small bit of notice too.

"And tell me, has the manager got you doing anything special?" quizzed the reporter.

"Like wha'?" asked Jigsaw.

"You know, training, dieting?" the hack encouraged.

Jigsaw scratched his head, pondering the question. "Bananas," he finally replied.

"Bananas?" asked the eager reporter, sensing a headline.

"Yeah. The boss says to get them into us, says they're perfect for hittin' the spot and fillin' a gap," Jigsaw helpfully explained.

Bingo! The reporter grinned as he scribbled down his notes in his own unique shorthand.

"That's grand, thanks. I better head, deadlines and all that nonsense," he said, tapping his hardback notebook. He normally used the tape-recorder on his phone but some fecker had dipped him the previous day on the Luas, forcing him to revert back to pen and paper, "And there's a lot of great material to be getting on with." He started to walk away.

"Remember," Jigsaw called out after him, "It's Jigsaw with a J, not a G."

The reporter flashed a weasel-like smile, gave the player the thumbs up and rushed off.

Davey retrieved a stray ball that had landed close to his gangly teammate. "Who's yer man?" he asked.

"Only a lad from the newspaper, was mad interested in the team. Seems like a genuine enough bloke, promised to give us a decent write up," Jigsaw naively answered.

Training continued in earnest until the roar of a powerful engine coupled with a car horn continuously being held down broke the peace. Mick's legs almost collapsed underneath him when he realised that it was his Porsche 911 and that the Assassin was the one driving it. The car did an elaborate handbrake turn, skidding to a halt next to the pitch. Al cut the engine and jumped out, all smiles.

"Wha' were the fuckin' chances, I ask ye," he said.

Fran knew that something was up when he glanced over at Mick and saw his pal's ashen face.

"Will ye get over here," the Assassin ordered, "and check out yer man in the boot."

Although Mick's feet felt like lead weights, he still found himself inexplicably moving towards the rear of the car.

"There I was, stopped at the traffic lights at the Whitehall junction when some sham pulls up in the lane next to me drivin' yer car," Al explained.

The other players were more than a little curious but were slow to encroach at first. Mick tried to brace himself for whatever he was going to see inside the trunk, hoping that whoever was in there was still alive at the very least.

"Ready?" said the Assassin.

Mick gave a reluctant nod. Al popped the boot revealing the mechanic who was gagged and bound. Apart from having a nasty bump on the side of his face he appeared to be otherwise intact. The rest of the team edged steadily closer.

"Now, ye migh've noticed that I haven't bothered to hide me identity," Al told his hostage as he began to deliver another one of his infamous sermons, "The reason for that is very simple, if I decide to let ye live that is." He had no intention of killing anyone for stealing a car of course, he wasn't that mad. But he had found from past experiences that if you convinced people that there was a good possibility that they were going to be murdered they would gladly settle for whatever deal was on offer. "There is nobody and I would like to emphasise the word nobody that I am afraid of. If ye try to identify me or him," he said, pointing at Mick then noticed that Baxter and the entire team were also in close proximity, "Or anyone of these fine gentlemen, I'm not only goin' to kill ye but I'm also goin' to slowly torture every single member of yer family. Now, have I made myself clear?"

The mechanic nodded vigorously as he glanced at the sixteen or so pairs of eyes which were staring down at him. Mick had to hold onto the car for support, afraid he'd topple over. Bile rose up from inside his gut and he was doing his utmost not to vomit.

"Isn't that..." Fran started to say before getting a sly kick from Davey followed by a quick shake of the head.

The Assassin turned to Fran, "You were sayin'?"

"Eh, isn't that the most pitiful sight ye've ever seen," Fran said, not fully sure what was going on.

"Got that righ', pal," the Assassin agreed. He switched his focus back to his prisoner. "Ye took somethin' that wasn't yers and unfortunately there are consequences."

Mick managed to gather himself. "I'd like to take care of this myself, if that's okay with you, Al?"

His teammate was suitably impressed. "I didn't think our college boy had it in him."

Mick made what he hoped was a convincing smile.

"Last chance for me to inflict the mother of all pain on him?" Al offered.

"I can handle this, thanks," said Mick.

After being freed, the terrified mechanic promised to not only store Mick's precious motor safely and for nothing but to also provide him with a better car than the banger he had first leant him. He also swore that he would never speak about the incident to another living soul for as long as he lived and had pleaded with Mick to make sure he was quits with the Assassin. Mick assured him that he would get it all squared away and to count his blessings that things hadn't ended up taking a turn for the worse. The incident demonstrated to Mick just how messed up things had become. Fran and Davey had discreetly cornered their pal, demanding answers after recognising the mechanic tied up in the boot leaving Mick no choice but to invite them around to his bedsit to confess.

To say the lads were stunned by Mick's revelations was an understatement. Davey couldn't get his head around the fact that his friend was pulling his plum and doing other peculiar things on a webcam and that people would then pay money for it. Mick explained that his customers were mostly rich, older, straight men who were curious or secretly gay and that 'Camming' was a safe way for them to get their kicks. Fran had questioned the legality of the whole setup but Mick had assured him that it was all above board. He further explained that he got sent presents by some of his clients or his 'friends' as he'd learned to call them, by having a wish list provided by one of the biggest online retailers where they could pick things to buy him, paid through tokens that were then changed into cash.

"There's some weirdo's out there," Davey had said, still having trouble getting his head around the whole thing.

Mick revealed that he didn't always have to take his clothes off, that some of his 'friends' just wanted to talk about how his day went, etc. He told the lads that he often just gave advice about their teenage sons or chatted away to others who were lonely. Mick had equated himself to the hot bartender in a club where you could look and flirt but couldn't touch. Some people, he found, couldn't handle real-life relationships preferring internet ones instead.

After the initial shock of Mick's misadventures, Fran and Davey had then become angry. They were absolutely furious that their pal hadn't come to them for help and were close to giving him a few slaps for good measure if the truth be told. Intervention, Irish style! Fran had ordered Mick to get out of the dingy bedsit straight away and to move in with him as there was plenty of room in his gaff. Mick declined the generous offer for the time being but was grateful all the same. Then Davey had a go off of his friend for not telling him about his financial difficulties. He said he'd have five grand for him by lunchtime the following day and that he wasn't in any rush to have it repaid. Mick at first declined the offer but Davey was persuasive. The loan, Mick told his friend, would at least give him some breathing space until he knew what he was going to do next. Davey had told Mick that there was also plenty of room in his house since his Ma had passed away especially if he didn't want to be listening to Fran's young wan crying all night. All three men laughed. Mick had made them promise not to tell the rest of the team about his unusual job and he knew he had nothing to worry about on that front.

Semi-Final: Sporting Les Behans' v Dundalk Dynamos

Moments before the semi-final was due to kick-off Baxter joined his players in a circle on the pitch. They were all linked together with their arms around the adjoining man's shoulders, facing one another. Davey was stood in the centre with his head slightly bowed. He made an elaborate gesture of blessing himself.

"In the name of the Father, the Son and the Holy Spirit," he said.

"D'ye not think yer takin' this religion thing a bit too far?" Podge said, laughing.

Baxter gave the sub-keeper a swift jab in the stomach.

"Fuck. Wha' was that for?" Podge asked.

"Show some respect'," Baxter said, chastising his player.

"Our Father who art in heaven," Davey said loudly. He then lowered his voice, "Etc. etc. etc."

"Ye don't even know the bleedin' prayer," blurted Podge, still smarting from his dig. He looked to his teammates for backup, "He doesn't even know the shaggin' words."

"Will ye just shut the fuck up. I'm after gettin' Father O'Brien to sponsor our end of season party," explained Davey, very close to decking the little bollox. He threw an eye over to the sideline where Fr. O'Brien and his colleague, Fr. O'Riordan, were standing, "We just need to bring a bit of religion back to the masses in return," Davey added, rehashing a phrase that Fr. O'Brien had delighted in using earlier.

The two priests were chuffed with themselves at the way Sporting Les Behans' had embraced the whole religious experience. Father O'Brien couldn't quite recall whether it was his or Davey's idea to sponsor the party but he was in no doubt that his parishioners would have no objections to covering the cost. The priest looked on as the Les Behans' blessed themselves and took up their various positions on the field.

"This could really catch on," Father O'Brien said, beaming from ear to ear. His fellow priest nodded enthusiastically in return.

The scoreboard read: Sporting Les Behans' 2 Dundalk Dynamos 2 after extra-time. Richie's absence after being recaptured by the guards was a huge loss for the team and the lads were fortunate to be still in the game if the truth be told. Their trusted goalie, Birdy, had been fantastic during the match, coming to the rescue on several occasions with some breathtaking saves. Both sides were now level in the dreaded penalty shootout with each team having already scored their first four penos. A Dynamos' player trudged towards the penalty spot with his head down trying his best to stay focused. In contrast, Birdy was marauding around his goal area like some sort of brooding big cat. The referee had in fairness done a good job in controlling the game without being overly involved and had allowed advantage to be played whenever he could. "Keeper," he said to Birdy.

The goalie raised a gloved hand and took up his position on the goal-line as the penalty taker placed the football on the spot. Birdy then started doing over-elaborate star jumps in an attempt to put his opponent off. The rest of the Les Behans' stood tall in the centre circle, linking each other while the Dundalk lads sat down in disjointed groups, some with their backs to the goal unable to watch the unfolding drama. The penalty taker took a few measured steps back, getting himself set to shoot but then changed his mind and returned to the ball. He picked it up, turned it over in his hands and replaced it once again.

"His bottle's gone," the Assassin said, carefully observing the proceedings.

On the sideline Father O'Brien looked up to the skies. "I know I shouldn't really be asking you for this kind of favour, Lord, but please make him miss."

The Dynamos' player glanced up at Birdy who was now doing his best Bruce Grobbelaar impersonation, his legs wobbling every which way as if they were made of jelly. It was all about inches. The penalty-taker blasted the ball high and over the crossbar. There was an audible groan from his teammates and their supporters, their cup run now no longer in their own hands.

"Told ye," the Assassin said.

The Sporting players all turned to Gitsy.

"Up to you now, ar kid. Do it for Richie," Baxter said, giving him some encouragement.

"No pressure then," replied Gitsy with his usual dry sense of humour.

He was totally unfazed as he strode towards the penalty area, placing the ball on the spot. The opposition goalie was eyeballing Gitsy, attempting to put him off but the Les Behans' player was far too busy trying to hold off a sneeze to notice. He searched under his sleeve for his handkerchief, but it was nowhere to be found. Instead he had to resort to pressing one nostril closed with his index finger while blowing hard through the other. A blob of mucus flew out and hit the football, sticking to it like glue. The Dynamos' keeper gagged, doing his best not to be sick and having to force himself not to look at the ball either. He tried to get the referee's attention to complain but hadn't the time as Gitsy took two steps back and smashed the ball into the back of the net with his powerful and trusted left foot. Game over.

As unbelievable as it was and against all the odds, Sporting Les Behans' were now into the cup final. The poor Dynamos' player ran to the referee to explain what Gitsy had done but when the football was recovered there was no trace of evidence and the lad just looked like a sore loser.

Baxter sat on the edge of the double bed, fumbling with the buttons on his good shirt as he tried his best to do it up. His head was pounding as if some little bugger with a jack hammer was trying to tunnel his way back out. These celebratory nights were really beginning to take their toll. He looked around and noticed for the first time just how filthy the bedroom was. There were dirty clothes strewn all over the kip and God knows what was mashed into the threadbare carpet.

"Where are ye goin?" coughed the peroxide blonde from where she was sprawled in a crumpled heap in the bed. Although only in her late thirties, the years hadn't been kind to her and she looked at least a decade older, "Thought we could spend the day in the sack, give us a chance to get to know each other that bit better."

"I can't," Baxter lied.

The woman sat up, holding a sheet to her ample chest, making an effort to hide her modesty, "Don't worry about it. If I'd a euro for every time a bloke couldn't get it up I'd be worth a fortune," she said.

Although the manager knew she meant well it didn't exactly inspire confidence in the trouser department.

"I've things to do," he said, unable to hide his annoyance.

The fake blonde flopped back down, pulling the covers up over her head. "Suit yerself, Mr. Softie," she said laughing before getting a fit of coughing.

"Classy," Baxter muttered.

He exited the bedroom as soon as he'd finished dressing, banging the door closed behind him in a huff. When he turned around he nearly leapt with the fright. There were three children staring back at him. He recognised the eldest boy as Derek, one of the lads who hung around the pitch. Derek was dressed in a hand-me-down school uniform that had definitely seen better days. A toddler with roaring red cheeks and a runny nose was strapped into a manky highchair. The young child quickly lost interest in the strange man and returned to his bowl of sugary cereal, trying his best to get the food into his mouth using his little fingers. The fact that there was no milk in the bowl didn't seem to bother him in the least. There was a girl of no more than seven years of age and she too didn't waste much time worrying about this latest visitor. She got back to her task in hand, scraping the remains of the butter from its plastic tub and dotting it onto a slice of toast. Baxter couldn't help but notice how dull and lifeless her long hair was. The girl began to subconsciously scratch her scalp in between buttering her bread. Baxter presumed her head was infested with biddies.

"Alright?" was the only word he could manage to say to the children.

Derek remained tight lipped, continuing to stare while his two siblings kept themselves busy trying to silence their bellies. Baxter shifted uneasily then reached into his trouser pocket and took out a twenty euro note. He dropped it on the table and quickly left, closing the paint chipped door. As he stood on the communal balcony, fishing a fresh piece of chewing gum from his pocket, he spotted Lenny tiptoeing out of a flat several doors away. The player was only wearing his boxers, carrying the rest of his clothes under one arm while holding his shoes in his other hand.

After the semi-final blowout it was time for the Sporting players to get their act together. Gathered in the truck container dressing room, most had changed into their training gear but a few stragglers were still lagging behind.

Fran was gingerly rubbing the bottom of his right foot. "Me feet are in rag order with blisters. That pitch is like concrete with the dry spell we're havin'."

Trigger took a jar of Vaseline from his kit bag and plonked it down on the bench next to his teammate.

"It would've been nice if ye'd at least bought me dinner first," Fran quipped.

"Rub it into the soles of yer feet before ye put yer socks on," said Trigger, "They'll be brand new."

"Ye learn somethin' new every day, thanks, bud."

Trigger smiled. He nodded his head towards the queue which had formed along the far wall.

"Business is brisk," he noted.

Fran unscrewed the lid of the lubricant. "Ye know wha' the lads are like, won't do anythin' on-line in case they leave an electronic footprint," he said.

"Big Brother's watchin'," Trigger said.

Leonard was sat behind a small table across from Charlie, ticking boxes on a form. Most of the other players were lined up behind him, holding paperwork of their own.

"A bloke I know was tellin' me that if I marry me elderly neighbour, who's dyin', I can claim her pension once she pops her clogs. Is that righ'?" asked Charlie.

"Are you serious?" Leonard said, taken aback.

"If there's an earner in it then why not?" Charlie bluntly replied, "Better than the money goin' back to that robbin' shower of bastards in government."

"Okay," said Leonard, wracking his brain, "I think you might be talking about the surviving civil partnership contributory pension."

"The bloke also said it's not means tested?" Charlie added.

Leonard raised an eyebrow. "This friend of yours seems to know a lot?"

"Got plenty of time on his hands. Currently doin' a six year stretch," said Charlie.

"Six years?" Leonard repeated, "What for?"

"Gettin' caught," said Charlie.

"No, I mean what is he in prison for?" Leonard asked.

"A misunderstandin'," explained Charlie.

"A misunderstanding?" Leonard said.

Charlie rubbed his nose, sniffing the tips of his fingers. "Yeah but the judge called it fraud."

Leonard didn't probe any further. "Yoyo, will you get me a form, please, for Charlie?"

Yoyo opened a press revealing stacks of various types of literature that Leonard had brought from the Social Welfare Office where he was posted.

"Which one?" asked Yoyo.

"Bottom left," said Leonard.

Yoyo retrieved the form and handed it to his teammate.

"Thanks."

Davey tilted his head, pausing for thought. He looked at Leonard. "Technically, is Yoyo now working?" he asked.

"Funny," said Yoyo.

Baxter was heading towards the container dressing room when Derek stepped out in front of him.

"There you are, lad," the manager cautiously greeted.

"We're not a charity," Derek informed Baxter as he attempted to hand back the twenty euro note that the manager had left on the table the previous morning.

"Of course not," Baxter said, a little stumped. Twenty quid was twenty quid after all and the boy and his siblings could clearly do with it.

"Look, I didn't realise it was your mother," Baxter meekly offered.

"It's always gonna be someone's Ma," said Derek.

"Suppose you're right," the manager agreed. He removed his tweed cap and scratched his head, "Tell you what. You can hold onto the few bob, we'll call it a down payment. I have a bit of work for you if you're interested."

"Doin' wha'?" Derek asked, suspicious of anything that sounded too good to be true.

"I've some whiskey that needs shifting," the manager half explained. Baxter entered the makeshift dressing room and looked around at his players, having a laugh and generally mucking about. "What's going on in here?" he roared like a man possessed, "Get your arses outside! It's not as if you don't need the practice."

The stunned lads left their forms on Leonard's desk and made their way outside as instructed without so much as a word. Leonard got to his feet to follow the boys but Baxter put a hand on his shoulder stopping him.

"Just a minute," the gaffer said, waiting for the last of his players to leave, "You know the way I have a few sprogs scattered around the place?"

Leonard nodded his head unsure of where the conversation was going.

"I'm not a hands-on type of father, think it helps to make them more independent," Baxter said, "Anyway, would I be entitled to a share of their children's allowance?"

Leonard was momentarily stuck for words. He knew that the boss was a bit of a rogue, but he didn't think that the man would stoop this low.

Leonard cleared his throat. "I don't like to tell anyone their business, but I think it's disgraceful that a parent would deny a child the monies which were meant to go towards their upkeep," he firmly said, surprising even himself.

"Couldn't agree more, lad," replied Baxter, "and that's why I'm looking for the cash, to make sure it gets spent on the kids."

"But..." Leonard began.

The manager smiled. "It's alright, Lenny, I've had my road to Damascus epiphany."

Leonard didn't look half as impressed as Baxter thought he would be.

"Okay, spit it out," the manager said.

"That's all well and good making sure that the children's allowance is spent on the child but the bigger question needs to be addressed here too."

"Which is?"

"If the men are man enough to make the babies then they should be man enough to take a more active role in their upbringing," Leonard said, not too sure how the gaffer would take it.

Baxter stroked his earlobe but said nothing.

The player decided to continue. "It's a copout blaming the women for not properly minding the children, but it can't be easy trying to do it all on their own. Afterall, it takes two to tango."

"That's a very fair point," Baxter said, unable to disagree with anything the other man had just said. If he was being honest, he never once considered what it must be like from the woman's point of view. He decided there and then that he was going to do something about it but wasn't sure what that would be, not yet anyhow.

The early morning cloud which had brought a light drizzle with it had petered out leaving a clear blue sky in its wake. Sporting Les Behans' were having a casual practice kick-about in the stadium that had been chosen to host the final, a stone's throw away from the city centre. Birdy made a couple of half-hearted saves from some handy shots and the manager was more than a little concerned.

"Is everything alright?" he asked his subdued goalkeeper.

Birdy reefed off his gloves, throwing them to the ground. "Family problems," he complained.

"I can relate to that," Baxter said, picking up the goalie's padded gloves. "Look, when I first met you, you told me that you just wanted to play footie. Now's your chance."

The keeper didn't look convinced.

The manager waved the gloves towards the rest of the team. "You don't want to let your new family down now, do you, lad?"

Baxter was fully aware that this was emotional blackmail, but he didn't really have a choice. Without their star keeper they hadn't a chance, especially if they were forced to stick Podge between the posts. Birdy surveyed the rest of his teammates as they kicked balls back and forth to one another, an air of determination in the camp. The manager held out the gloves.

"Okay," Birdy eventually agreed, accepting his gloves.

"Good lad," cajoled the experienced manager before strolling the short distance over the finely cut grass surface to where Fran was standing, "I'm like a flipping social worker these last few days," he confided, "I even had to go around to Podge's house after he rang me in a panic, to rescue him."

"Righ'," said Fran, only half listening.

"He'd only gone and locked himself in his bedroom and Sharon was going ballistic, trying to break the bloody door down. Apparently, she'd found a pack of three condoms in his jacket pocket but with one missing and she thought that poor Podge had an aul mare on the go."

"Sure who'd touch that ugly fucker?" Fran said but not in a mean-spirited way.

"Isn't that exactly what I said to Sharon and she nearly took the head clean off of me. I had to explain to her that I was the one who told him to cut down on the grub and that's why he was losing all the weight. Davey then had to ring her about the rubbers, something about keeping the sheets clean. Bugger if I know what that's all about and frankly, I don't want to know either but everything's sorted now, thank Christ."

Fran forced a smile, but it didn't fool the boss.

He put a hand on his centre-half's shoulder. "You know if you're not up to this game the rest of the lads will understand. Can't be easy having your little girl taken away from you like that."

"I'll be grand," said Fran, trying to put a brave face on things, "The match will help to keep me mind occupied."

"Sound. Your brother will be a massive loss tonight."

"I know."

"Fair play to him for battering that kiddy fiddling coach," said Baxter, his cheeks flushing with anger, "Castration will be too good for the low-life."

"There's no need. Apparently the paedo died a few years ago," Fran revealed.

"Pity."

"Better believe it."

Baxter removed a newspaper from the inside pocket of his heavy coat. "Did you see the papers this morning?"

"No," said Fran, having very little interest in current affairs at the moment when his own world was crashing down about him.

The manager opened up a page with a photo of the Sporting team splashed across it wearing the stolen dresses and under the headline: 'Les

Behans' Stuff Themselves With Bananas'.

"You'd have to wonder how these so-called reporters make half this crap up," Baxter said, shaking his head in bewilderment.

"God only knows," Fran agreed.

In another corner of the pitch Yoyo discreetly handed the Assassin a small container of tablets.

"Don't overdo it," the amateur chemist sternly advised, "They'd drop a bleedin' horse."

"Good man, Yoyo," thanked the Assassin, "And I won't be forgettin' this in a hurry."

"Yoyo," Baxter called out.

The player immediately thought that he'd been sussed giving the tablets to Al and was preparing himself for a bollocking.

The Assassin said, "I better stash these for later on," before heading for the dressing room leaving Yoyo to face the gaffer alone.

"What's up, Boss?" Yoyo innocently asked.

Baxter looked around to make sure there was no one else in earshot. "This is strictly between you and me, do you hear?"

"No prob," the player tentatively answered.

"There's nothing wrong with me, like," Baxter said.

Yoyo didn't answer.

"It's just that I need something stronger than our usual blue friends, have a busy few days ahead of me."

"Stronger than Viagra?" laughed Yoyo.

The manager put his finger to his lips, glancing around. "Shush."

"Ye need to chill, Boss. Anyway, I thought you were given up sleepin' around."

"I never said that," Baxter replied, "Am just going to be more responsible from now on. I'm going to try and find a regular girlfriend and hopefully settle down."

"And pigs will fly."

The manager looked cross. "Have you got something that'll do the job, yes or no?"

"Of course, but aren't ye forgettin' one thing?"

"What's that?" Baxter asked, impatiently.

"I can't give ye any, ye've put a chemical ban in place."

The manager remembered his edict but that was before it had impacted on him personally. "We're into the final now so that no longer stands."

"A bit like yer mickey," Yoyo couldn't resist from saying.

Baxter pointed at his player and said, "You're going to get old too, someday – if you don't die of an overdose in the meantime."

The player was shocked but Baxter then flashed a friendly smile.

"I'll sort ye out after the match," Yoyo said, giving in.

Mr. Quinn stepped out through the small door set within the large prison gates. He looked up at the clear blue sky, a rarity in this part of the world but hopefully a good omen for things to come. It was great to be free even if it had taken a lot longer than his expensive, poncey brief had promised. He'd have to put the shits up the legal eagle to remind the prick that he was his number one client and not to be getting complacent. 'What was his kid's name again? Clarke. Nah. Kieran.' He shook his head, 'Karl. That was it. Karl the diabetic. Now what would happen if poor little Karl accidently got too much insulin?' The heavy door was shut behind the newly-released prisoner bringing him back from his meanderings. He didn't bother turning around. He took out his mobile, hit a number from memory and put the phone to his ear. After several moments he took it away again, checked the screen and frowned. An automated voice told him to leave a message. The gang boss ended the call without saying a word. Moments later, a taxi pulled up next to the kerb and the driver's window lowered.

"Mr. Quinn?" asked the Assassin.

Quinn looked around cautiously, the fear of being whacked prominent in his mind. It wouldn't have been the first time some poor fucker got snuffed only moments after being released.

"Stevo sent me," the Assassin explained, sensing Quinn's reluctance, "Said he apologises for not being here in person, but he needed to tie up a few lose ends first, said ye'd know the score."

Al then nodded towards the back seat of his cab. There were several large bottles of cider sat in a metal bucket surrounded by ice. Charlie's hot sister, Simone, who was dressed like an expensive tart was also waiting for the crime boss. She gave him a coy smile.

"Left somethin' for ye to get the party started," the Assassin said, doing his best not to overdo things.

The taxi bullied its way through the usual dense city traffic doing its best to blend in. Al glanced into his rear view mirror every few minutes, making sure that Quinn was being kept occupied. The newly released convict swigged greedily from one of the chilled bottles of cider as he laughed and joked with his gorgeous date. At one stage he ran his hand a little too high up Simone's smooth leg for her liking. She crossed her fine pins angering the gangster but when she whispered something suggestive in his ear he was all smiles again. Although repulsed by the lecher's advances she didn't let on. She gave the Assassin a discreet wink to assure him that she had everything under control. Al knew that Simone was playing a blinder, especially after having previously confided in him that she was gay.

He relaxed a small bit even though he was still concerned at how long it was taking for the tablets which Yoyo had earlier supplied, to knock Quinn out. Al hadn't told his teammate who the tablets were intended for and Yoyo knew better than to ask. There was no need to complicate things. After another ten minutes of aimless driving through areas Al knew for certain didn't have adequate CCTV, Quinn finally conked out mid-sentence. The Assassin stopped his car at the next red light and allowed Simone to slip out and make herself scarce. The lights turned green and he smoothly pulled away again, merging with the rest of the southward bound traffic.

The fucker was a lot heavier than the Assassin had anticipated and it took all of his considerable strength to drag Quinn through the deserted wooded area. He left him slumped against a tree next to the hole that the Runner from his taxi had previously dug, weeks earlier. Faint rustling in the undergrowth alerted Al to the presence of another person but he wasn't unduly worried. A few branches parted and Stevo appeared, taking care to step over a patch of tangled briars.

"Long time no see," Stevo said.

"Must be the guts of five or six years," the Assassin replied.

Stevo pulled at the cuff of one of his snug fitting leather gloves more out of habit than necessity. "Almost eight, believe it or not," he said.

"The good aul days."

Both men smiled.

The Assassin looked down at the heavily sedated crime boss. "Wha' were ye doin' involved with a scumbag like that?" he asked, spitting on the ground next to Quinn.

"Needed the work, ye know the story," Stevo said.

"Too righ'. How d'ye find out he was gonna whack ye?"

"His idiot nephew was shootin' his mouth off and some of the crew got wind of it. They were already startin' to get edgy about the whole setup and Quinn's obsession with rubbin' yer mate out, well that was the straw that broke the camel's back."

"So we're all square with Richie, he doesn't have to be lookin' over his shoulder anymore?"

Stevo smiled and said, "The threat ends here."

"Wanna hand?" Al asked, looking down at the unconscious crime boss.

"Nah, ye've done enough already, thanks."

"That's wha' friends are for."

The former associates exchanged smiles.

"Make sure yer alibi's water tigh', be a lot of interest with this one," Stevo advised.

"Already sorted," the Assassin said. He turned and started to walk back to his car.

"Al?" Stevo called out.

The Assassin checked over his shoulder.

"Best of luck with the game tonigh'."

Chapter 23

The Final: Sporting Les Behans' v Dalymount Hibernians

Hundreds of fans, wearing all manner of Sporting Les Behans' merchandise, including replica jerseys, t-shirts, hats and the obligatory blow-up sex dolls, squeezed their way through the turnstiles into the brightly lit stadium. A small group of hot women, waving plastic rainbow flags, had taken up a central position in one of the covered stands. They were all performers from the local pole dancing club where Charlie's sister, Simone, was one of the star attractions. The club was also a place frequented by the majority of the Sporting team. The ladies felt it was good to publicly show their support in return even though if the truth be known they felt pity for the lads. Davey had been able to import most of the merchandise on the cheap from China through a connection he'd made at his favourite local takeaway but he'd been forced to source the Gay Pride stuff closer to home where thankfully people were a lot more understanding.

Derek and his young pals had been brought into the fold to sell the goods on a commission only basis on some very favourable terms, for Davey that was. An invaluable life lesson that he was passin' on for half nothin' was how he'd sold it to them! He knew there'd be enough profit to have given the kids a bigger slice of the pie but he didn't want to ruin them. They'd have to serve their apprenticeship first just as he had done all those years ago.

Derek had suggested a supporter's club membership, directed primarily at the younger lads. He reckoned there'd be a huge demand to join, especially if it was being sold to them as being part of the Sporting Ultras. 'Cha-ching!' thought Davey, already liking this membership concept. So, regardless of tonight's result, he knew he was already onto a winner.

Not too far away from the stadium, Richie lay in his prison bunk catching sound bites of the crowd chanting every time the warm breeze blew in his direction. He was staring at the ceiling contemplating the game when a heavyset warder shuffled into his cell.

"The Governor wants a word," the screw said, somewhat out of breath.

The football stadium was packed to the rafters. Derek's gang of kids had grown enormously and was now easily one hundred strong. With the last of the football paraphernalia offloaded it was time to enjoy the big game. They held their outstretched arms high above their heads, chanting as loudly as their developing lungs would allow. "Les Behans'," followed by clap, clap, clap, "Les Behans'," clap, clap, clap. Simone arrived at the game later than her colleagues after doing a private dance as part of a rider for a well-known rock band who were playing in the capital. She found the aging rockers very sweet and extremely generous with the tips and they had insisted on her joining them for some green tea after her performance. All very rock and roll, baby and nice work if you could get it. Her evening attire now consisted of skin-tight leather trousers and a figure hugging black top. She looked as if her outfit had been vacuum-packed around her curvaceous figure and was immediately spotted by both sets of players who were warming up on the field of play.

"They're some weapons of mass distraction," the Assassin said appreciatively about Simone's ample breasts.

"Could take yer eyes out with them nips," Trigger commented.

"Ah lads, that's me sister," said Charlie, defending his sibling's honour.

Mick, being a connoisseur of the female form, was equally impressed. "Built for sin," he said.

"Suppose," Charlie conceded.

Mrs. Flynn held Laura safely in her arms as she moved closer to the side of the pitch after spotting Fran doing his stretching exercises. She grabbed the attention of a steward who was standing on the opposite side of the advertising hoarding.

"Young fella, will ye get that man for me, please," she asked, pointing towards Fran.

The steward was about to refuse but had a change of heart when he looked into the older woman's eyes. She reminded him of his own mother who had recently passed away.

"No prob," he said instead. He jogged over to Fran, had a quick word then nodded back towards Mrs. Flynn. Laura was so excited when her Daddy came rushing over that she jumped into his arms almost catching him off-guard. He gave her a big kiss and hugged her tightly, nearly squeezing the life out of her tiny frame.

"I don't make mistakes, well, not that often," began Mrs. Flynn, her tone an awful lot kinder than of late, "Yer her Dad and her rightful place is with ye. I'd like to get to know her better though, if that's okay? Maybe she could sleep over now and again?"

"Of course. Thanks," Fran humbly said. He was almost in tears and was doing his utmost to keep it altogether. He turned to Laura, "Be a good girl now and mind yer Granny while yer Da plays his match."

Mrs. Flynn gave Fran a grateful smile as he handed back the precious cargo.

The substitutes, Jigsaw, Podge, Split and Huey had just taken up their positions on the Perspex covered bench when a mobile phone rang, playing the lyrics 'Hey, did you happen to see the most beautiful girl in the world?' The subs turned to where the song was emanating from. Podge. The sub keeper wore a sheepish expression.

"It's me new ringtone for Sharon," he whispered.

"You've changed yer tune," joked Split.

The rest of the lads groaned.

"Changed yer tune, d'ye get it?" said Split, delighted with his latest pun.

"Better shut bleedin' up or you'll be gettin' it," warned Podge in a hushed voice, "Sharon's sittin' righ' behind us."

The subs all turned around and saw Podge's missus, her mobile stuck to her ear, sitting several rows back, glaring at them.

Podge answered his phone in a sickly sweet tone, "Howya darlin'."

Nobody recognised English international, Johnny Carter, as he slipped anonymously into a seat in the stand hoping to meet up with his former teammate, Richie Reilly. He'd discovered that Richie played for the Sporting outfit but hadn't been informed that his former youth teammate was now languishing in a prison cell approximately five hundred metres down the road. One of the kids who was selling the Les Behans' merchandise had done a double take when Johnny had purchased a baseball cap and scarf from him outside the ground but the young entrepreneur was too busy trying to earn a crust to care and quickly moved on to his next victim. Time was money. Johnny felt like a ton weight had been lifted off of his shoulders since his television revelations and he was determined to get his act together and to try and make amends. Apologising to Richie would be a major step forwards in that regard.

The cup final wasn't long started when the Assassin, intent on making his presence felt, went straight through the back of a Hib's player, levelling him just outside the box. The Assassin's mother who was sitting close to the Sporting Les Behans' dugout jumped to her feet.

"Go easy, Alphonsus, it's only a game," she urged in her high pitched voice.

The Sporting substitutes glanced at one another and grinned. The Assassin was livid.

Out on the pitch Charlie turned to Gitsy. "Alphonsus," he mimed, trying not to laugh. The lads had always presumed that the Assassin's real name was Alan. Even at school he was always called Al and no teacher had ever dared asking him to elaborate further. It just went to prove that every day was a learning day.

The Assassin's tackle was brutal, but the referee decided to give the offending player the benefit of the doubt as the match had only just begun. In his experience the vast majority of players were a bundle of nerves at the start of a big game, especially one of this magnitude. Giving a card this early on had a major bearing on how many lads would be left on the pitch at the end of the ninety minutes, so unless some fella was decapitated a good talking to would suffice. Al knew he was a lucky boy to only receive a verbal warning from the man in black and promised to relax, blaming his doctor's recent decision to increase his medication for his mistimed tackle. The official was about to add a smart comment but luckily managed to catch himself in time. There was something very unsettling about the big man's dark, steely eyes.

Dalymount Hibernian's organised their free kick while Sporting Les Behans' sorted out their defence. The Hib's playmaker struck the ball sweetly with the inside of his left boot sending it floating over the Sporting wall. Birdy was first to react. He climbed high using his left knee for extra elevation as well as protection and plucked the football out of the air but inexplicably let it slip from his hands on landing. An alert opposition player pounced on the rare mistake and poked the ball home. A gift at any level. The Hibs' supporters went mental as the players mobbed the goal scorer.

Baxter was seething on the sideline. "A simple bloody ball," he muttered, "The boy can collect them in his sleep."

Mick walked up to Birdy as he retrieved the ball from the back of the net.

"Unlucky, keeper. Don't worry about it, there's plenty of time left," he said, trying to console the man between the sticks.

Birdy lashed the ball against the back of the net in anger. "No good enough! No good enough!" he shouted.

"The Les Behans' are gettin' rightly stuffed," commented Gonzales from his vantage point in the wheelchair section of the stadium.

The Dalymount side had most of the possession early on and had just won their second corner. Both sets of players were jostling with one another in the box, the attackers trying to make that all important extra yard of space. The ball was whipped in at the near post but Paddy Power read it well and jumped the highest, clearing it from the danger zone with a powerful header. Unfortunately for Paddy he landed heavily, going over on his right ankle and collapsing to the ground in agony. The referee immediately blew his whistle and signalled towards the Sporting Les Behans' bench allowing for medical assistance to enter the field of play. Baxter ran onto the pitch with Podge in tow, carrying water bottles and the all-important magic spray. Podge distributed the water to his fellow teammates, but the referee was having none of it and told the players to go to the sideline if they wanted a drink.

Baxter crouched down next to the injured Power. "How bad is it?" he asked.

"Think it's broke, Boss," said Power, his face etched with pain.

"Looks banjoed alrigh'," the Assassin agreed.

"I'll get me sister," said Charlie. He glanced over towards the stand trying to find her familiar face.

Baxter looked at his player questioningly.

"She's an expert in all that stuff. The new girls are always fallin' off poles," Charlie explained. He spotted his sister in the crowd along with the rest of the girls, still madly waving their rainbow flags and beckoned for her to come join him with a flailing arm.

Baxter looked to his weakened subs bench, considering his options but was struggling to be inspired. "Split, warm up!" he shouted after finally making his decision.

An elderly steward kindly helped Simone onto the pitch while copping a feel of her toned behind as she passed. She turned around, all smiles and gave the steward a peck on the cheek and as the fans cheered she discreetly planted the heal of her leather boot down on top of the steward's foot using all her weight.

"Don't touch wha' ye can't afford, ye dirty aul man," she advised before making her way over to the injured player, admiringly watched every single step of the way by both sets of players. As she bent down and examined Power's ankle everyone got a flash of the sparkling pink thong that she was wearing.

An excited young Hibernian's player nudged his teammate. "Why can't we get a physio like that?" he complained.

The mood in the Les Behans' dressing room at half-time was downbeat to say the least.

Paddy Power sat in a corner with his raised foot wrapped in an icepack.

Spittle flew from Charlie's mouth as he cursed, "Three fuckin' nil."

"They seem to have so much time on the ball," moaned Mick.

"Come on, lads, there's still another half to go. We didn't come this far just to make up the numbers now, did we?" said Baxter, trying to give his players a much-needed lift. "Did you see the amount of head-bangers out there that came to support us? At least give them something to shout about. I'm going to shake things up a bit, make a few changes. Gitsy, you're coming off to make way for Jigsaw. We're reverting back to two up front. Lenny, Davey, I want you to keep switching wings, drag your markers all over the shop."

There was an official sounding knock on the door. Everyone looked up only to see Richie pop his cheeky head around.

"Anyone got a spare pair of boots?" he asked.

The entire team apart from Fran, got to their feet and made their way over to their star player, gratefully welcoming him back. After a few moments of soaking up the greetings Richie sat down next to his smiling brother.

"Ye didn't escape again did ye?" Fran asked, light-heartedly.

"Nah. Out on T.R.," Richie explained, "Think the Governor took pity on yis. That and the fact he's a massive Rover's fan."

The Sporting lads went back out for the second half with a spring in their step. Although Split was disappointed to be taken off to make way for Richie, he didn't cause a fuss, putting the team first. Birdy spotted his uncle, the ringmaster, with the rest of his relations and friends from the circus. They were still wearing their various circus outfits as they hurriedly took their seats in the packed stand. His uncle saw Birdy and came straight to the advertising hoarding at the side of the pitch.

"Why you here?" asked Birdy, unsure.

"For you," explained the ringmaster. "We just finished the show. Look, I understand why you left but you have to see it from my side. Things are tough. I have to take all the bookings I can, otherwise..." the ringmaster looked back at the rest of his people, "...there'll be no circus."

"I know," Birdy said, "but it is best share worries. We'll work together." Both men smiled and shook hands before pulling each other closer and firmly embracing.

Baxter looked on from a distance, happy that his keeper had made up with his uncle. He then caught the eye of a dark-haired beauty who was with the circus crowd. She was dressed in a sparkling, silver, figure hugging dress with a delicate white cardigan thrown over her sallow shoulders. Baxter gave a barely discernible nod and got a coy smile in return.

The second half got underway with both teams getting stuck in from the off. Richie intercepted a long ball, pretended to spread it out wide to the left but instead changed direction sending the Hibs' player the wrong way.

"Go on, my son," urged Johnny Carter, rising from his seat in the stand, the excitement getting the better of him.

Richie then threaded a pass through the proverbial eye of a needle to Leonard who was tearing up the wing. Leonard expertly cushioned the ball with his bootlaces without breaking stride and just as the defender came across to block him, the winger cut the ball back and banged in a high cross. Jigsaw caught it perfectly on his chest, pushing it slightly ahead of himself. This gave him ample space to line up the shot.

"Bury it!" Baxter roared.

"Shoot!" screamed the supporters.

"Use the force," whispered Davey.

Jigsaw imagined himself holding the heavy, Russian made machine gun from Trigger's hidden bunker. He pointed it at the Hibernian's keeper who was now dressed as the paper target from the firing range. Jigsaw then hit the ball with venom. It struck the keeper square in the face knocking him off his feet and flat onto the ground. Everyone in the stadium seemed to make a collective 'ooh' sound, feeling the prone, shot-stopper's pain. The ball smashed against the crossbar and rebounded to Trigger, the coolest man on the field, who powered it home with his noggin. The Sporting supporters went bananas. The Hibs' physio and some other medical personnel sprinted onto the pitch to where the keeper lay, motionless.

Trigger put an arm around Jigsaw's shoulder. "Did ye not remember our practice session in the bunker, when I told ye it was all about stayin' calm?" he asked.

"I did but got a bit mixed up," Jigsaw replied. "Went for the head shot."

The game was delayed for a short period while the opposition keeper was stretchered off to a rousing, sympathetic applause from both sets of supporters. His understudy unexpectedly took to the field, fixed his gloves and got set for action. Sporting Les Behans' had Hibs on the ropes, throwing everything at them.

"I had the pleasure of seein' the Les Behans' earlier this year, comin' from behind," Gonzales excitedly reported. He gave a dirty wink to a neighbouring female, wheelchair-bound supporter, but she was having none of it and rolled a few feet away.

With ten minutes to go and three-one down, things didn't look great though. Hibs launched a counterattack and their top striker with the pretty boy looks and the one-hundred-euro haircut found himself in acres of space. He was one-on-one with Birdy and a fourth goal seemed inevitable. The ball was curled beautifully with his left foot towards the top far corner. The shot had goal written all over it and the sports journalists present were already busily writing the headlines. Birdy had a different idea, however. He quickly adjusted his feet, shuffling sideways in order to reduce the distance he'd need to dive if he had any hope of making the save. Miraculously, he somehow managed to get a fingertip to the ball, pushing it spectacularly onto the upright. An absolute worldy save.

The Hibs' striker couldn't believe his eyes as he dropped to his knees, holding his head in his hands but still careful not to ruin his expensive hairdo. The Sporting crowd were ecstatic while the circus troupe erupted into wild applause.

The proud ringmaster was up on his feet. "That's my nephew!" he shouted to nobody and everybody at the same time.

Mick raced back and was first to the rebounding ball from Birdy's spectacular save. He collected it and found Richie who had also sprinted back to help. Richie put his foot on the ball and looked up to see what was on. Realising that his options were limited he decided to take matters into his own hands. He weaved his way up the pitch, ghosting past several players with ease using his electrifying pace. As he crossed the halfway line the opposition midfielder made a desperate lunge, trying to get something on the football or the man. Giving away a free this far out wouldn't have been the end of the world.

"Man on!" roared Fran.

Richie, who was well aware of the opposition player's presence, read the situation and deftly lifted the ball between his two feet, evading the tackle and leaving his opponent sliding past in disbelief. No sooner had Richie landed when a defender came racing towards him. Richie spotted him out of the corner of his eye and did a turn that Cruyff would have been proud of leaving his opponent for dead. The Sporting player was now at the edge of the box with the goal at his mercy. He pretended to slip the ball to Leonard who was running off his shoulder. The last Hibs' defender bought the dummy and was unable to readjust his feet in time as Richie skipped past and blasted an unstoppable shot into the opposition net out of reach of the despairing, replacement keeper's dive.

The stadium erupted.

Johnny Carter stood up and applauded Richie, undoubtedly the best youth player he had ever seen, and he had seen a lot of very talented youngsters over the years. He felt pangs of guilt knowing in his heart that the lad would have been a superstar if it wasn't for him.

Not long after Sporting's second goal, the final whistle was inevitably blown. The Les Behans' just couldn't get the equaliser and had lost by the narrowest of margins, three goals to two. They had received a standing ovation from both sets of fans as well as the opposition team before making their way back to the dressing room. Every man to the last had emptied the tank for the cause.

While the dream was over Baxter couldn't have been prouder of his lads. He went around to each and every single one of them, shaking their hands and thanking them for the tremendous effort they'd put in all season. There was a cautious knock on the door and Baxter opened it half expecting to see some journalist or reporter mooching for a quote for tomorrow's sport's edition. He immediately recognised Johnny Carter but was dumbfounded to find the international player standing in front of him.

"Hi, I'm Johnny. Can I come in for a minute?" Mr. Carter politely asked.

Baxter, still unable to get any words out, stood aside and motioned for the soccer star to enter. The entire room went quiet, not sure what would happen next. They had all seen the televised interview. Richie slowly rose to his feet and walked over to Johnny. Without the need to say a single word the two former youth teammates warmly embraced.

Chapter 24

The end of season party was sponsored, as promised, by the generous Father O'Brien and his unsuspecting congregation. Frank the Publican's bar was the venue for the bash and nothing was spared. There was even a humongous pig being cooked on a spit courtesy of the local butcher who was also a massive fan of the team. When Charlie heard that there was a spit roast out in the newly installed beer garden, he made a beeline for the area, no doubt picturing a completely different sort of feast.

Frank the Publican was relieved that he had heeded the Assassin's sage advice in hiring half a dozen bouncers to help with crowd control such was the volume of people who had turned up to show their support. Al had personally vetted the security staff and was happy that they were up to the job, appointing Hego from the flats as head doorman. Live and let live being one of Al's many mottos.

Birdy's uncle, the ringmaster, had generously loaned one of his larger circus tarpaulins to Frank, enabling him to cover the entire yard at the back of the pub in case the weather decided to act up. The makeshift beer garden was designated a fan zone and was jam packed. This allowed the many madcap followers to be able to have a gargle and to feel that they were in the thick of things while at the same time keeping them out of the boozer. The players in fairness took turns to mingle with the supporters and were more than obliging with the requests for photos and autographs. This is what Sporting Les Behans' was all about, community. And sure if they could make a few quid on the side then more power to them.

Davey negotiated his way through the heaving bodies piled up at the bar counter. Frank had just finished pulling several fresh pints of stout, allowing the turbulent, caramel coloured swirls to settle into creamy topped blackness.

"I have a confession," Davey announced.

"Shouldn't ye be talkin' to yer favourite priest then?" the publican said, nodding towards Father O'Brien who was chatting away to some of the guests and seemed to be really enjoying himself.

"Think ye missed yer callin'," Davey replied.

"Am not that big into the whole religion thing if I'm bein' honest."

"As a comedian."

Frank smiled. "You were about to confess?" he said.

"I was indeed. There was never a sham called Les Behan," said Davey.

"I know."

"Ye do?"

"Yeah," said Frank.

Davey arched his eyebrows. "And ye never said a word?"

"Had a feelin' that sponsorin' a team with a name like that would be good for business." Both men surveyed the packed bar.

Davey shook his head slowly and said, "Ye cute Culchie."

"Yer more than welcome," said Frank, accepting the compliment. "How are things goin' with you and the young lass from the hills of Donegal?" he asked, nodding towards Lily.

Davey's girlfriend was busy having the craic with Fran and Tracey.

"She's a bleedin' mad yoke but sound at the same time if ye know wha' I mean," answered Davey, "It's probably just as well I can only understand the half of wha' she says to me."

"And vice versa?"

"Without doubt."

"She seems like a really nice girl."

"Yeah, helped me out big time with me Ma dyin' and all that. Got me to see this bloke and he told me I was dyslexic."

"So Davey, yer not a feckin' eejit after all," quipped Frank. Although he'd only known the player these last few months, they had built up a great rapport and he felt he could say anything to him. He'd also learned that Davey was a very shrewd operator and definitely nobody's fool.

"Well, I'm not an ordinary eejit in anyway," Davey laughed, not in the slightest bit insulted. You needed skin like a rhino if you wanted to survive in this part of the world. "By the way, it's Les now, Les Behan."

"Sorry?"

"I changed me name by deed pole," Davey revealed.

"Are ye takin' the piss?" Frank said.

"No, honestly," Davey confessed. "I hadn't got a choice. There was a complaint made about the team name and they were gonna throw us outta of the cup so wha' else could I do?"

"Yer completely off yer rocker," said Frank, shaking his head.

Jigsaw accidently bumped into Wendy who was standing alone with her drink in hand, waiting for Mick to return from the bathroom.

"I'm very sorry," Jigsaw immediately apologised.

"It's okay. I didn't spill any," she said, referring to her dry white wine. "I'm Wendy by the way."

She offered him her hand but Jigsaw didn't take it. He just stood there looking, making her feel very uncomfortable. She shifted from one foot to the other praying that her partner would return as soon as possible.

"Ye don't usually hear birds bein' so honest," Jigsaw finally explained. "Get windy meself, especially after a good feed of stout."

Wendy forced a smile, made her excuses and shuffled away. Mick came back from the toilets not a minute too soon.

"Everything okay? Seen you chatting to Jigsaw," he commented.

"Is he all there?" she discreetly asked of the tall striker.

Mick rubbed his chin, looking thoughtful. "Jigsaw? Let's just say he's a few pieces short of the complete picture," he said affectionately, "but he's a really nice guy."

Sharon and Podge were standing in a corner all by themselves. Podge was sipping his drink while his missus was lashing down the pints in between casting a condescending eye around the room. She settled her sights on Mick and Wendy.

"Is that his Ma?" she asked sarcastically, making no attempt to keep her voice down.

"Will ye ever shut the fuck up," whispered Podge, absolutely mortified.

"Who d'ye think yer talkin' to?" Sharon said, loud enou[ ] above the party music.

Several people glanced their way.

"Please," urged Podge, desperate for things not to escalate, espe[ ] here in front of his teammates.

Sharon pointed at Baxter who was in the company of Birdy's beaut[ ] dark haired cousin from the circus, the one who had caught his eye at t[ ] final. "And what's he bleedin' like, the dirty aul man, chasin' that young wan."

Baxter and his new friend were flirting outrageously.

"Maybe they're in love," Podge suggested.

"And wha' would you know about love, ye fuckin' simpleton?" Sharon said, sneering while putting the emphasis on the word 'love'.

"Fuck all as it turns out," muttered Podge.

"Wha' was that?" his other half demanded, grabbing a clump of material from around the chest area of her husband's top with her masculine hand.

"Nothin', Sharon. Absolutely nothin'," the downtrodden subgoalie conceded.

The Assassin stood with his back against a far wall witnessing the scene. Watching unsuspecting people from a distance was a hobby of his but not in a stalking kind of manner. The way people behaved naturally revealed an awful a lot about them. He planted his finished pint glass on a shelf, wiped his mouth with the back of his hand and strolled over to the not so happy couple.

"Howya, Sharon. I saw your sister a few minutes ago but she had to leave in a hurry," he said.

"Me sister?" asked Sharon, confused. She only had a brother.

"Yeah, Cinderella," said Al, bursting into laughter.

Podge froze, fearing the worst but his partner laughed as well. If she was hurt by the ugly sister reference, she didn't let on.

"D'ye fancy headin' outside for a smoke?" the Assassin asked her, completely ignoring Podge.

haron was all smiles. "Of course," she said. "Be nice to be in the company real man for a change." She cocked her head to one side, smirked at her flated husband and left with Al, the most dangerous man she knew.

Rather than going out the back to the smoking area Al led Sharon around the other side of the pub where it was much quieter. He caught hold of a section of red and white safety tape which was blocking off a dimly lit area and beckoned Sharon forward. She hesitated but only for a split second then ducked under the tape with Al following. He retrieved a cigarette box from his pocket and offered Sharon a smoke. She took it and rolled it between her fingers and thumb.

"I was hopin' for somethin' a lot bigger," she said.

Al smiled. "And I wouldn't like to disappoint a lady." He took a phone from his pocket and held it aloft. "Let's get a selfie first."

Sharon felt like a teenager. She'd always had a thing for Al, his raw strength and his 'I couldn't give a flyin' fuck about anyone' attitude. The fact that he'd a huge muscular arse also helped. She hoped that the saying 'It took a big hammer to drive a big nail' was true. Nudging in beside Al she gave her best pout for the camera. The Assassin examined the photo.

"I'll get that printed and give it to me brother," he said.

Sharon looked puzzled.

"So he can put it on the mantelpiece to keep the kids away from the fire," Al added.

"Yer a mad bastard," said Sharon, thinking he was joking.

The Assassin laughed and said, "Go back a bit and I take one of ye on yer own."

Sharon reluctantly retreated a few steps.

When the Assassin came back into the boozer Podge was still waiting next to the counter where he'd left him, looking like a lost soul.

"Two pints, Frank!" Al shouted above the dim.

Podge looked forlornly at his teammate, presuming that he had just given his missus one, albeit a very quick one.

Al rested his hand on Podge's shoulder. "I've a bit of good news for ye."

His teammate said nothing.

"Yer missus is goin' away for a while and yer also gonna get a nice few quid," Al said.

Podge didn't understand. Was Sharon running away with his teammate? And if so was Al going to give him some sort of compensation?

"I could be wrong," the Assassin said, "but I'd say a broken leg, maybe two and at least a half dozen cracked ribs. Not to mention the head injury but she was always fucked up in that department so there'll be no change there."

Frank set two pints down in front of Al.

"Thanks, bud," said the Assassin. "Ye migh' wanna call an ambulance. Podge's wife is after fallen through the rotten timber coverin' the hole ye were tellin' me about a while back."

"Wha'!" said Podge, already making a move for the exit.

The Assassin caught hold of him by the scruff of the neck and pulled him back. "Where d'ye think yer goin'?" he asked.

"To help Sharon."

"Think again. Yer gonna enjoy the rest of the nigh' and probably the next coupla months too by the looks of it."

"I'll ring for an ambulance," the publican said, "but I just need to serve the rest of the thirsty customers first." He went back to pulling pints as if it was the most natural thing in the world to do.

Podge's lower lip started to quiver. "But..."

"But nothin'," said Al. "Now enjoy yer pint and let the medics do their job. I'll put ye in touch with me solicitor tomorrow about the claim." He poured a large amount of his pint down his throat like it was going out of fashion. "And ye should think about gettin' counsellin'. That's a very toxic environment to be livin' in."

Podge was in a daze and was barely able to take in what his friend was advising.

The Assassin licked his lips then said, "I know everyone is made differently but if Sharon was my mot I'd be after takin' a long drive up the woods and gettin' me shovel dirty but that's just me."

The Gardaí raided Scully's place after his fingerprints were found on the revolver at the safe house, the scene of the failed hit. The thug was caught hiding under his bed, terrified, clutching a bag of suspicious looking tablets. He was handcuffed and shoved into the back of a waiting squad car but was secretly relieved to be lifted. Since his uncle's disappearance, his old associates wanted nothing to do with him. Worse still was that he'd heard through the grapevine that he was going to be rubbed out.

He decided that he was going to confess to possessing drugs, the small amount he'd earlier counted out into the plastic bag and would hopefully be only put away for a short spell. This was his best option under the circumstances until his uncle resurfaced to post bail. With the backing of the gang boss he'd wipe out the rest of the chicken-shit crew. They hadn't a clue what loyalty meant, and he'd be the man to show them all. Cunts. He'd put together his own gang and then he'd be able to call the shots himself. The Gardaí were still searching for Mr. Quinn but weren't having much luck. They didn't realise just how right they were when their spokesman announced at a recently held press conference that 'They were still pursuing several lines of enquiry in establishing the whereabouts of Eddie Quinn, the ruthless crime lord, believed to be directly responsible for at least a dozen gangland hits in the capital. It seems as if he has disappeared underground.'

A fashion photographer busily snapped away with his expensive Japanese made camera.

"Magnifique. Le camera adores you, baby," bullshitted the fake Frenchman who was really from a small village in North County Dublin and who grew tomatoes and lettuce for a living.

Mick had not surprisingly received his marching orders from his estate agents' job after the safe house carry on and was now selling his body instead, so to speak. He had given up the camming as he'd found it too intrusive and couldn't deal with the issues which it presented. If people had personal problems, they should ring the Samaritans. Earning money was still a priority to support his lavish lifestyle so when Wendy had suggested he pose in colourful lingerie for the alternative catalogues scene he decided what the hell. He'd also moved into her luxury apartment, rent free, another bonus, where she encouraged him to bring home younger women who they could both have a go at corrupting. Wendy's icebreaker to the guests was always the same, 'Two's company but three is allowed.' As the cameraman clicked and flashed, Wendy, who was watching all hot and bothered from the wings, gave her man the thumbs up.

A group of reformed alcoholics and Davey sat on hard plastic chairs arranged in a circle. The Christian man tipped his head towards the Sporting Les Behans' player who coughed before rising to his feet. He was in a kind of purgatory knowing that if he didn't keep his end of the bargain in attending the meetings the Christian lad he'd assaulted would press charges.

"Look, I'm tired of all the deceit," Davey said. "I lied. I don't have a drink problem."

The reformed alcoholics shook their heads in a collective show of disappointment.

"Tut, tut, tut, Roger. Oh sorry, I forgot. It's really Davey," the Christian man said.

Davey let out a loud sigh and said, "It's actually Les, now."

The Christian man turned to a fellow member who'd been on the wagon almost ten years. "Going to need all of the Almighty's help with this one," he predicted.

Sporting Les Behans', togged out in their spotless new football kit, stood behind a long table holding an array of power tools. They had been inundated with requests to join them since their cup final appearance and exposure in the various media forms. They'd also had a shit load of sponsors falling over themselves, offering plenty of cash. Lenny was appointed treasurer not because he was good with sums, which he was, but because nobody else on the team was trusted enough. The front of the table was draped with a banner that read 'Thompson Power Tools' in bold, black writing. The whole thing was being filmed for an advert to be shown in Australia where they'd apparently a better sense of humour and weren't as caught up on the whole PC palaver. On the instruction of the director, an arty farty, grey-haired dude, the entire team spoke their well-rehearsed line in unison. "Thompson power tools, as recommended by Sporting Les Behans', everywhere."

Richie served the remainder of his sentence in prison, well almost, he was allowed out early for good behaviour. Johnny Carter had pulled a lot of strings and got Richie a coaching job with his old club back in England. Despite the unsavoury incident with the perverted coach back when the lads were only teenagers, the club had never involved the police, so no crime had ever been reported. A damage limitations exercise had been enacted by the worried directors, the result being that Richie was offloaded while the paedo was paid a substantial sum of money to keep his trap shut.

Richie was now working hard towards getting his coaching badges. He oversaw a group of young footballers engaged in various drills intended to improve their footwork and decision making, essential ingredients of any good ball player. They were very lucky to have the use of the immaculately kept sports pitches in such a safe environment. The public outcry regarding sex offenders in sport and the subsequent procedures that had been put in place had now ensured this. There was talk that Sporting Les Behans' would get the chance to come over and use the top-class facilities and maybe even play a pre-season friendly against the premiership outfit. If it happened, God help them, the premiership team that was.

Fran sat on the old couch on top of the truck container dressing room with Laura resting on his knee. He was watching Baxter preside over a training session with a large number of local kids. High above, Derek's younger sister was about to throw a dirty nappy over the balcony but stopped short when she noticed her brother and his pals playing on the pitch below. They all seemed to be enjoying themselves and she could clearly hear Derek laughing wholeheartedly, something she'd never heard him do before. She decided not to dump the nappy and instead walked the short distance to the communal shoot that led to the huge metal bins on the ground floor.

"Baxter had his hands full with the new recruits, the Junior Les Behans'. Rough diamonds in need of a small bit of polishing was how the manager thought of them now. He wouldn't allow anyone to criticise them, encouragement was the new name of the game. The local council had agreed to invest a substantial sum of money into improving the changing facilities and the playing surface and were also tendering for the construction of a small all-weather pitch. The players themselves had unanimously decided to set aside some of the money earned from the sponsorship deals to go towards the redevelopment of the community centre where it was planned to organise cookery and literacy classes for the adults as well as a homework club for the kids.

The team had also agreed to cover all the costs involved in entering the young lads into the schoolboys' leagues. The name Junior Les Behans' would probably have to be changed though before the powers that be would allow them to play. Davey had suggested Baxter's Boys which wasn't a bad idea seems how the boss probably owned half of them. If the team had a choice at the start of the year as to where the new home ground would have been, it definitely wouldn't have been here. But ye have to make the most of wha'ever life throws at ye, I suppose, and I know from speakin' to the other players they wouldn't have it any other way now. In fact, they can't wait for another season at the Stadium of Light. The plan is to qualify for Europe although gettin' visas for some of the lads migh' prove tricky. But wha'ever happens, it's gonna' be bleedin' deadly!"

Fran Reilly

The End

337

Sporting Les Behans' Team

1. Patrik 'Birdy' Nagy – Goalkeeper

2. Paddy Power – Full-Back

3. Al 'The Assassin' Caffrey – Centre-Back

4. Fran Reilly – Centre-Back

5. Charlie – Full-Back

6. Yoyo – Right Wing

7. Davey Byrne – Left Wing

8. Mick Young – Midfielder

9. Trigger – Striker

10. Jigsaw – Striker

11. Huey Campbell – Midfielder

12. Split The Wind – Left Wing

13. Richie Reilly – Midfielder

14. Leonard (Lenny) – Right Wing

15. Gitsy – Full-Back

16. Podge – Sub Goalkeeper

Pa Baxter – Manager

Gonzales – Commentator

Les Behan – Mascot

Sporting Les Behans' cup run:

First Round Qualifier: Newton Rangers 1-1 Sporting Les Behans'

First Round Qualifier (Replay): Sporting Les Behans' 5-0 Newton Rangers

Second Round Qualifier: St. Marks F.C. 0-6 Sporting Les Behans'

First Round: Sporting Les Behans' 3-0 Glasnevin Celtic

Second Round: Transport United 1-5 Sporting Les Behans'

Third Round: Sporting Les Behans' 4-1 Ballyer Boys

Fourth Round: Real Roscrea 4-8 Sporting Les Behans'

Fifth Round: United Dunboyne 1-3 Sporting Les Behans'

Sixth Round: Sporting Les Behans' 4-2 Galway City F.C.

Quarter Final: Sporting Les Behans' 2-1 Cork Rovers

Semi Final: Sporting Les Behans' 2-2 Dundalk Dynamos
(AET) Penalties 5-4.

Final: Dalymount Hibernians ?-? Sporting Les Behans'

About The Author

Paddy was born in 1971 in the heart of Dublin's Inner City and was educated at St. Paul's CBS (Brunner). He qualified as an Amenity Horticulturist from the National Botanic Gardens, Glasnevin in 1992 and now lives in Killarney. He is a referee with the FAI for his sins. His father, Paddy Snr is the current Vice President of the IABA while his mother, Joanie is a carer for the elderly. Paddy is one of six siblings along with Maria, Siobhan, Stephen (deceased), Deirdre & Elaine. This is Paddy's debut novel. He has written and performed three short plays to date: Sam Who? - The Irish Hangover (2014); Bar Flies (2018) & A Fishy Tale (2019) as well as writing the poem, Journey Through Immortality (2017) for the short film Immortal Souls.